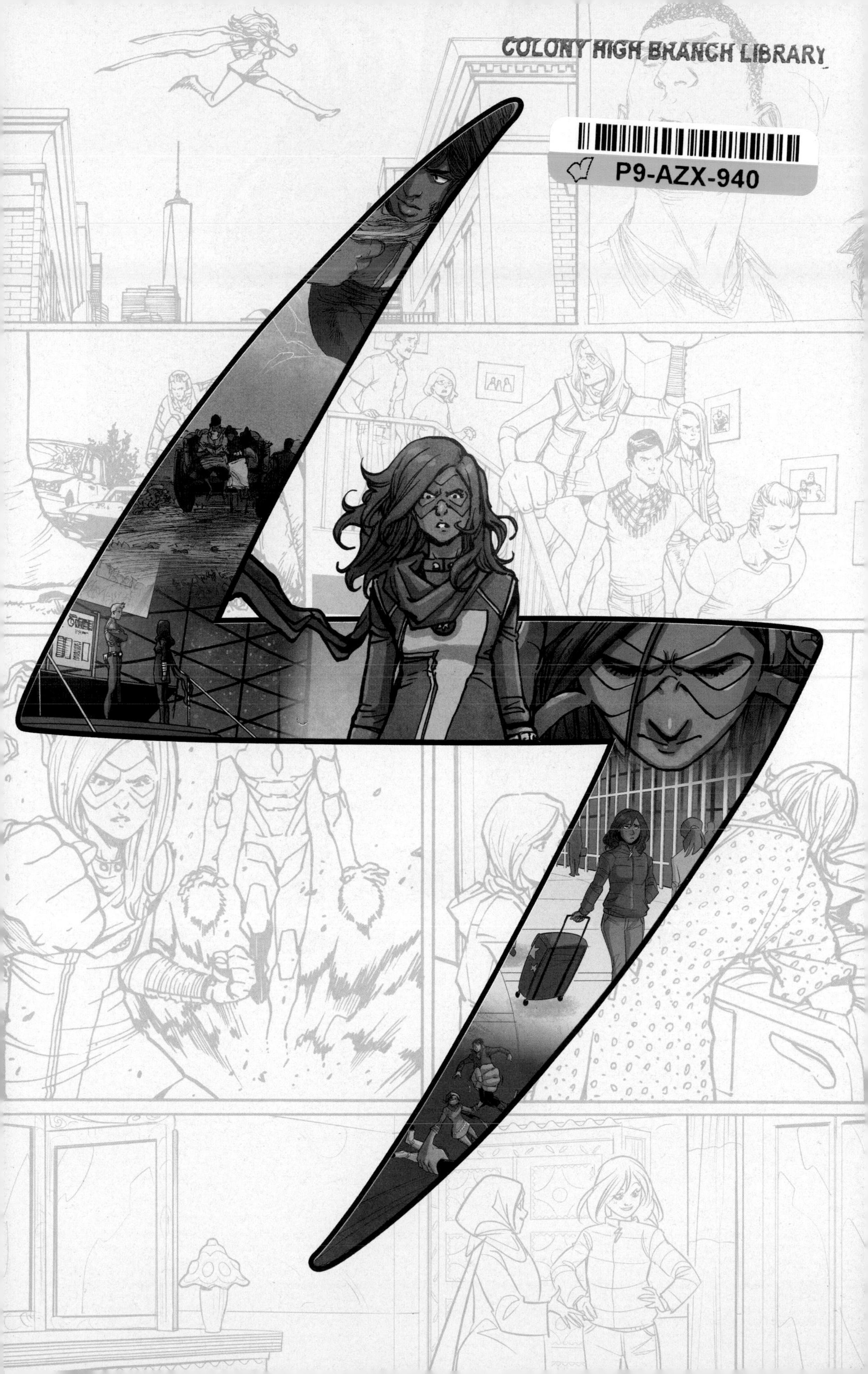

MS. MARVEL VOL. 6: CIVIL WAR II. Contains material originally published in magazine form as MS. MARVEL #7-12. First printing 2016. ISBN# 978-0-7851-9612-9. Published by MARVEL WORLDWIDE, INC., a subsidiary of MARVEL ENTERTAINMENT, LLC. OFFICE OF PUBLICATION: 135 West 50th Street, New York, NY 10020. Copyright © 2016 MARVEL No similarity between any of the names, characters, persons, and/or institutions in this magazine with those of any living or dead person or institution is intended, and any such similarity which may exist is purely coincidental. **Printed in Canada.** ALAN FINE, President, Marvel Entertainment; DAN BUCKLEY, President, TV, Publishing & Brand Management; JOE QUESADA, Chief Creative Officer; TOM BREVOORT, SVP of Publishing; DAVID BOGART, SVP of Business Affairs & Operations, Publishing & Partnership; C.B. CEBULSKI, VP of Brand Management & Development, Asia; DAVID GABRIEL, SVP of Sales & Marketing, Publishing; JEFF YOUNGQUIST, VP of Production & Special Projects; DAN CARR, Executive Director of Publishing Technology; ALEX MORALES, Director of Publishing Operations; SUSAN CRESPI, Production Manager; STAN LEE, Chairman Emeritus. For information regarding advertising in Marvel Comics or on Marvel.com, please contact Vit DeBellis, Integrated Sales Manager, at vdebellis@marvel.com. For Marvel subscription inquiries, please call 888-511-5480. **Manufactured between 10/21/2016 and 11/28/2016 by SOLISCO PRINTERS, SCOTT, QC, CANADA.**

10 9 8 7 6 5 4 3 2 1

MS. MARVEL

writer
G. WILLOW WILSON

artists
ADRIAN ALPHONA (#7, Flashback Art #8-11),
TAKESHI MIYAZAWA (#8-11)
& MIRKA ANDOLFO (#12)

color artists
IAN HERRING with IRMA KNIIVILA (#8)

letterer
VC's JOE CARAMAGNA

cover art
CAMERON STEWART

assistant editor
CHARLES BEACHAM

editor
SANA AMANAT

collection editor
JENNIFER GRÜNWALD
associate managing editor
KATERI WOODY
associate editor
SARAH BRUNSTAD
editor, special projects
MARK D. BEAZLEY
vp production & special projects
JEFF YOUNGQUIST
svp print, sales & marketing
DAVID GABRIEL

editor in chief
AXEL ALONSO
chief creative officer
JOE QUESADA
publisher
DAN BUCKLEY
executive producer
ALAN FINE

PREVIOUSLY

AFTER A STRANGE TERRIGEN MIST DESCENDED UPON JERSEY CITY, KAMALA KHAN GOT POLYMORPH POWERS AND BECAME THE ALL-NEW...

MS.MARVEL

AFTER A FEW CALAMITOUS MONTHS OF SOLO SUPER HERO WORK MADE A MESS OF HER PERSONAL LIFE, MS. MARVEL WAS FORCED TO CALL IN BACKUP TO SAVE HER CITY FROM THE MINDLESS MONSTERS SHE ACCIDENTALLY CREATED. KAMALA LEARNED THAT EVEN THE BEST HEROES REQUIRE A LITTLE HELP SOMETIMES.

WITH THINGS FINALLY SETTLING DOWN IN JERSEY CITY, AND HAVING FOUND SOME BALANCE IN HER LIFE, KAMALA'S ABLE TO ENJOY SOME OF THE SIMPLER PLEASURES OF BEING IN HIGH SCHOOL…

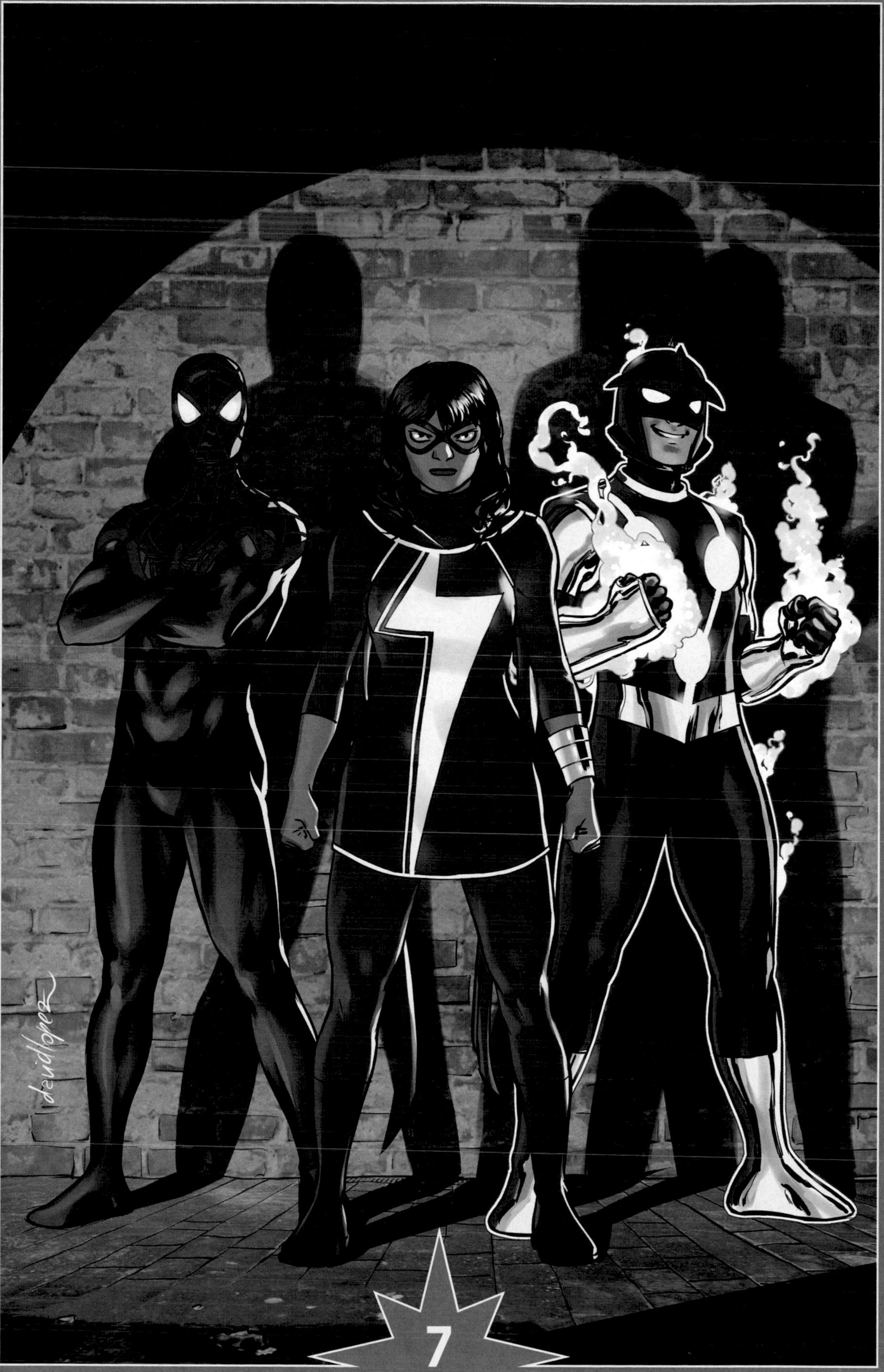
7

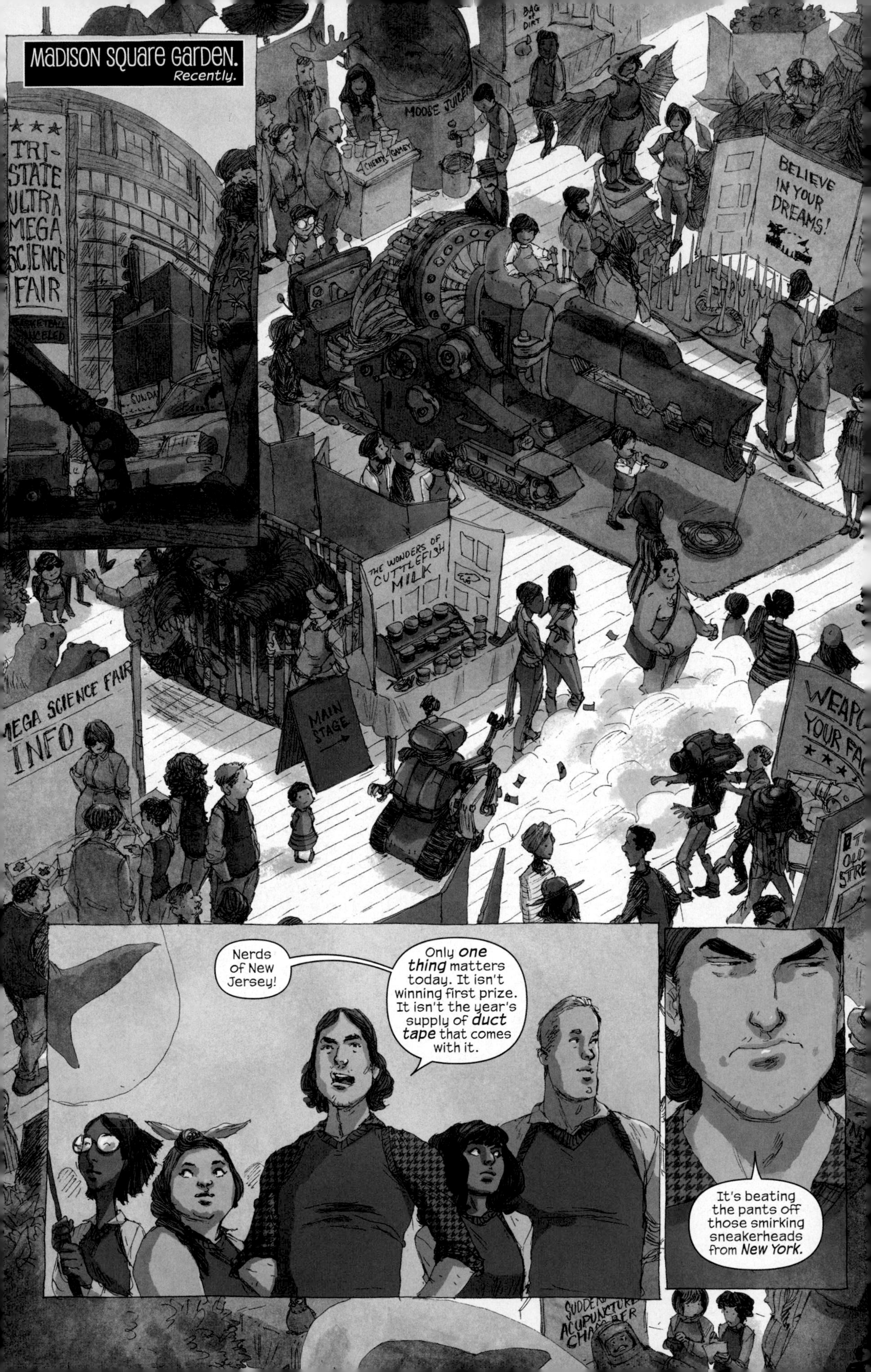
MADISON SQUARE GARDEN.
Recently.
TRI-STATE ULTRA MEGA SCIENCE FAIR
MOOSE JUICE
BAG of DIRT
BELIEVE IN YOUR DREAMS!
THE WONDERS OF CUTTLEFISH MILK
MAIN STAGE
MEGA SCIENCE FAIR INFO
Nerds of New Jersey!
Only one thing matters today. It isn't winning first prize. It isn't the year's supply of duct tape that comes with it.
It's beating the pants off those smirking sneakerheads from New York.

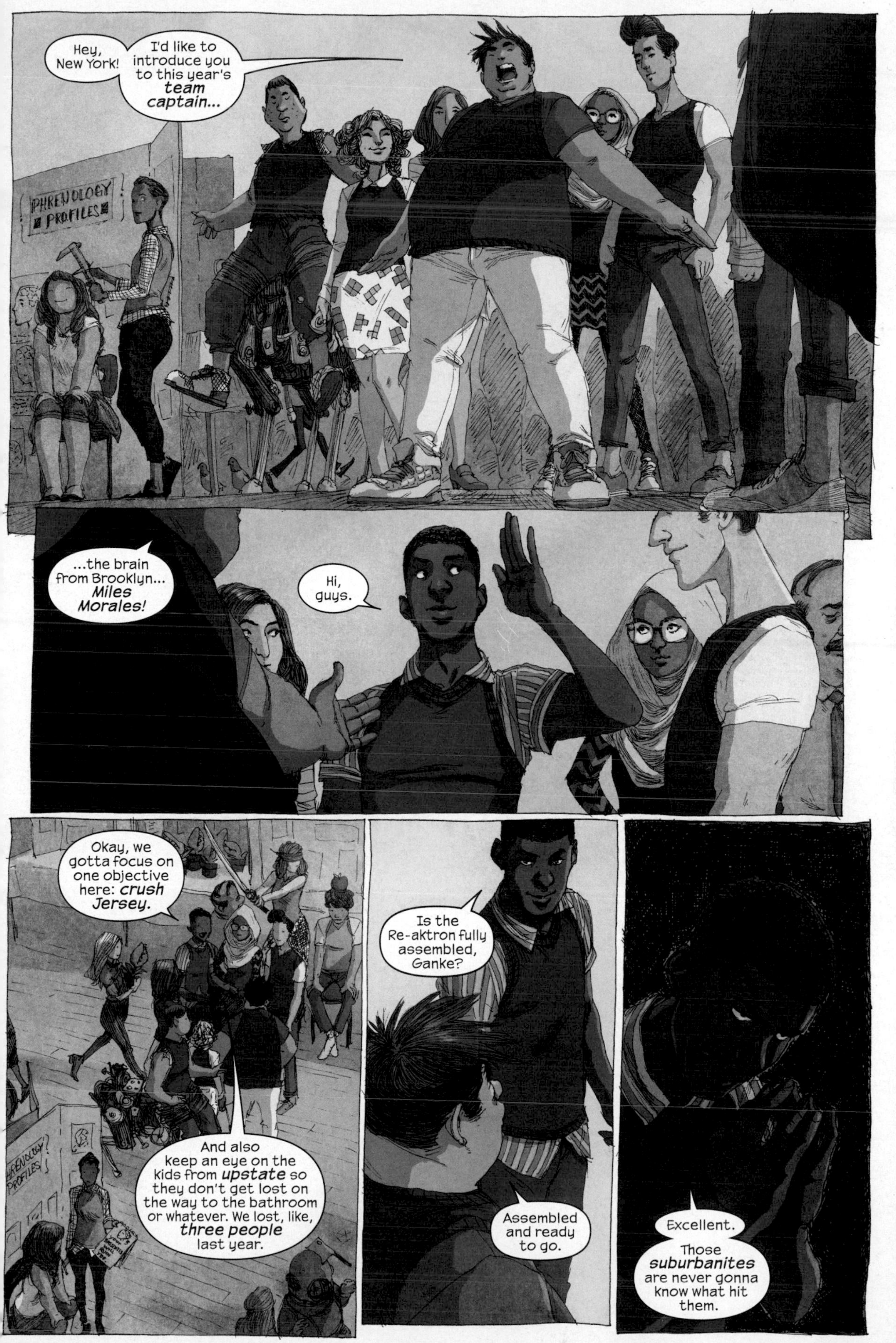
Hey, New York!
I'd like to introduce you to this year's team captain...
PHRENOLOGY PROFILES
...the brain from Brooklyn... Miles Morales!
Hi, guys.
Okay, we gotta focus on one objective here: crush Jersey.
And also keep an eye on the kids from upstate so they don't get lost on the way to the bathroom or whatever. We lost, like, three people last year.
PHRENOLOGY PROFILES
Is the Re-aktron fully assembled, Ganke?
Assembled and ready to go.
Excellent.
Those suburbanites are never gonna know what hit them.

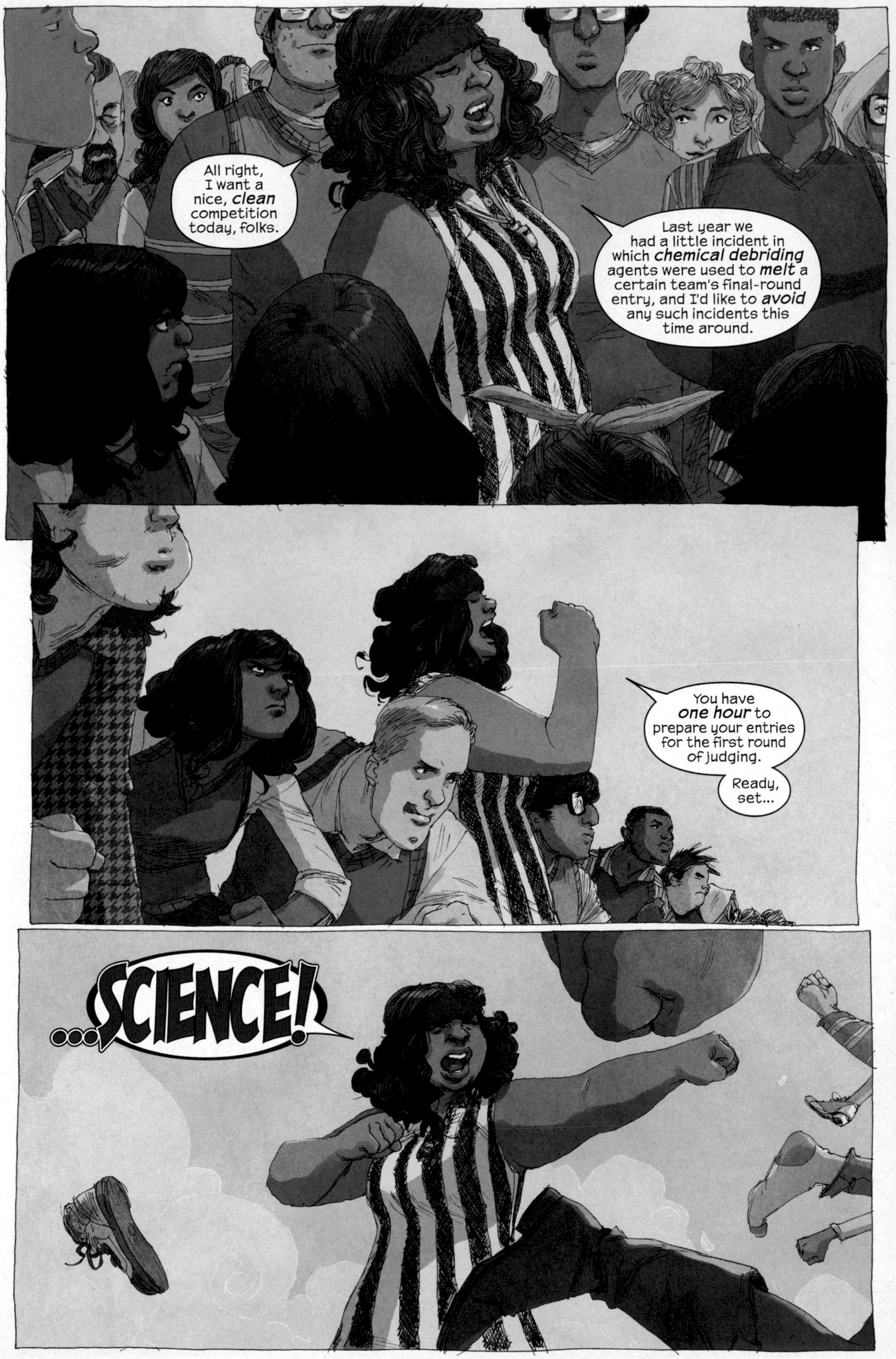
All right, I want a nice, clean competition today, folks.
Last year we had a little incident in which chemical debriding agents were used to melt a certain team's final-round entry, and I'd like to avoid any such incidents this time around.
You have one hour to prepare your entries for the first round of judging.
Ready, set...
...SCIENCE!

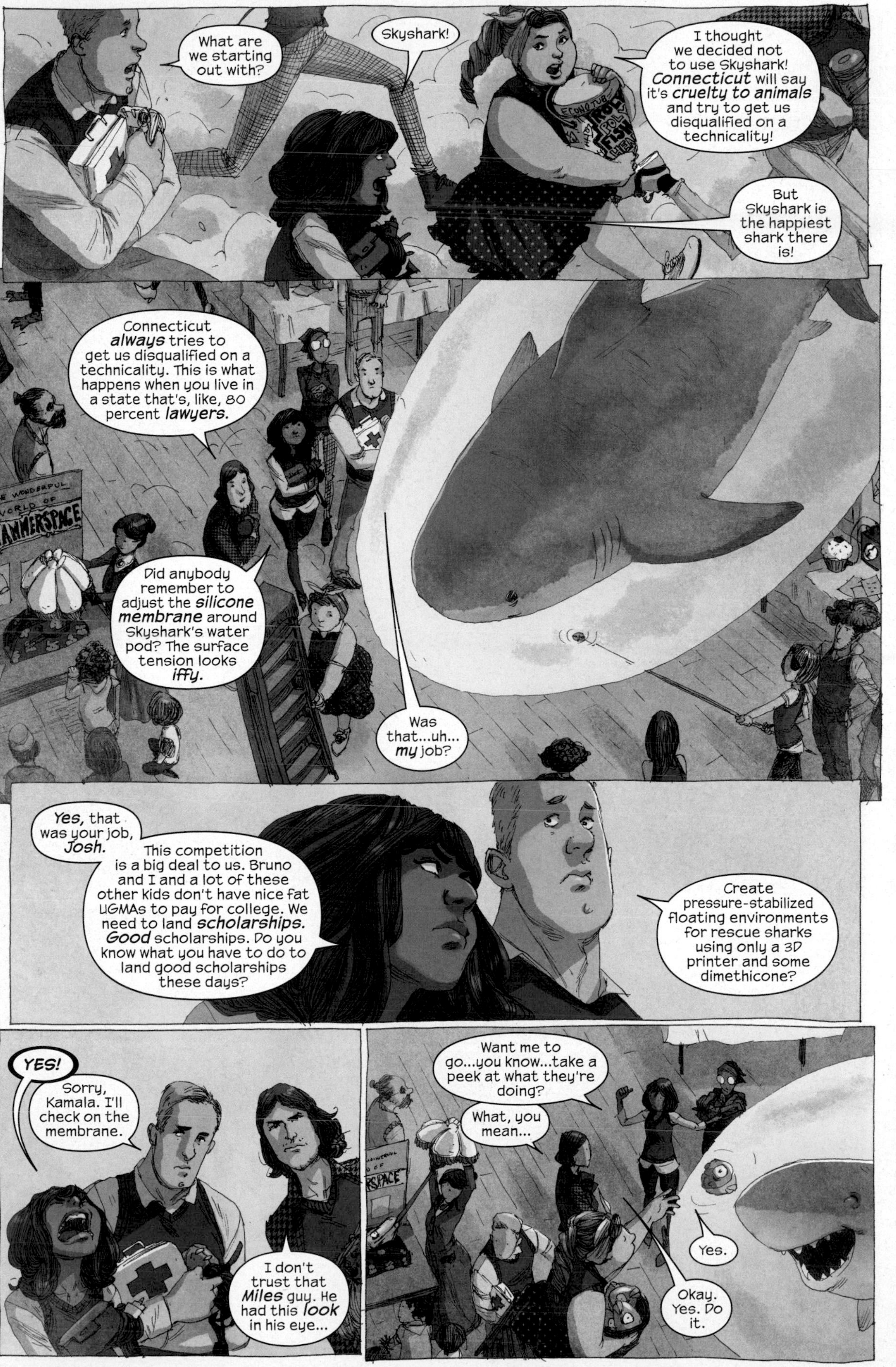
What are we starting out with?
Skyshark!
I thought we decided not to use Skyshark! Connecticut will say it's cruelty to animals and try to get us disqualified on a technicality!
But Skyshark is the happiest shark there is!
Connecticut always tries to get us disqualified on a technicality. This is what happens when you live in a state that's, like, 80 percent lawyers.
THE WONDERFUL WORLD OF HAMMERSPACE
Did anybody remember to adjust the silicone membrane around Skyshark's water pod? The surface tension looks iffy.
Was that...uh... my job?
Yes, that was your job, Josh.
This competition is a big deal to us. Bruno and I and a lot of these other kids don't have nice fat UGMAs to pay for college. We need to land scholarships. Good scholarships. Do you know what you have to do to land good scholarships these days?
Create pressure-stabilized floating environments for rescue sharks using only a 3D printer and some dimethicone?
YES!
Sorry, Kamala. I'll check on the membrane.
I don't trust that Miles guy. He had this look in his eye...
Want me to go...you know...take a peek at what they're doing?
What, you mean...
Yes.
Okay. Yes. Do it.

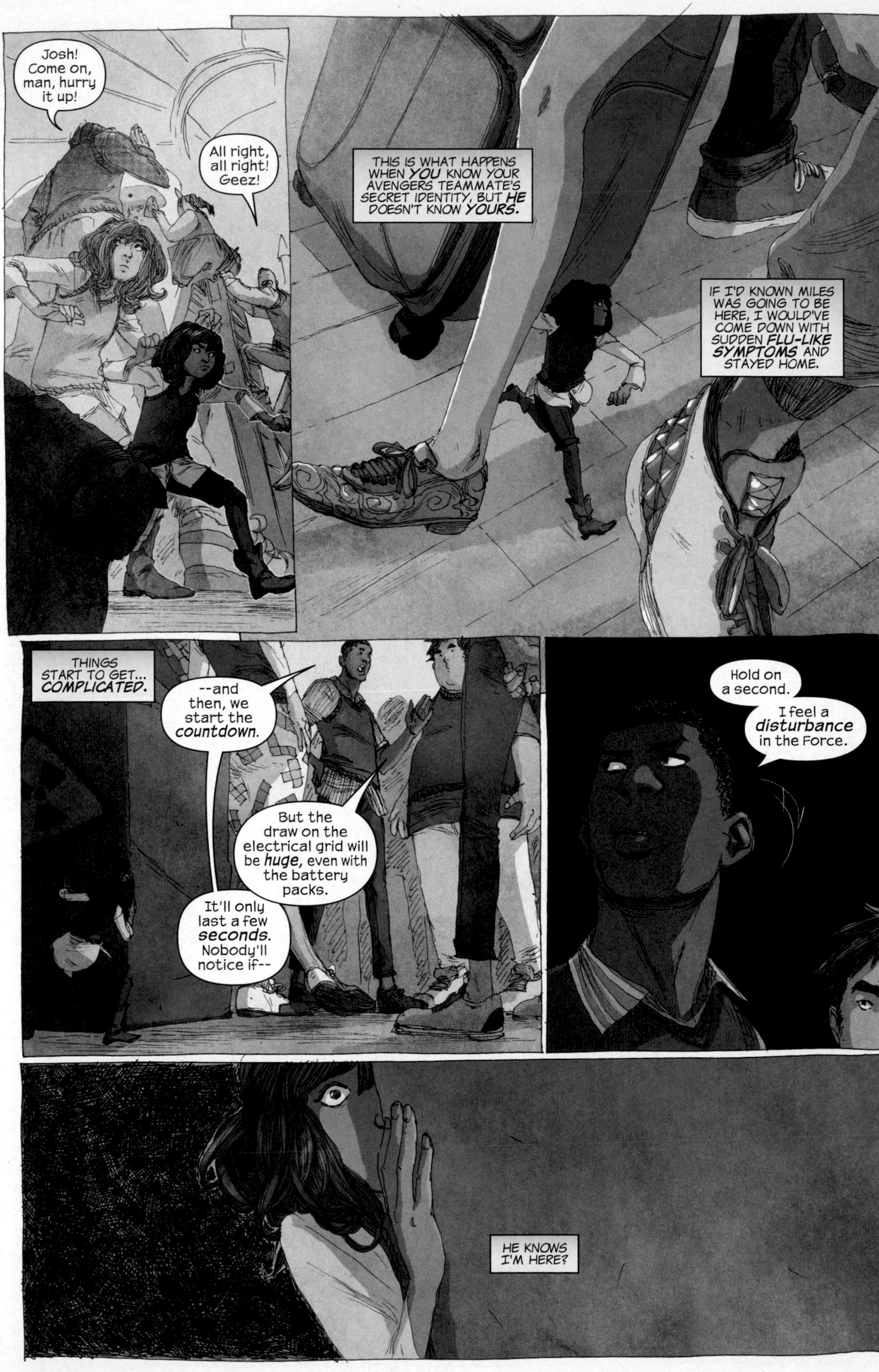
Josh! Come on, man, hurry it up!
All right, all right! Geez!
THIS IS WHAT HAPPENS WHEN YOU KNOW YOUR AVENGERS TEAMMATE'S SECRET IDENTITY, BUT HE DOESN'T KNOW YOURS.
IF I'D KNOWN MILES WAS GOING TO BE HERE, I WOULD'VE COME DOWN WITH SUDDEN FLU-LIKE SYMPTOMS AND STAYED HOME.
THINGS START TO GET... COMPLICATED.
--and then, we start the countdown.
But the draw on the electrical grid will be huge, even with the battery packs.
It'll only last a few seconds. Nobody'll notice if--
Hold on a second.
I feel a disturbance in the Force.
HE KNOWS I'M HERE?

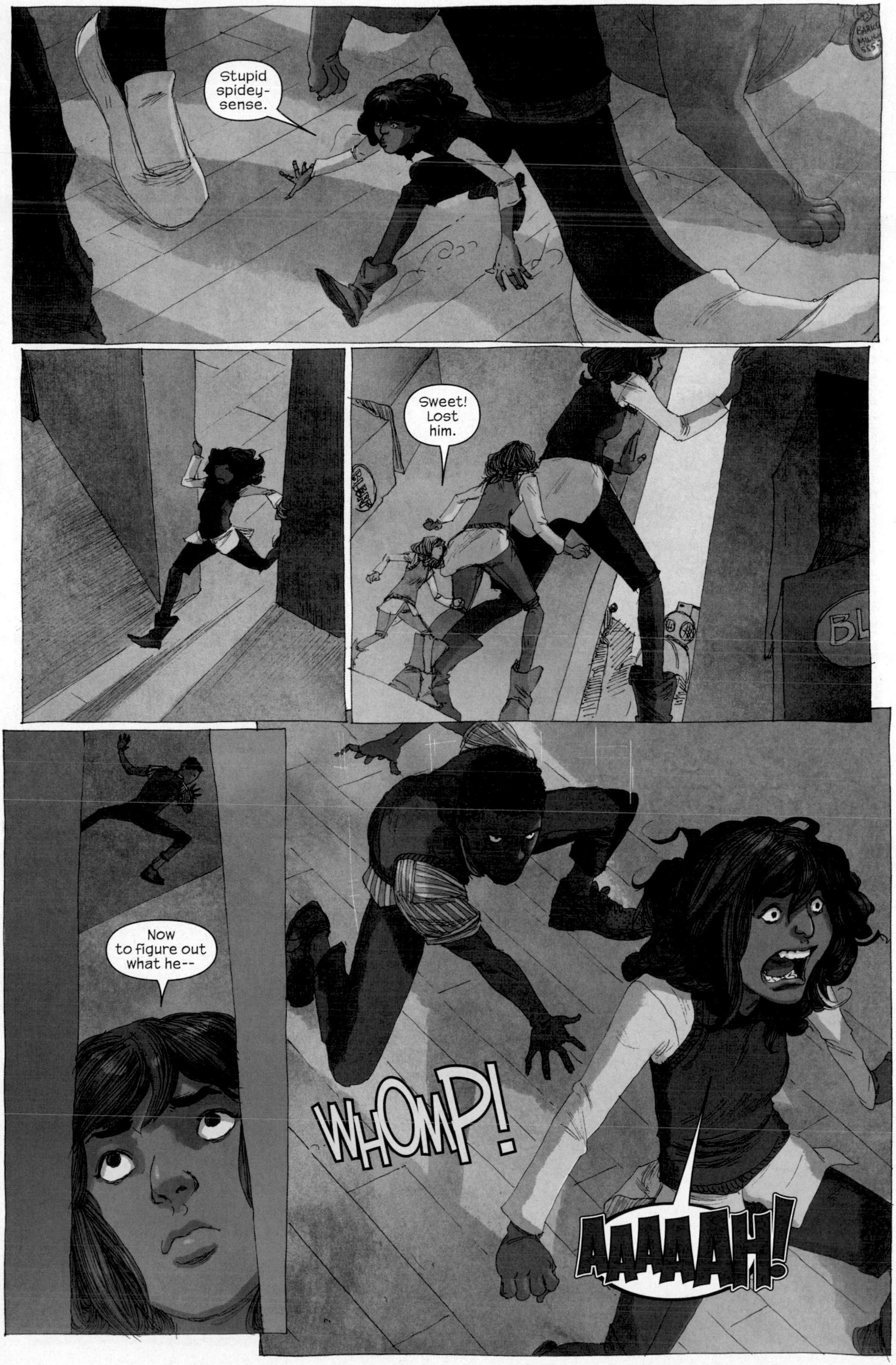
Stupid spidey-sense.
Sweet! Lost him.
Now to figure out what he--
WHOMP!
AAAAAH!

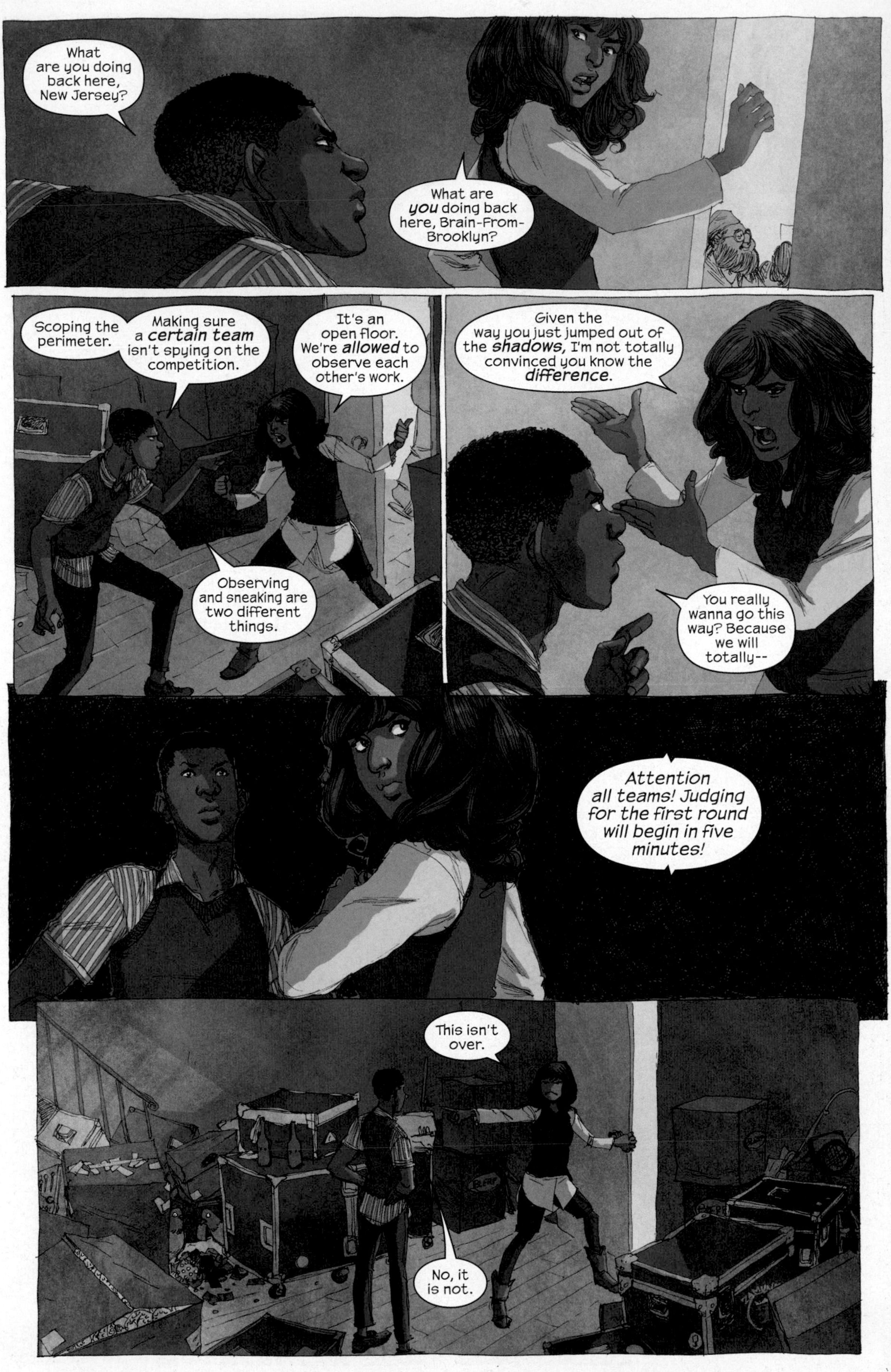
What are you doing back here, New Jersey?
What are you doing back here, Brain-From-Brooklyn?
Scoping the perimeter.
Making sure a certain team isn't spying on the competition.
It's an open floor. We're allowed to observe each other's work.
Observing and sneaking are two different things.
Given the way you just jumped out of the shadows, I'm not totally convinced you know the difference.
You really wanna go this way? Because we will totally--
Attention all teams! Judging for the first round will begin in five minutes!
This isn't over.
No, it is not.

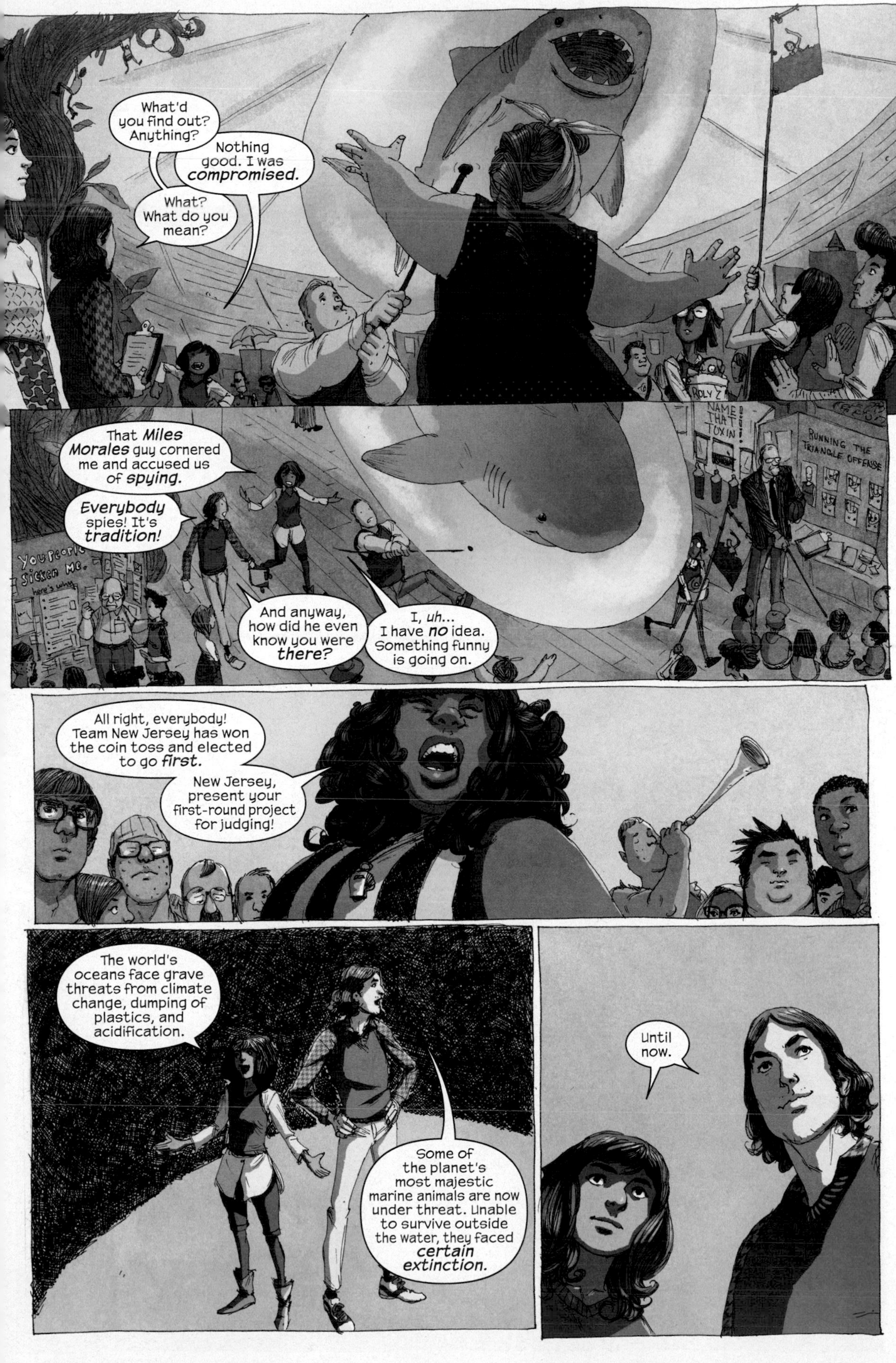

What'd you find out? Anything?
Nothing good. I was compromised.
What? What do you mean?
That Miles Morales guy cornered me and accused us of spying.
Everybody spies! It's tradition!
And anyway, how did he even know you were there?
I, uh... I have no idea. Something funny is going on.
NAME THAT TOXIN
RUNNING THE TRIANGLE OFFENSE
You people sicken me. here's why
ROLY Z
All right, everybody! Team New Jersey has won the coin toss and elected to go first.
New Jersey, present your first-round project for judging!
The world's oceans face grave threats from climate change, dumping of plastics, and acidification.
Some of the planet's most majestic marine animals are now under threat. Unable to survive outside the water, they faced certain extinction.
Until now.

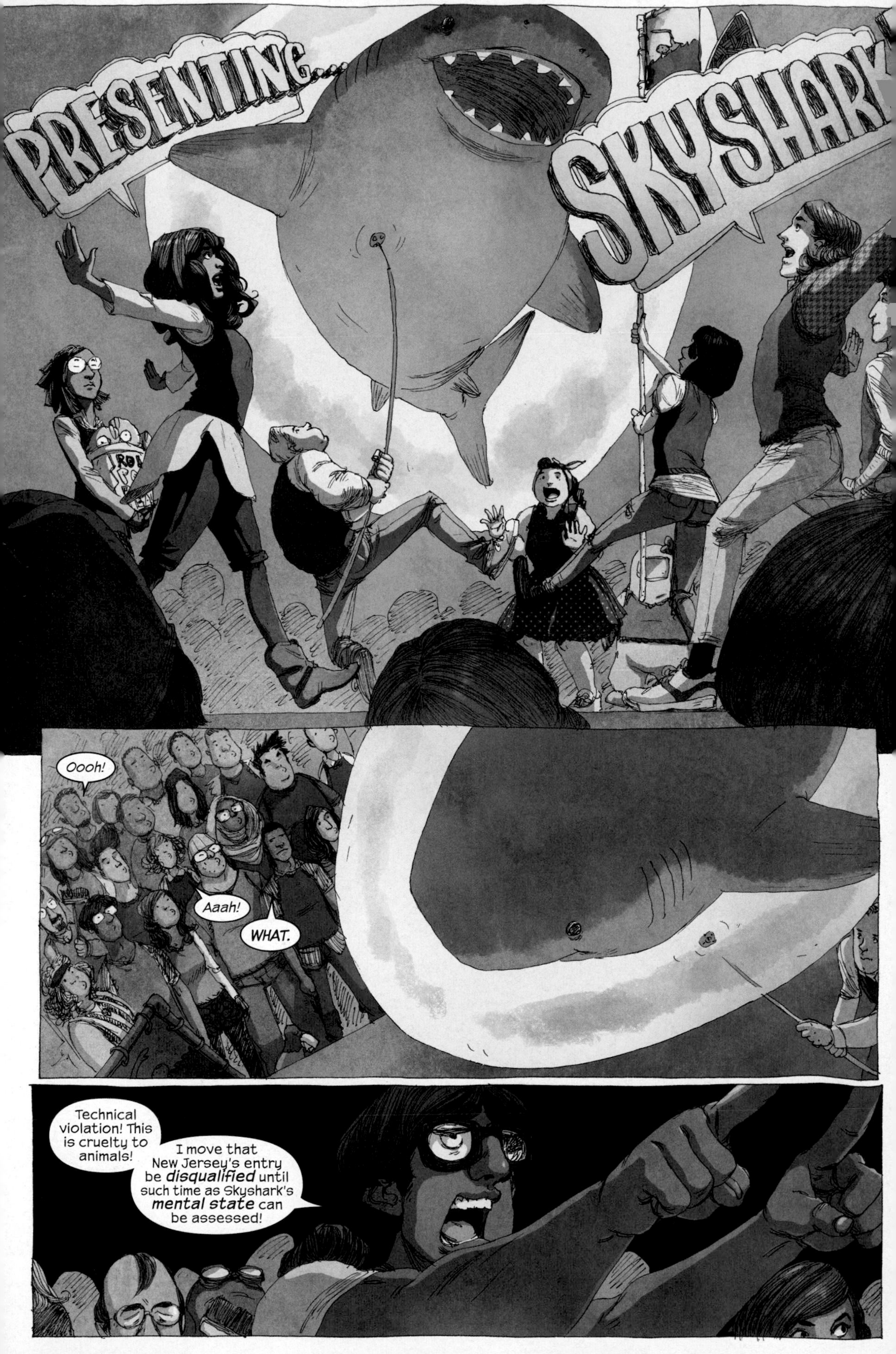
PRESENTING...
SKYSHARK!
Oooh!
Aaah!
WHAT.
Technical violation! This is cruelty to animals!
I move that New Jersey's entry be *disqualified* until such time as Skyshark's *mental state* can be assessed!

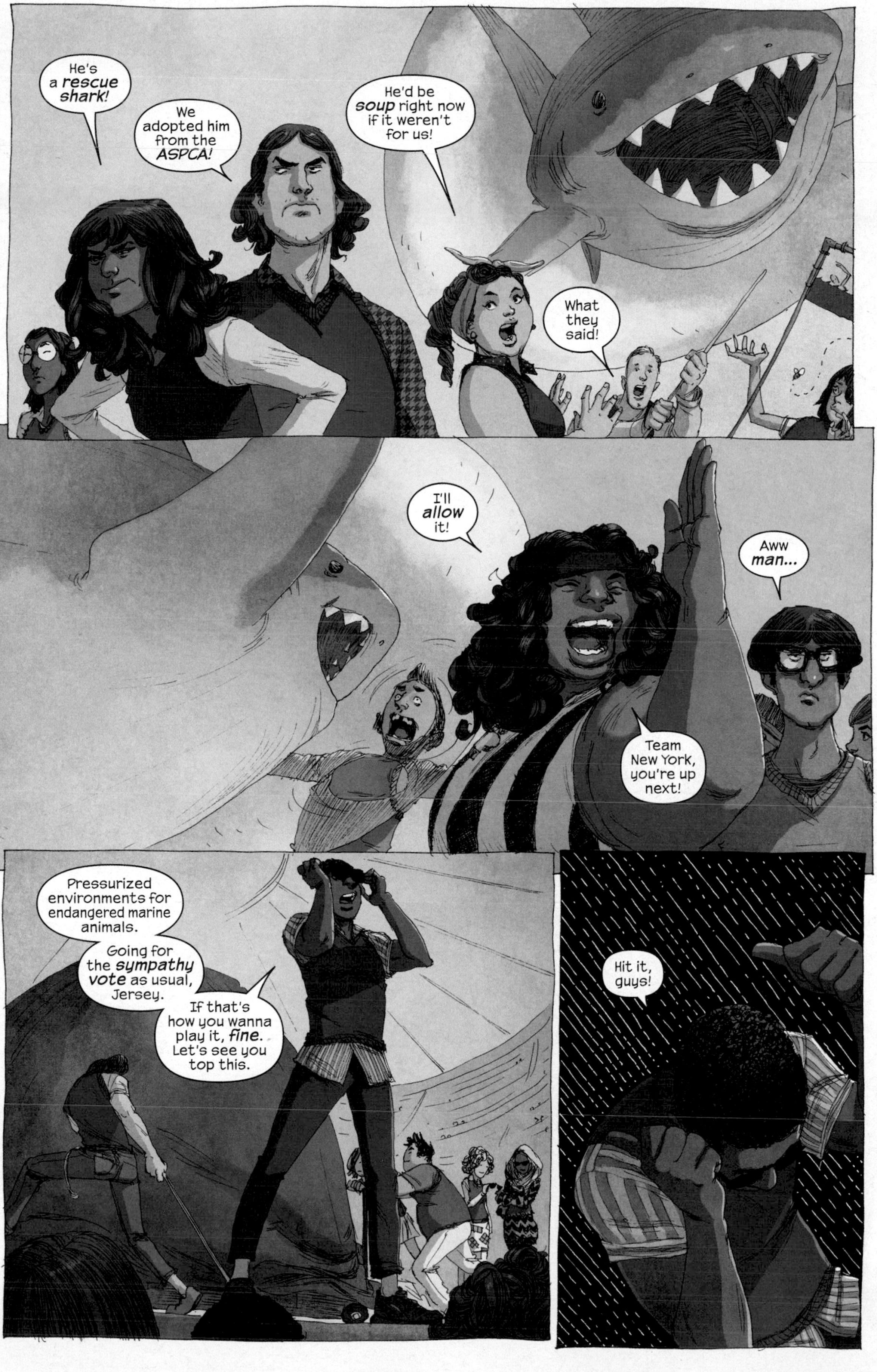
He's a rescue shark!
We adopted him from the ASPCA!
He'd be soup right now if it weren't for us!
What they said!
I'll allow it!
Aww man...
Team New York, you're up next!
Pressurized environments for endangered marine animals.
Going for the sympathy vote as usual, Jersey.
If that's how you wanna play it, fine. Let's see you top this.
Hit it, guys!

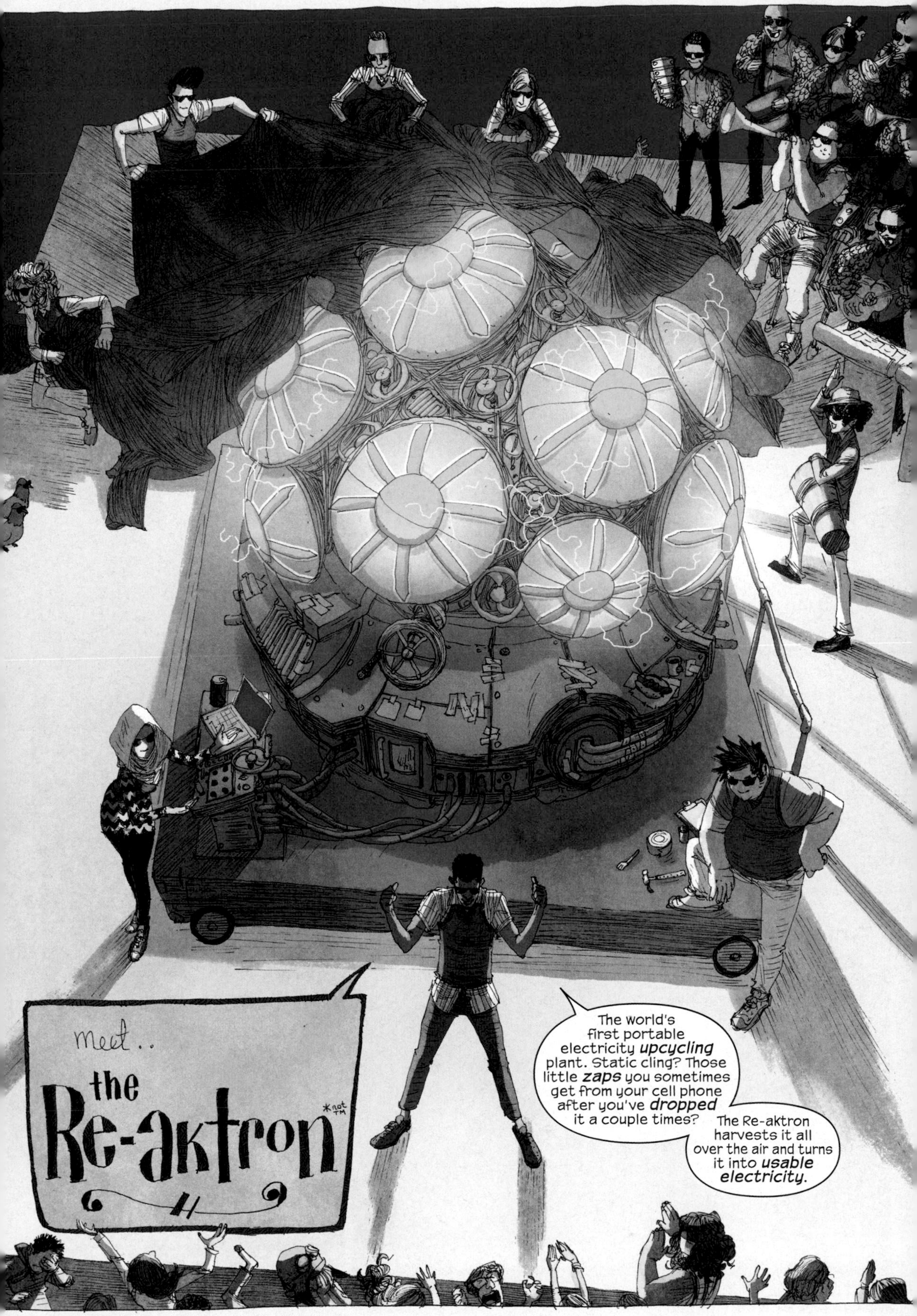
Meet..
the
Re-aktron
*not TM
The world's first portable electricity upcycling plant. Static cling? Those little zaps you sometimes get from your cell phone after you've dropped it a couple times?
The Re-aktron harvests it all over the air and turns it into usable electricity.

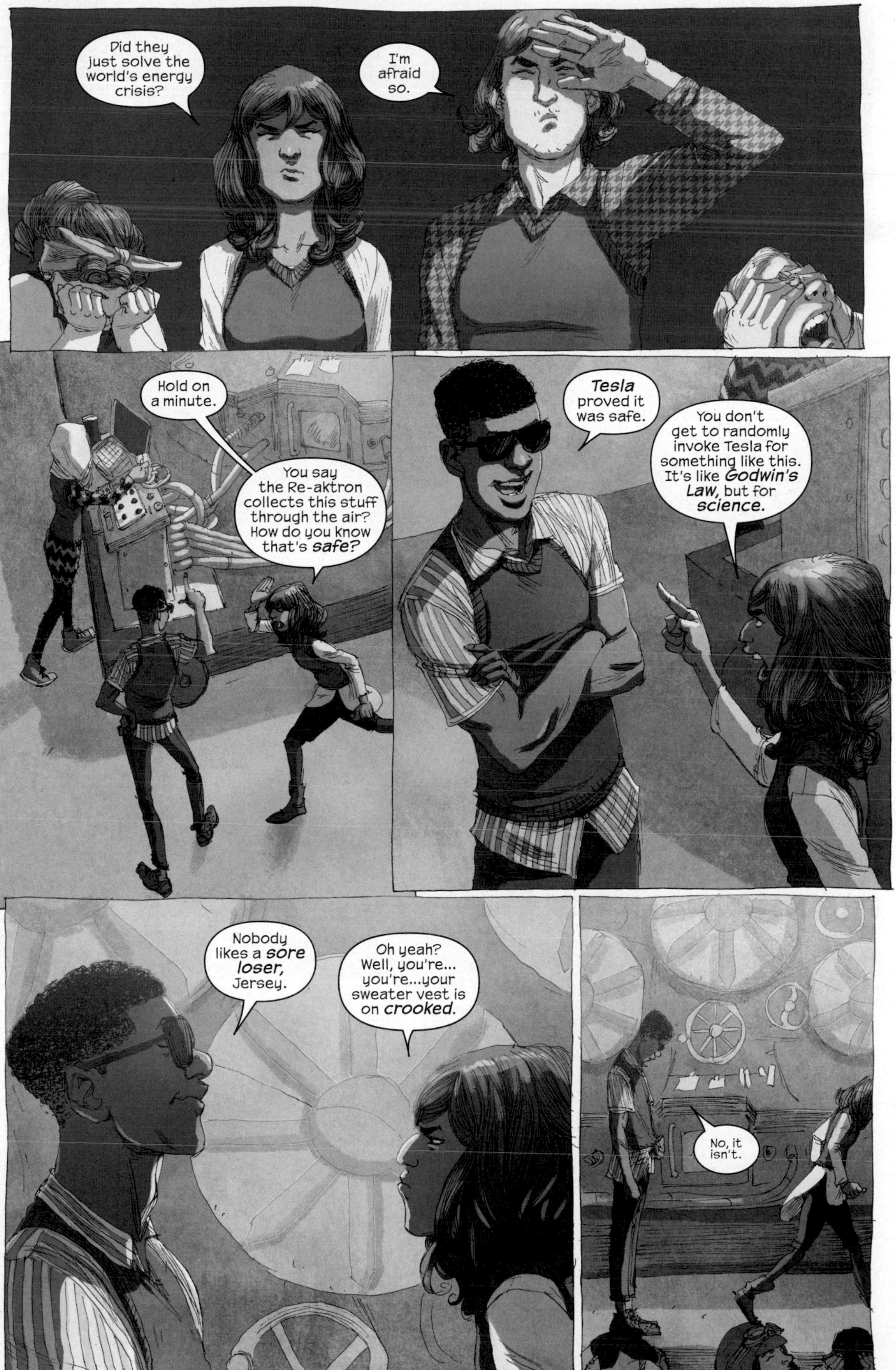
Did they just solve the world's energy crisis?
I'm afraid so.
Hold on a minute.
You say the Re-aktron collects this stuff through the air? How do you know that's *safe?*
Tesla proved it was safe.
You don't get to randomly invoke Tesla for something like this. It's like *Godwin's Law,* but for *science.*
Nobody likes a *sore loser,* Jersey.
Oh yeah? Well, you're... you're...your sweater vest is on *crooked.*
No, it isn't.

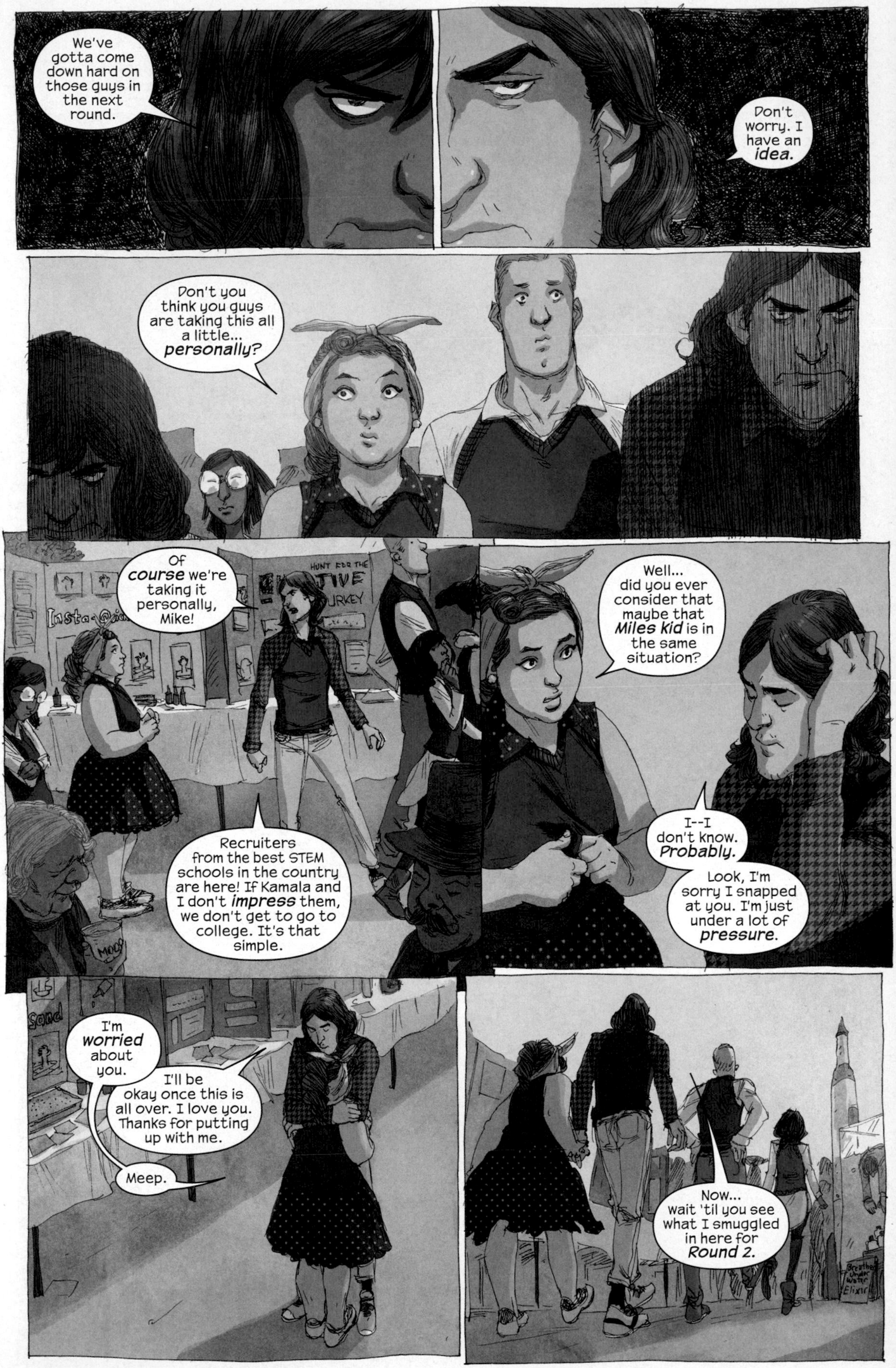
We've gotta come down hard on those guys in the next round.
Don't worry. I have an *idea.*
Don't you think you guys are taking this all a little... *personally?*
Of *course* we're taking it personally, Mike!
Recruiters from the best STEM schools in the country are here! If Kamala and I don't *impress* them, we don't get to go to college. It's that simple.
Well... did you ever consider that maybe that *Miles kid* is in the same situation?
I--I don't know. *Probably.*
Look, I'm sorry I snapped at you. I'm just under a lot of *pressure.*
I'm *worried* about you.
I'll be okay once this is all over. I love you. Thanks for putting up with me.
Meep.
Now... wait 'til you see what I smuggled in here for *Round 2.*

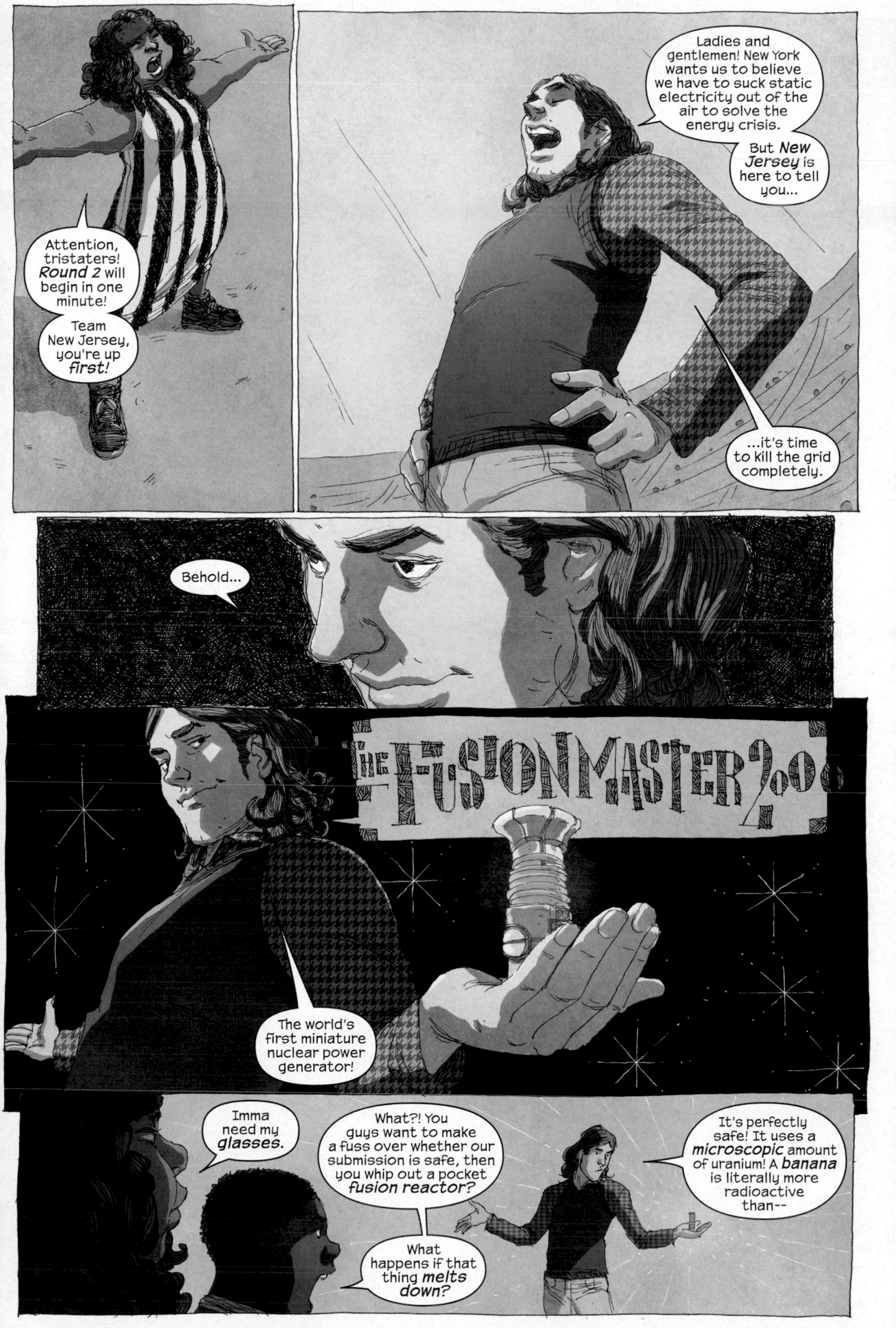
Attention, tristaters! *Round 2* will begin in one minute!
Team New Jersey, you're up *first!*
Ladies and gentlemen! New York wants us to believe we have to suck static electricity out of the air to solve the energy crisis.
But *New Jersey* is here to tell you...
...it's time to kill the grid completely.
Behold...
THE FUSIONMASTER 2.0
The world's first miniature nuclear power generator!
Imma need my *glasses.*
What?! You guys want to make a fuss over whether our submission is safe, then you whip out a pocket *fusion reactor?*
What happens if that thing *melts down?*
It's perfectly safe! It uses a *microscopic* amount of uranium! A *banana* is literally more radioactive than--

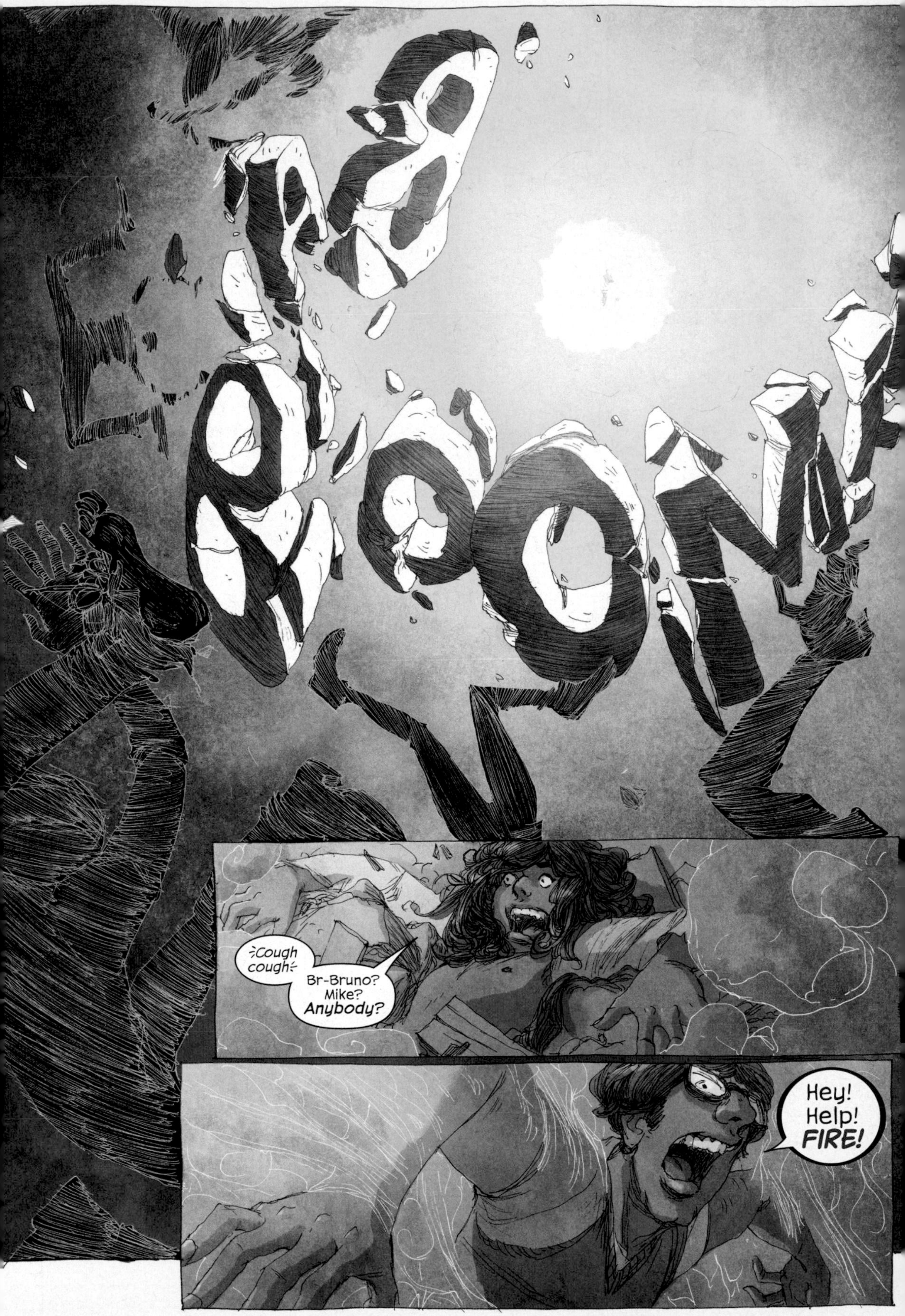
Cough cough
Br-Bruno? Mike? *Anybody?*
Hey! Help! ***FIRE!***

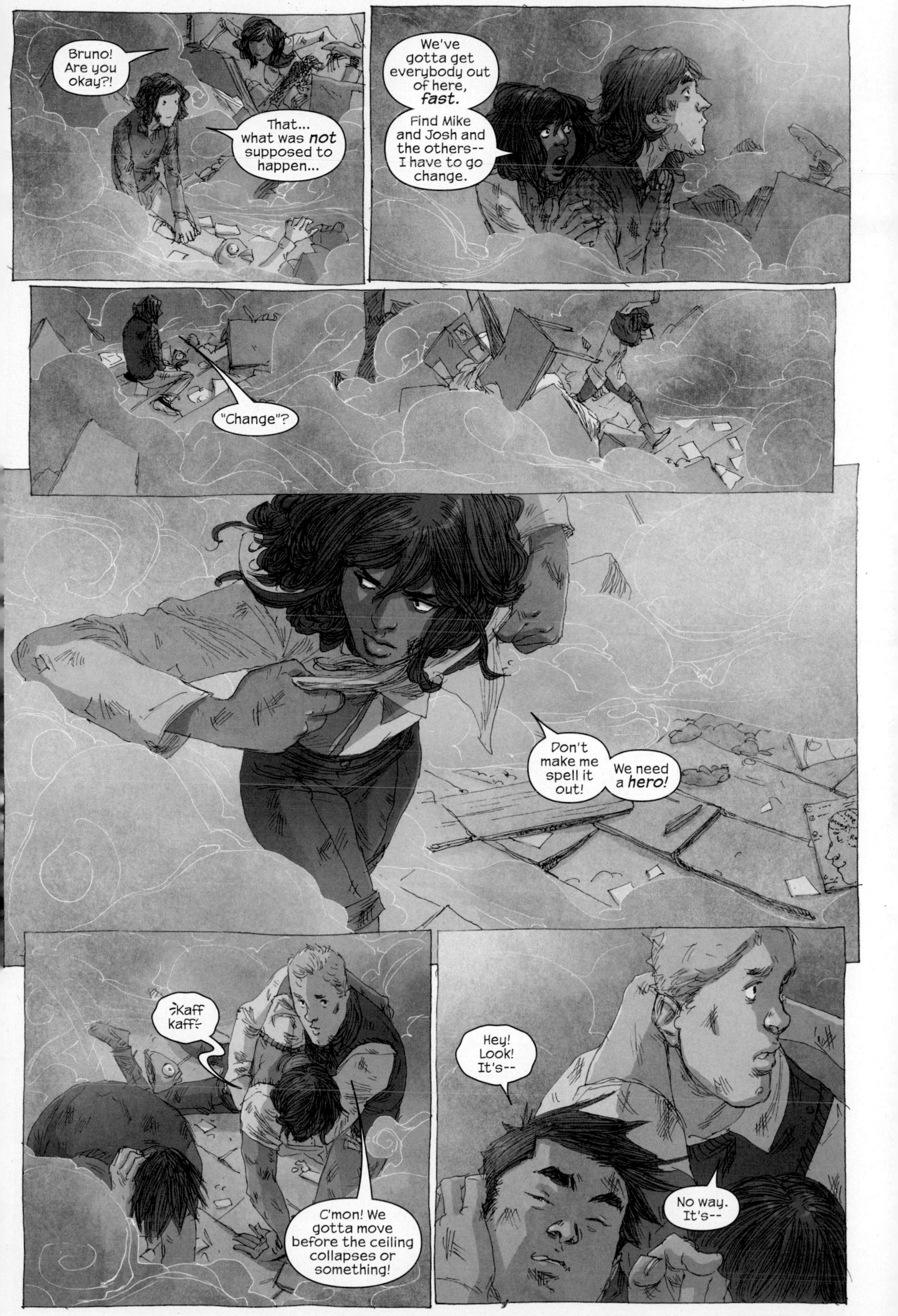

Bruno! Are you okay?!
That... what was not supposed to happen...
We've gotta get everybody out of here, fast.
Find Mike and Josh and the others-- I have to go change.
"Change"?
Don't make me spell it out!
We need a hero!
-Kaff kaff-
C'mon! We gotta move before the ceiling collapses or something!
Hey! Look! It's--
No way. It's--

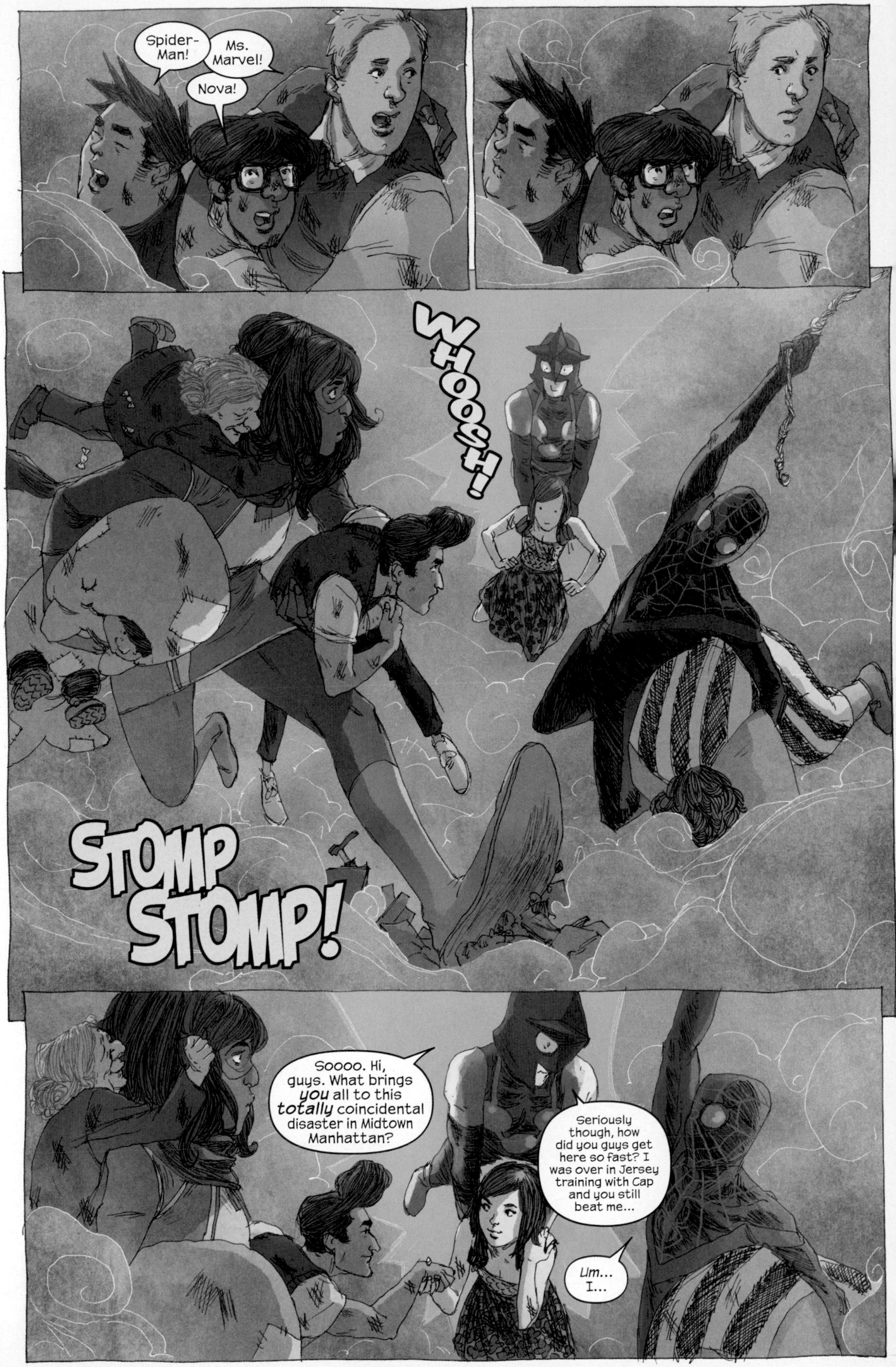
Spider-Man!
Ms. Marvel!
Nova!
WHOOSH!
STOMP STOMP!
Soooo. Hi, guys. What brings *you* all to this *totally* coincidental disaster in Midtown Manhattan?
Seriously though, how did you guys get here so fast? I was over in Jersey training with Cap and you still beat me...
Um... I...

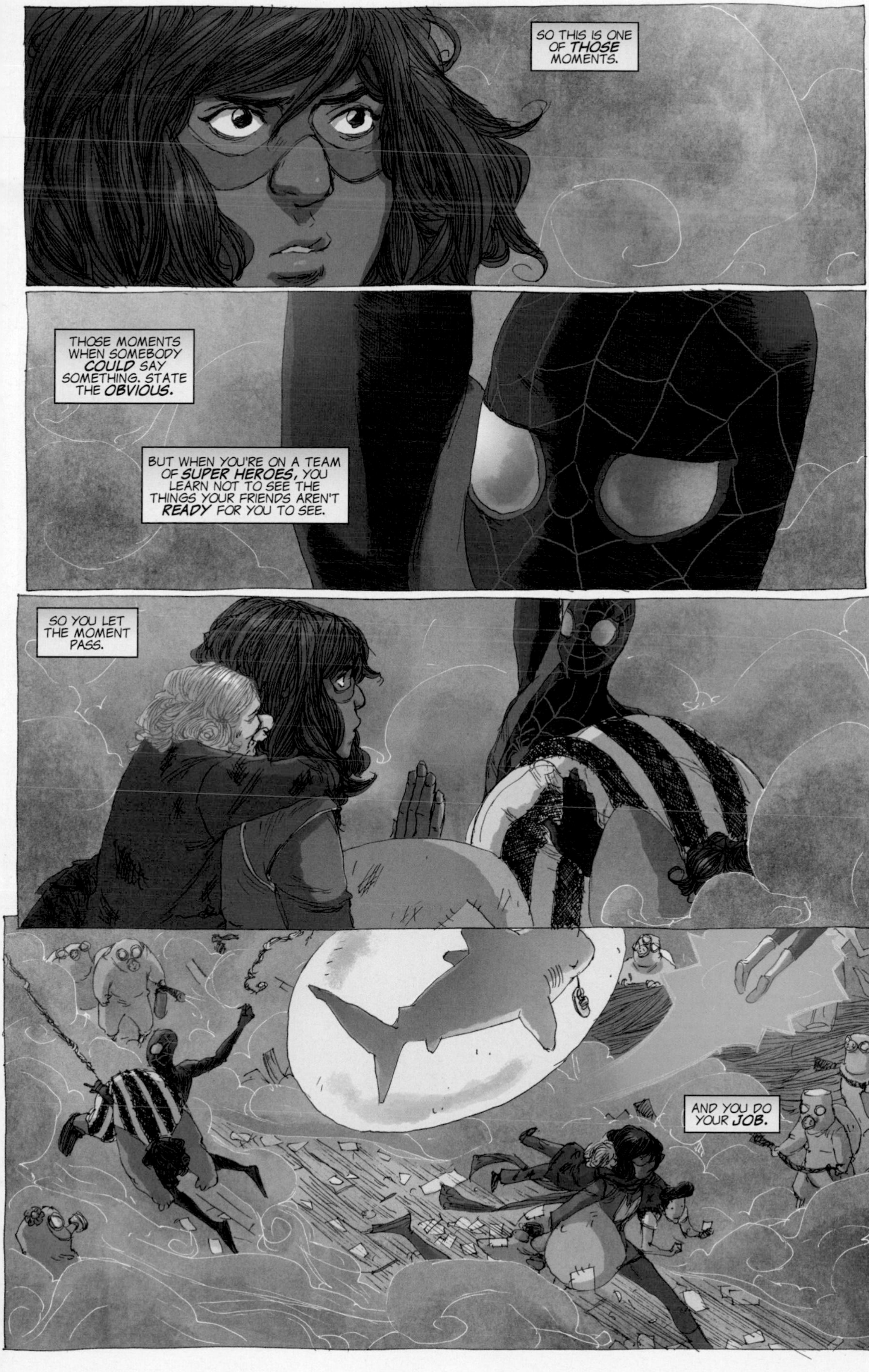
SO THIS IS ONE OF THOSE MOMENTS.
THOSE MOMENTS WHEN SOMEBODY COULD SAY SOMETHING. STATE THE OBVIOUS.
BUT WHEN YOU'RE ON A TEAM OF SUPER HEROES, YOU LEARN NOT TO SEE THE THINGS YOUR FRIENDS AREN'T READY FOR YOU TO SEE.
SO YOU LET THE MOMENT PASS.
AND YOU DO YOUR JOB.

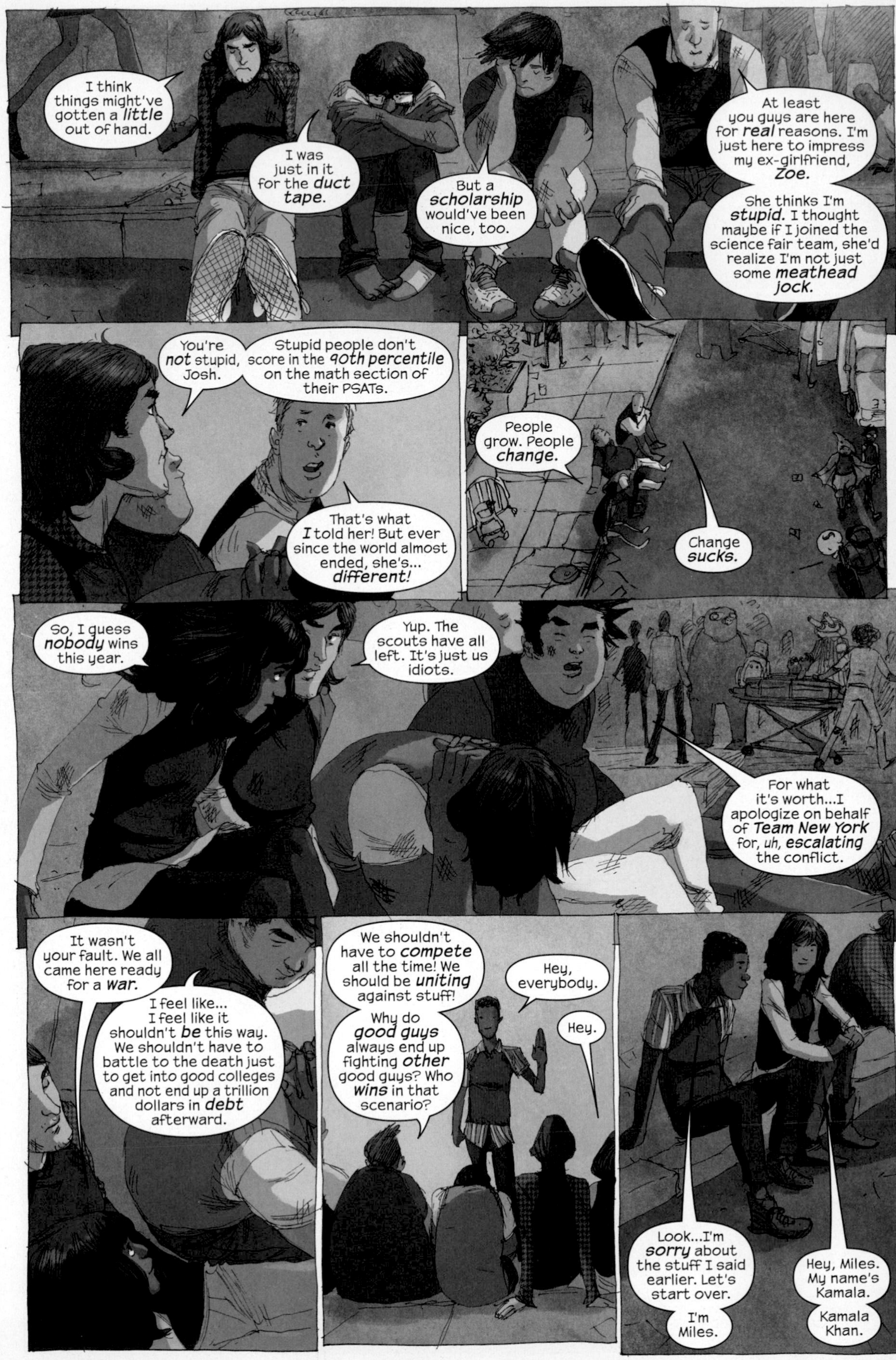
I think things might've gotten a *little* out of hand.
I was just in it for the *duct tape*.
But a *scholarship* would've been nice, too.
At least you guys are here for *real* reasons. I'm just here to impress my ex-girlfriend, *Zoe.*
She thinks I'm *stupid.* I thought maybe if I joined the science fair team, she'd realize I'm not just some *meathead jock.*
You're *not* stupid, Josh.
Stupid people don't score in the *90th percentile* on the math section of their PSATs.
That's what *I* told her! But ever since the world almost ended, she's... *different!*
People grow. People *change.*
Change *sucks.*
So, I guess *nobody* wins this year.
Yup. The scouts have all left. It's just us idiots.
For what it's worth...I apologize on behalf of *Team New York* for, *uh, escalating* the conflict.
It wasn't your fault. We all came here ready for a *war.*
I feel like... I feel like it shouldn't *be* this way. We shouldn't have to battle to the death just to get into good colleges and not end up a trillion dollars in *debt* afterward.
We shouldn't have to *compete* all the time! We should be *uniting* against stuff!
Why do *good guys* always end up fighting *other* good guys? Who *wins* in that scenario?
Hey, everybody.
Hey.
Look...I'm *sorry* about the stuff I said earlier. Let's start over.
I'm Miles.
Hey, Miles. My name's Kamala.
Kamala Khan.

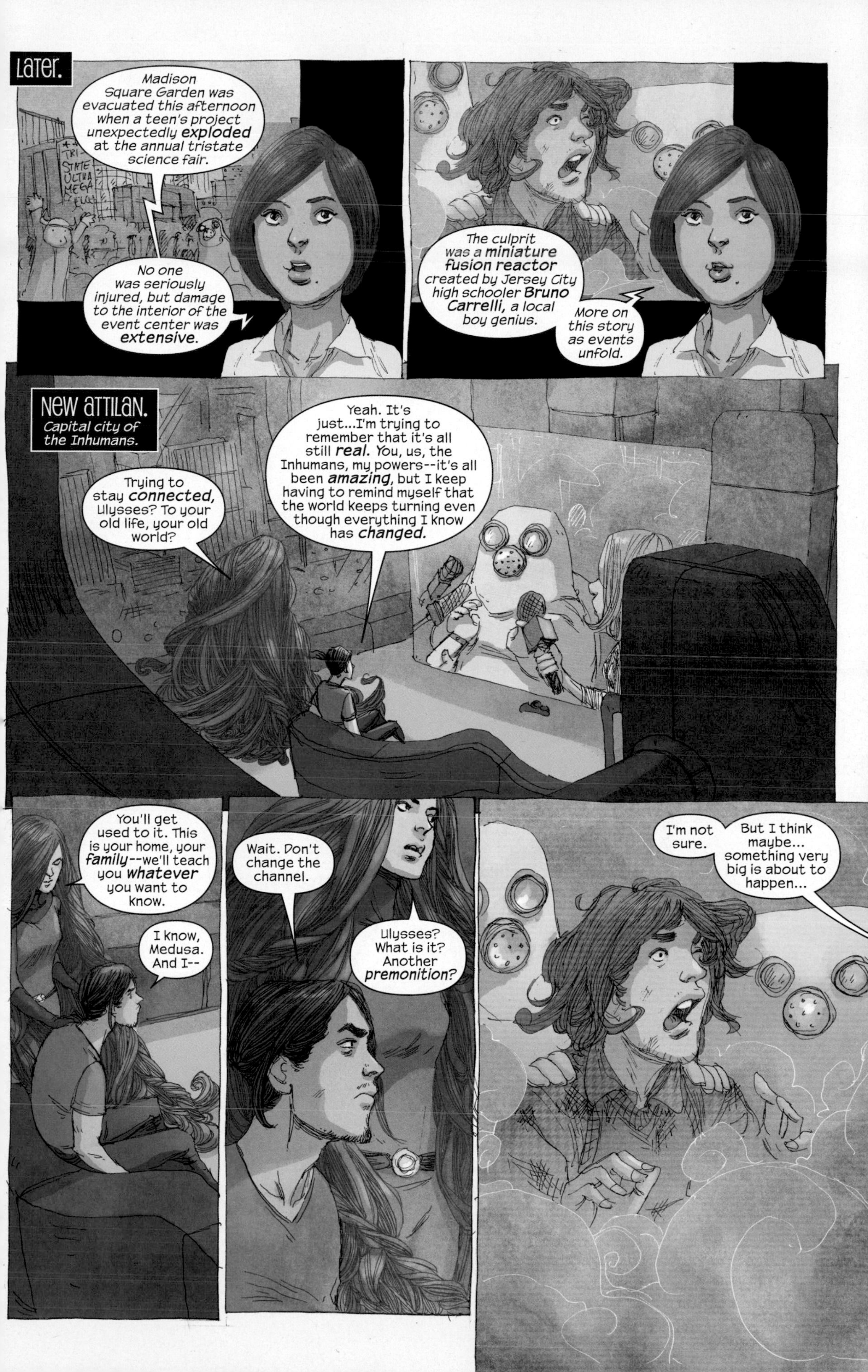
LATER.
Madison Square Garden was evacuated this afternoon when a teen's project unexpectedly exploded at the annual tristate science fair.
No one was seriously injured, but damage to the interior of the event center was extensive.
The culprit was a miniature fusion reactor created by Jersey City high schooler Bruno Carrelli, a local boy genius.
More on this story as events unfold.
NEW ATTILAN. Capital city of the Inhumans.
Trying to stay connected, Ulysses? To your old life, your old world?
Yeah. It's just...I'm trying to remember that it's all still real. You, us, the Inhumans, my powers--it's all been amazing, but I keep having to remind myself that the world keeps turning even though everything I know has changed.
You'll get used to it. This is your home, your family--we'll teach you whatever you want to know.
I know, Medusa. And I--
Wait. Don't change the channel.
Ulysses? What is it? Another premonition?
I'm not sure.
But I think maybe... something very big is about to happen...

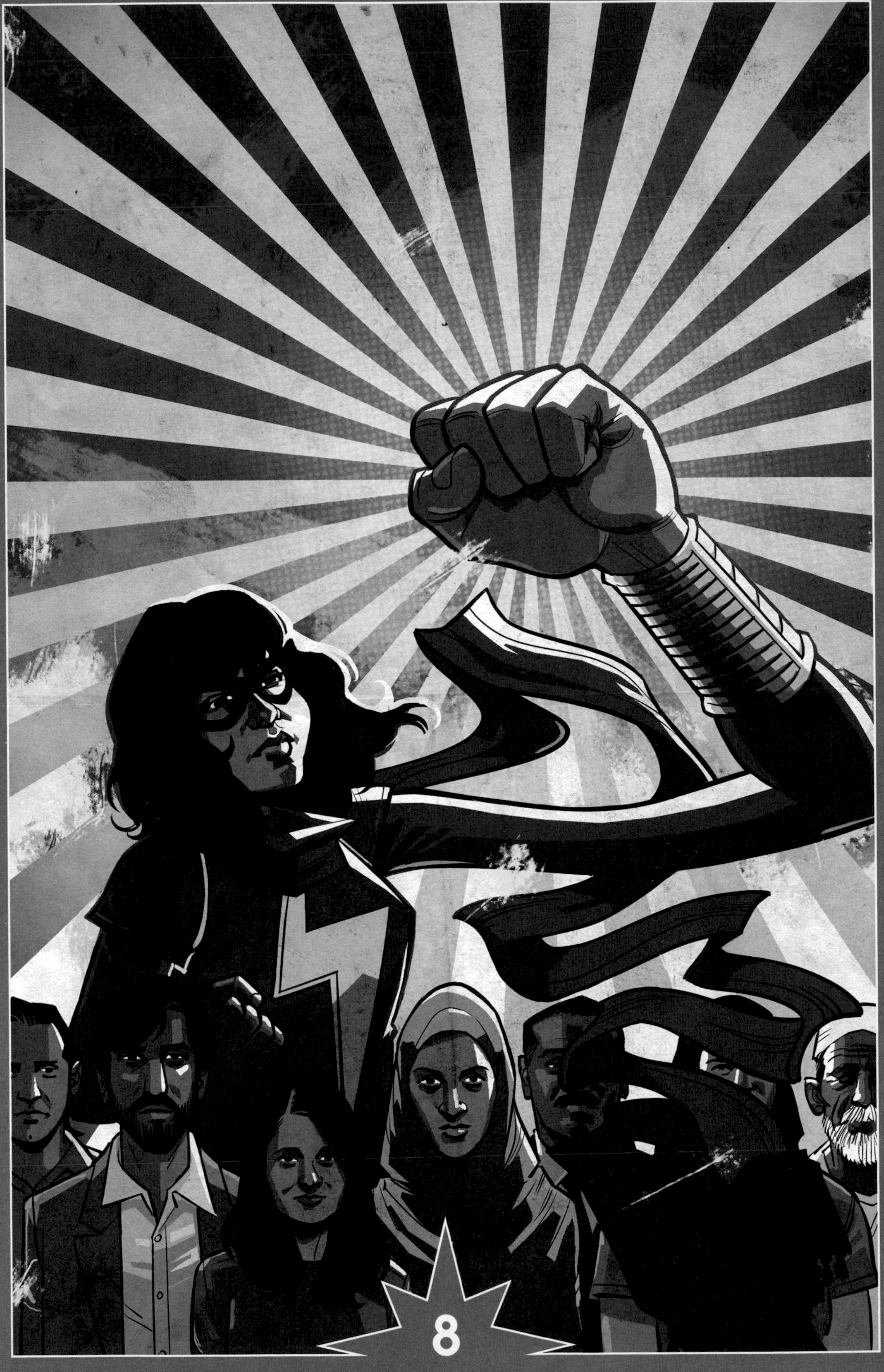
8

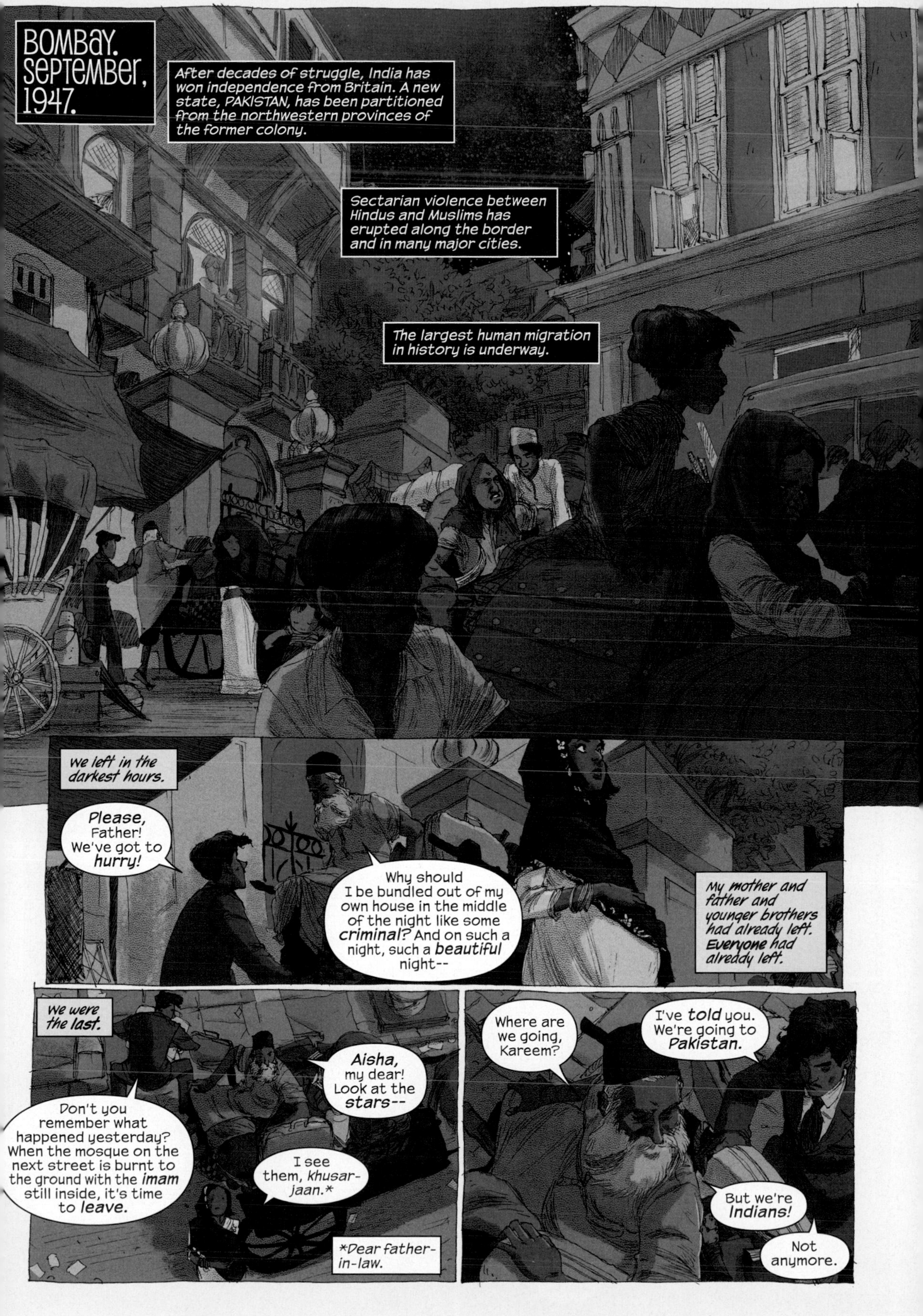

BOMBAY. SEPTEMBER, 1947.
After decades of struggle, India has won independence from Britain. A new state, PAKISTAN, has been partitioned from the northwestern provinces of the former colony.
Sectarian violence between Hindus and Muslims has erupted along the border and in many major cities.
The largest human migration in history is underway.
We left in the darkest hours.
Please, Father! We've got to hurry!
Why should I be bundled out of my own house in the middle of the night like some criminal? And on such a night, such a beautiful night--
My mother and father and younger brothers had already left. Everyone had already left.
We were the last.
Aisha, my dear! Look at the stars--
Don't you remember what happened yesterday? When the mosque on the next street is burnt to the ground with the imam still inside, it's time to leave.
I see them, khusar-jaan.*
*Dear father-in-law.
Where are we going, Kareem?
I've told you. We're going to Pakistan.
But we're Indians!
Not anymore.

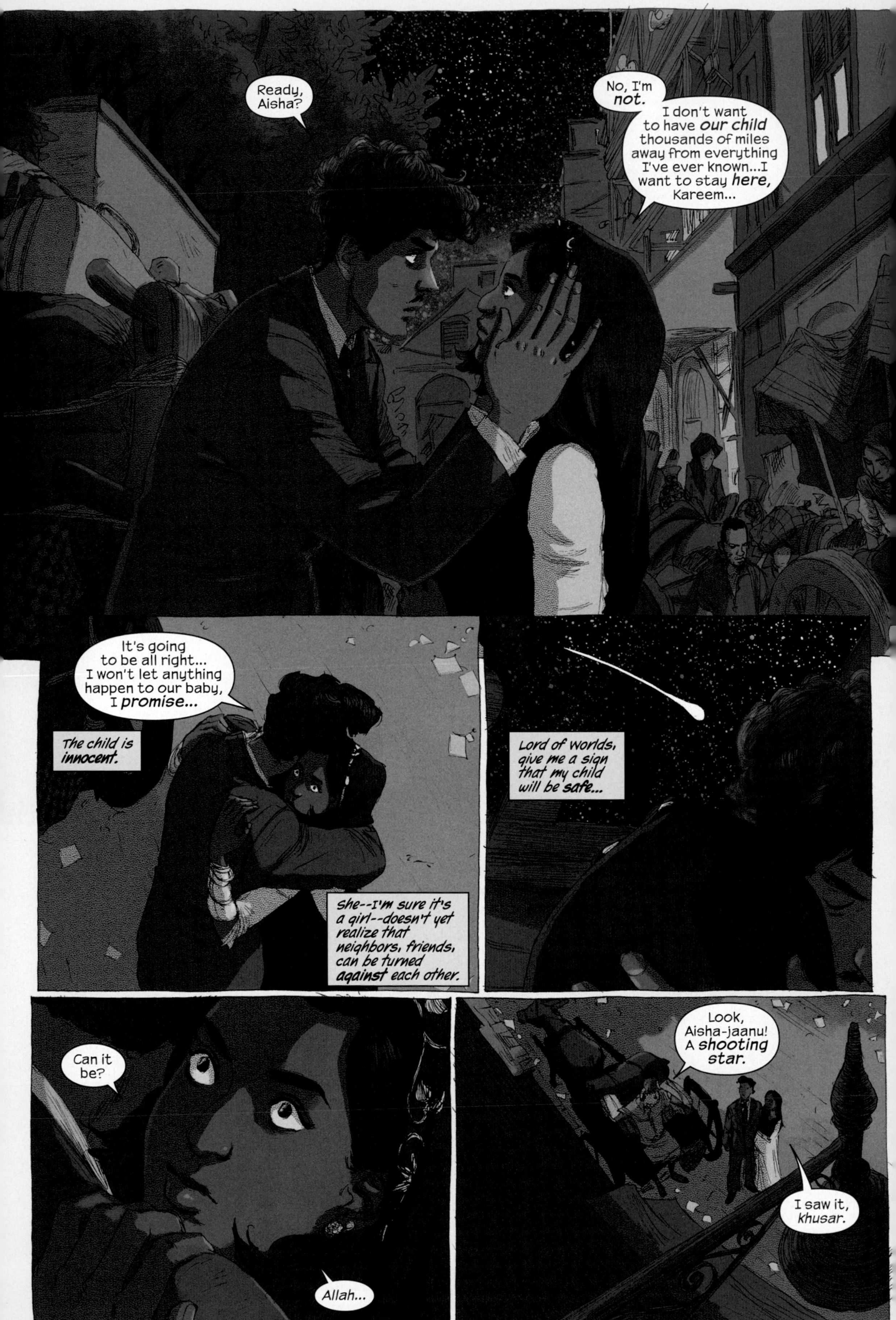

Ready, Aisha?
No, I'm not.
I don't want to have our child thousands of miles away from everything I've ever known...I want to stay here, Kareem...
It's going to be all right... I won't let anything happen to our baby, I promise...
The child is innocent.
She--I'm sure it's a girl--doesn't yet realize that neighbors, friends, can be turned against each other.
Lord of worlds, give me a sign that my child will be safe...
Can it be?
Allah...
Look, Aisha-jaanu! A shooting star.
I saw it, khusar.

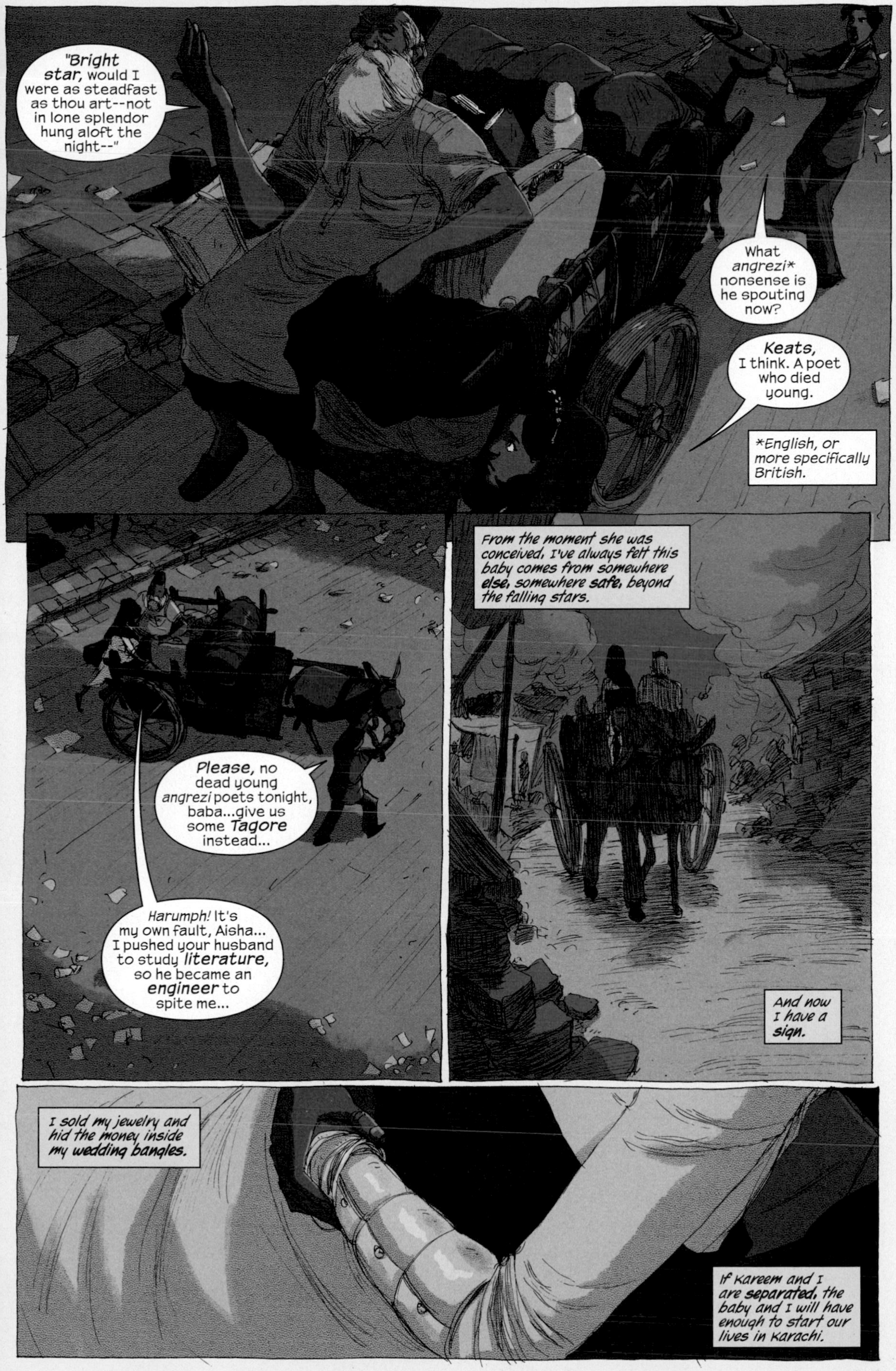
"Bright star, would I were as steadfast as thou art--not in lone splendor hung aloft the night--"
What angrezi* nonsense is he spouting now?
Keats, I think. A poet who died young.
*English, or more specifically British.
Please, no dead young angrezi poets tonight, baba...give us some Tagore instead...
Harumph! It's my own fault, Aisha... I pushed your husband to study literature, so he became an engineer to spite me...
From the moment she was conceived, I've always felt this baby comes from somewhere else, somewhere safe, beyond the falling stars.
And now I have a sign.
I sold my jewelry and hid the money inside my wedding bangles.
If Kareem and I are separated, the baby and I will have enough to start our lives in Karachi.

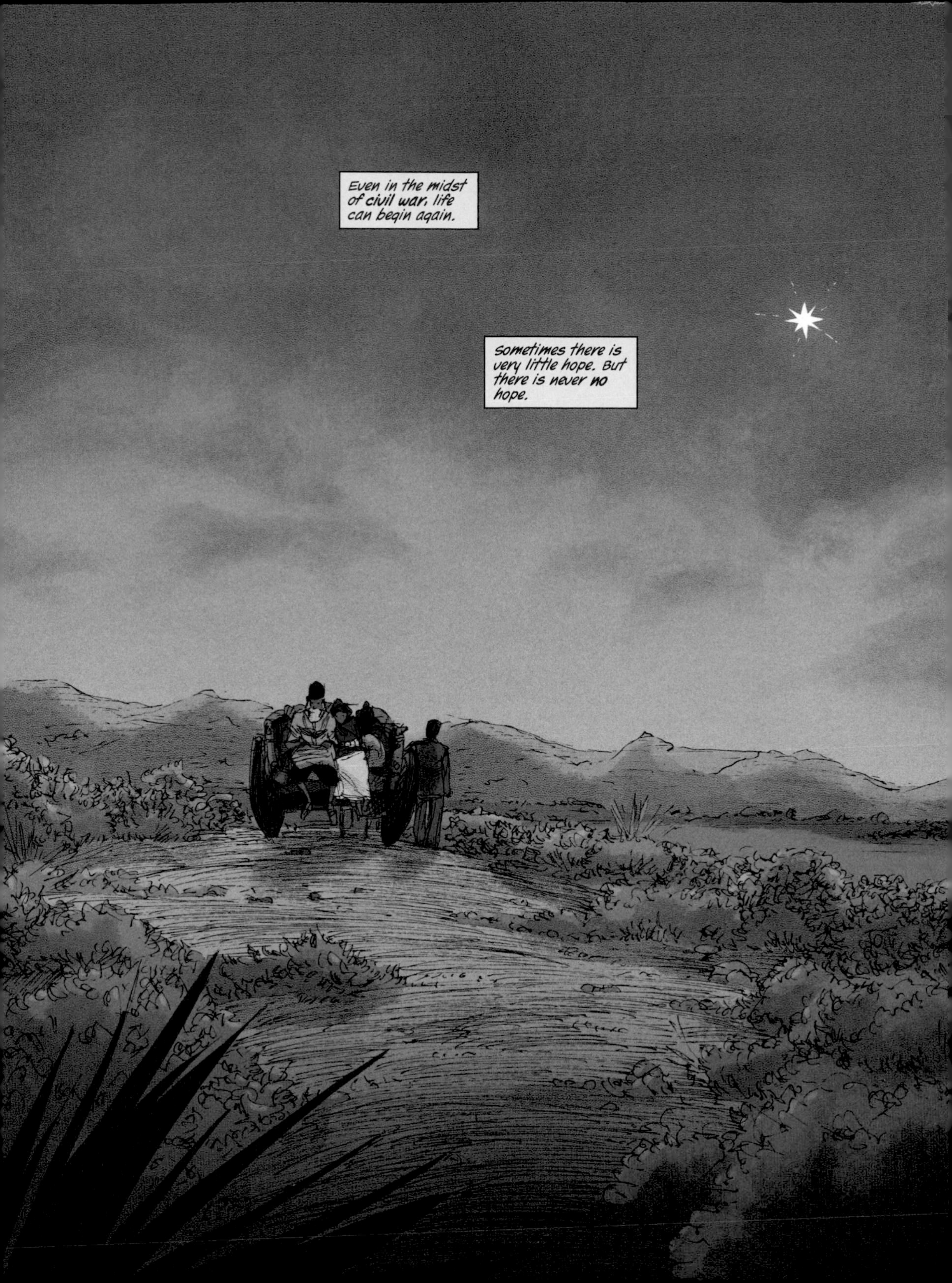
Even in the midst of civil war, life can begin again.
Sometimes there is very little hope. But there is never no hope.

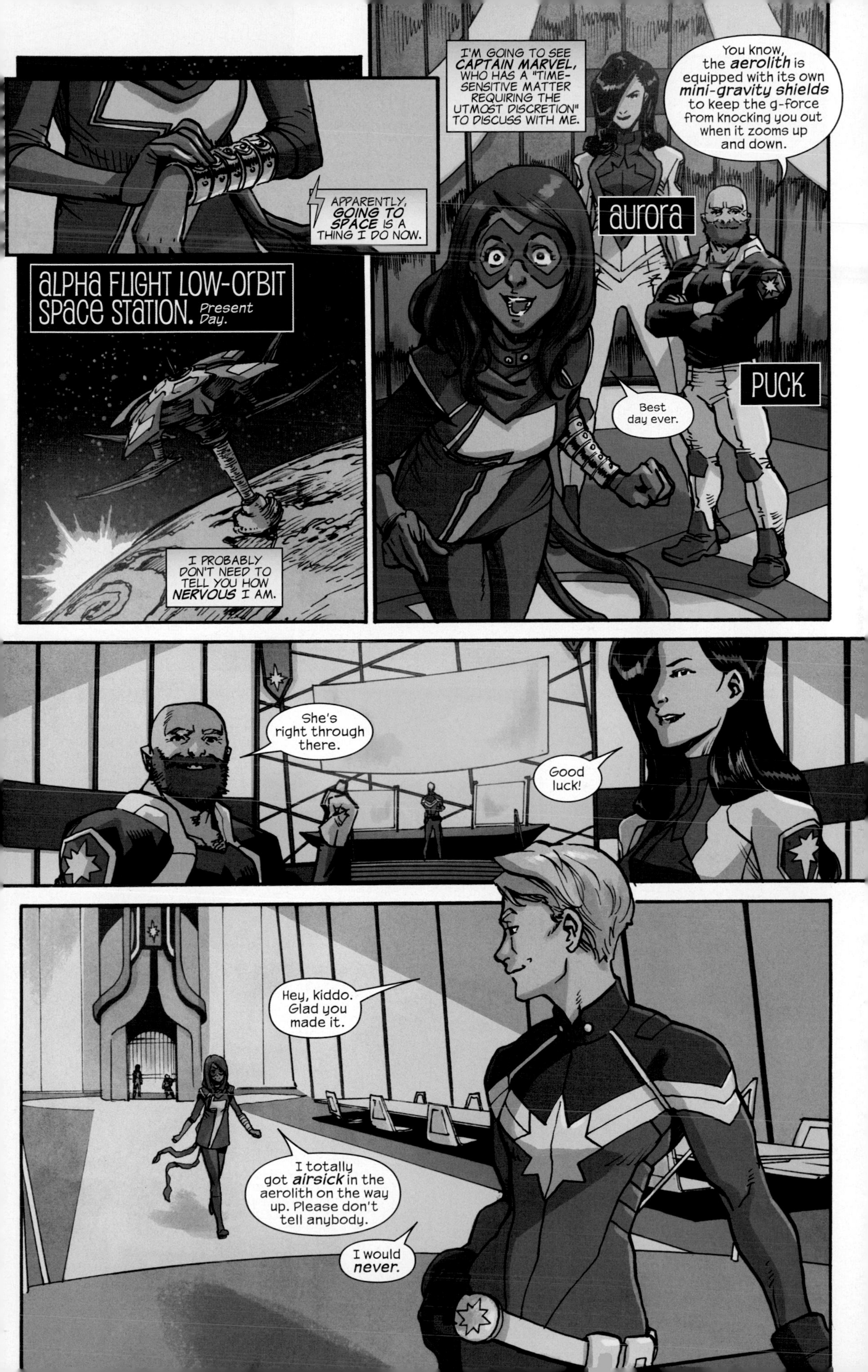

APPARENTLY, GOING TO SPACE IS A THING I DO NOW.
ALPHA FLIGHT LOW-ORBIT SPACE STATION. Present Day.
I PROBABLY DON'T NEED TO TELL YOU HOW NERVOUS I AM.
I'M GOING TO SEE CAPTAIN MARVEL, WHO HAS A "TIME-SENSITIVE MATTER REQUIRING THE UTMOST DISCRETION" TO DISCUSS WITH ME.
You know, the aerolith is equipped with its own mini-gravity shields to keep the g-force from knocking you out when it zooms up and down.
AURORA
PUCK
Best day ever.
She's right through there.
Good luck!
Hey, kiddo. Glad you made it.
I totally got airsick in the aerolith on the way up. Please don't tell anybody.
I would never.

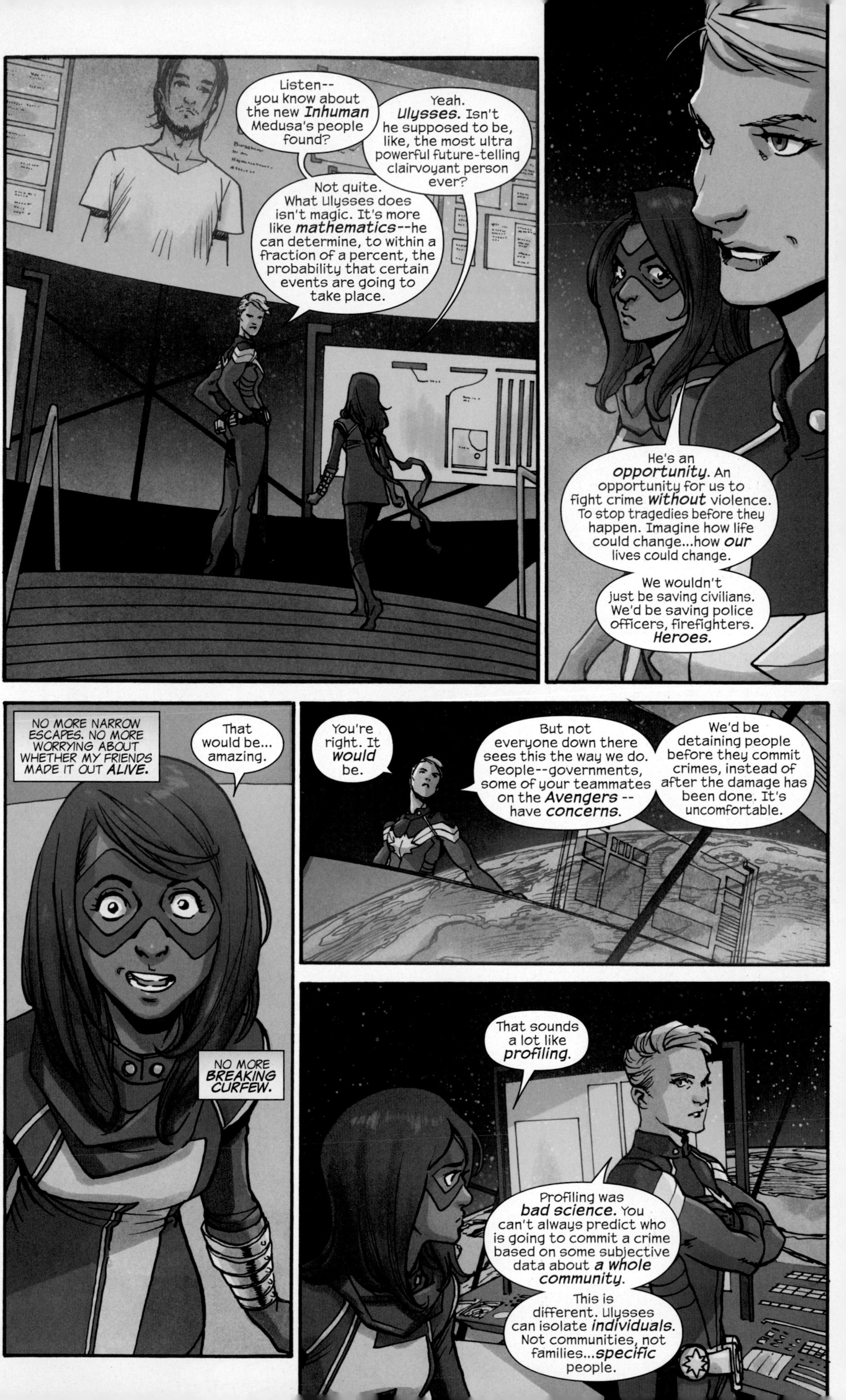
Listen-- you know about the new Inhuman Medusa's people found?
Yeah. Ulysses. Isn't he supposed to be, like, the most ultra powerful future-telling clairvoyant person ever?
Not quite. What Ulysses does isn't magic. It's more like mathematics--he can determine, to within a fraction of a percent, the probability that certain events are going to take place.
He's an opportunity. An opportunity for us to fight crime without violence. To stop tragedies before they happen. Imagine how life could change...how our lives could change.
We wouldn't just be saving civilians. We'd be saving police officers, firefighters. Heroes.
NO MORE NARROW ESCAPES. NO MORE WORRYING ABOUT WHETHER MY FRIENDS MADE IT OUT ALIVE.
That would be... amazing.
NO MORE BREAKING CURFEW.
You're right. It would be.
But not everyone down there sees this the way we do. People--governments, some of your teammates on the Avengers -- have concerns.
We'd be detaining people before they commit crimes, instead of after the damage has been done. It's uncomfortable.
That sounds a lot like profiling.
Profiling was bad science. You can't always predict who is going to commit a crime based on some subjective data about a whole community.
This is different. Ulysses can isolate individuals. Not communities, not families...specific people.

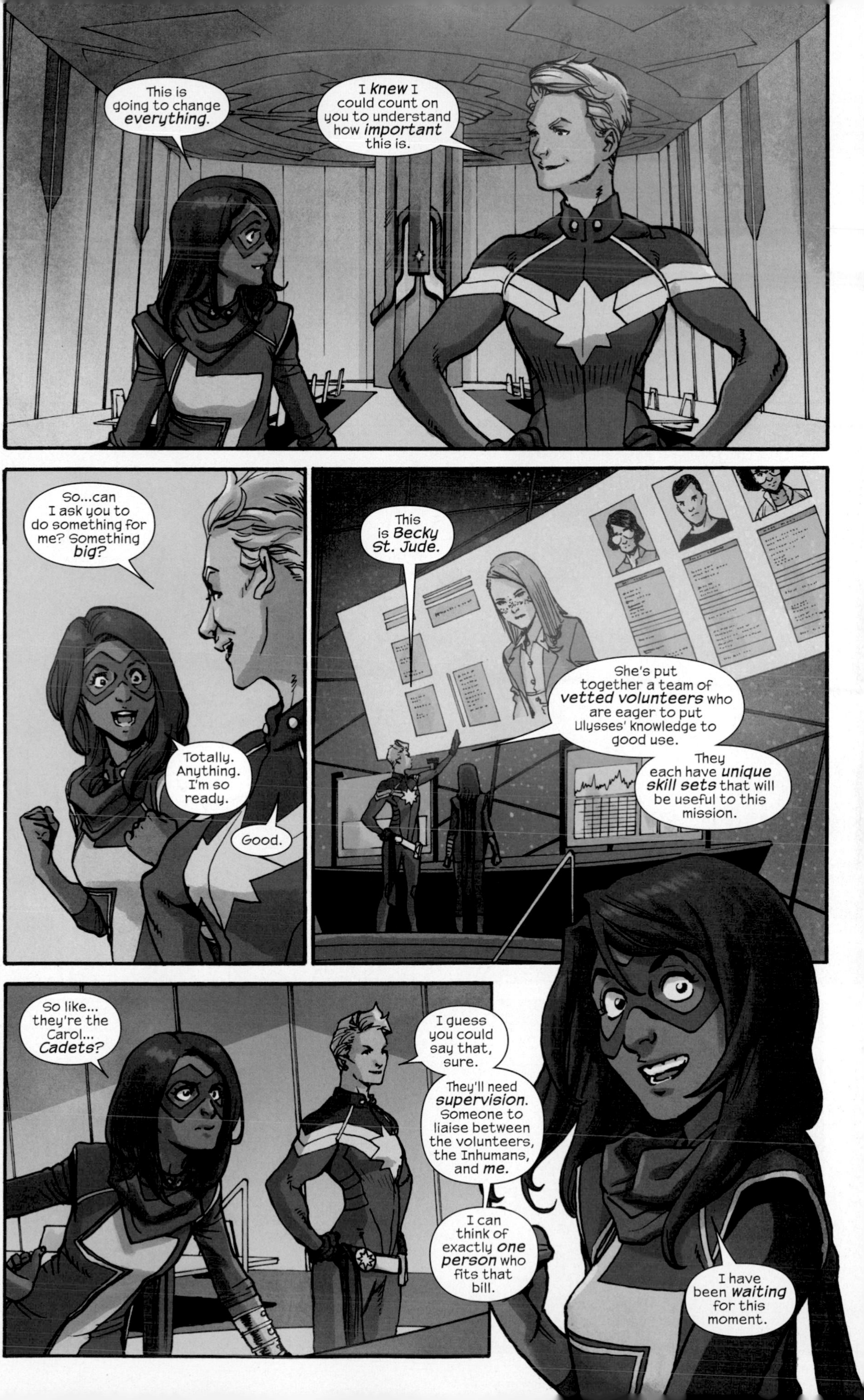
This is going to change *everything*.
I *knew* I could count on you to understand how *important* this is.
So...can I ask you to do something for me? Something *big*?
Totally. Anything. I'm so ready.
Good.
This is *Becky St. Jude.*
She's put together a team of *vetted volunteers* who are eager to put Ulysses' knowledge to good use.
They each have *unique skill sets* that will be useful to this mission.
So like... they're the Carol... *Cadets*?
I guess you could say that, sure.
They'll need *supervision*. Someone to liaise between the volunteers, the Inhumans, and *me*.
I can think of exactly *one person* who fits that bill.
I have been *waiting* for this moment.

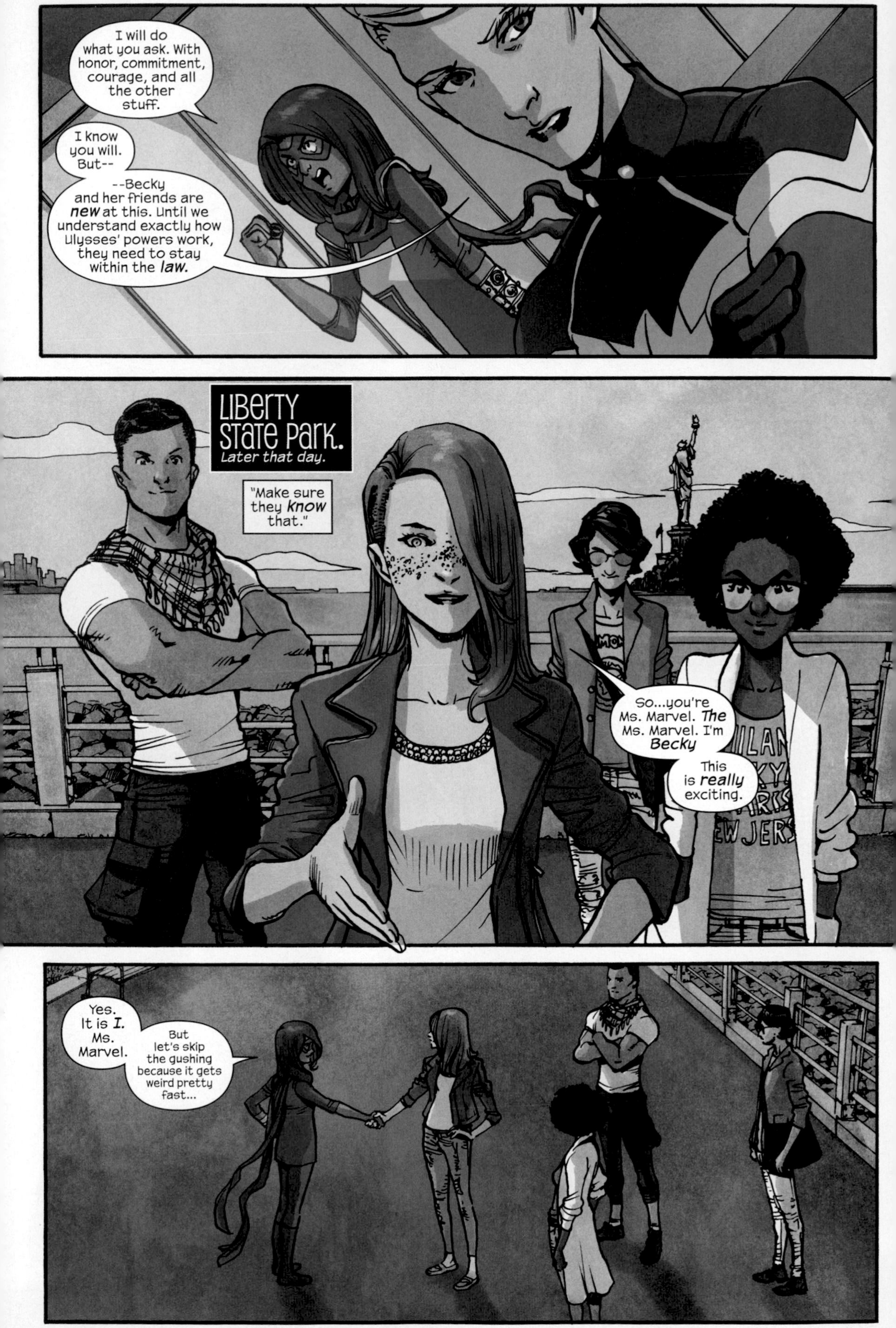

I will do what you ask. With honor, commitment, courage, and all the other stuff.
I know you will. But--
--Becky and her friends are *new* at this. Until we understand exactly how Ulysses' powers work, they need to stay within the *law.*
LIBERTY STATE PARK.
Later that day.
"Make sure they *know* that."
So...you're Ms. Marvel. *The* Ms. Marvel. I'm *Becky*
This is *really* exciting.
Yes. It is *I.* Ms. Marvel.
But let's skip the gushing because it gets weird pretty fast...

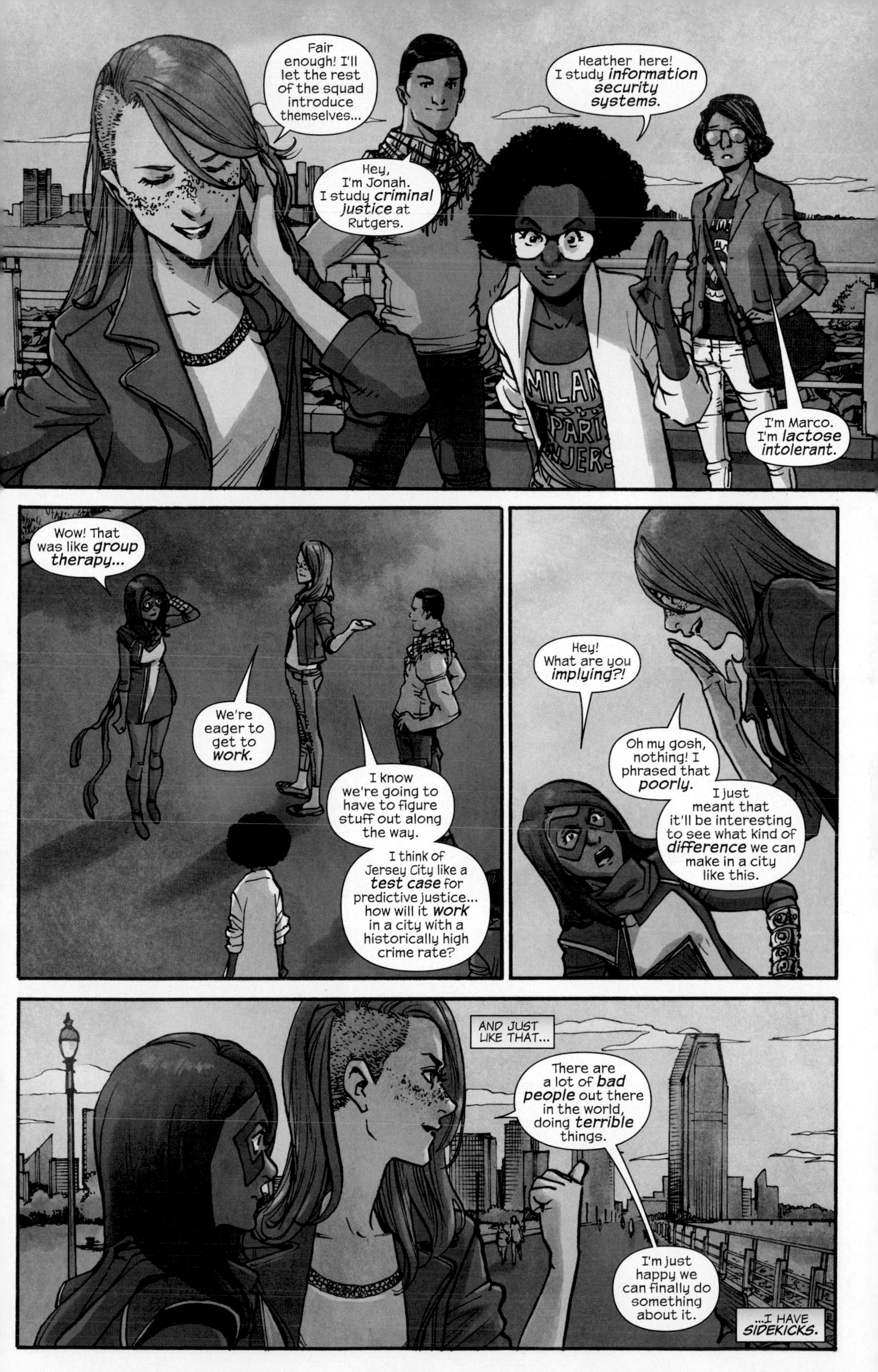

Fair enough! I'll let the rest of the squad introduce themselves...
Hey, I'm Jonah. I study *criminal justice* at Rutgers.
Heather here! I study *information security systems.*
I'm Marco. I'm *lactose intolerant.*
Wow! That was like *group therapy...*
We're eager to get to *work.*
I know we're going to have to figure stuff out along the way.
I think of Jersey City like a *test case* for predictive justice... how will it *work* in a city with a historically high crime rate?
Hey! What are you *implying?!*
Oh my gosh, nothing! I phrased that *poorly.*
I just meant that it'll be interesting to see what kind of *difference* we can make in a city like this.
AND JUST LIKE THAT...
There are a lot of *bad people* out there in the world, doing *terrible* things.
I'm just happy we can finally do something about it.
...I HAVE *SIDEKICKS.*

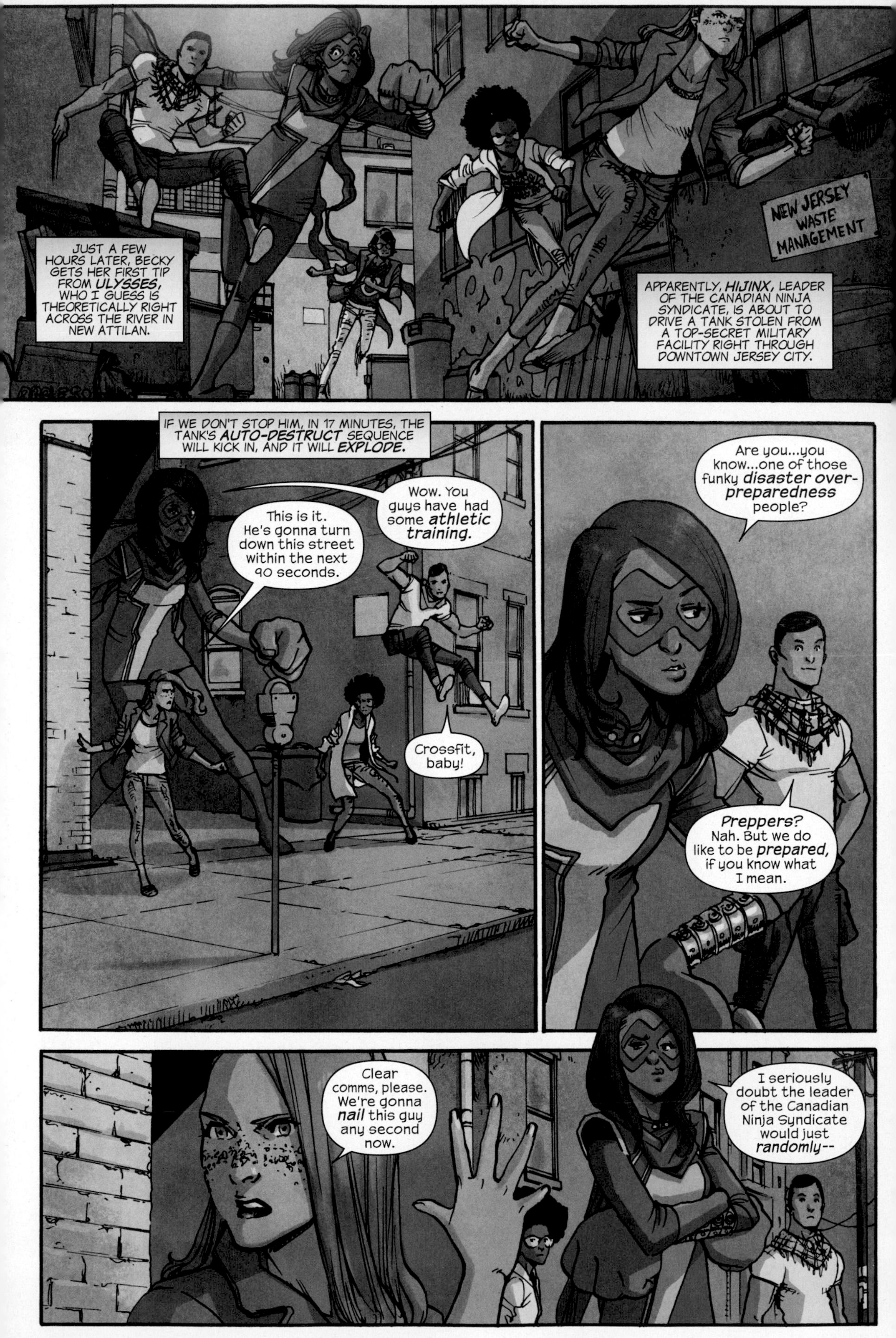
JUST A FEW HOURS LATER, BECKY GETS HER FIRST TIP FROM ULYSSES, WHO I GUESS IS THEORETICALLY RIGHT ACROSS THE RIVER IN NEW ATTILAN.
NEW JERSEY WASTE MANAGEMENT
APPARENTLY, HIJINX, LEADER OF THE CANADIAN NINJA SYNDICATE, IS ABOUT TO DRIVE A TANK STOLEN FROM A TOP-SECRET MILITARY FACILITY RIGHT THROUGH DOWNTOWN JERSEY CITY.
IF WE DON'T STOP HIM, IN 17 MINUTES, THE TANK'S AUTO-DESTRUCT SEQUENCE WILL KICK IN, AND IT WILL EXPLODE.
This is it. He's gonna turn down this street within the next 90 seconds.
Wow. You guys have had some athletic training.
Crossfit, baby!
Are you...you know...one of those funky disaster over-preparedness people?
Preppers? Nah. But we do like to be prepared, if you know what I mean.
Clear comms, please. We're gonna nail this guy any second now.
I seriously doubt the leader of the Canadian Ninja Syndicate would just randomly--

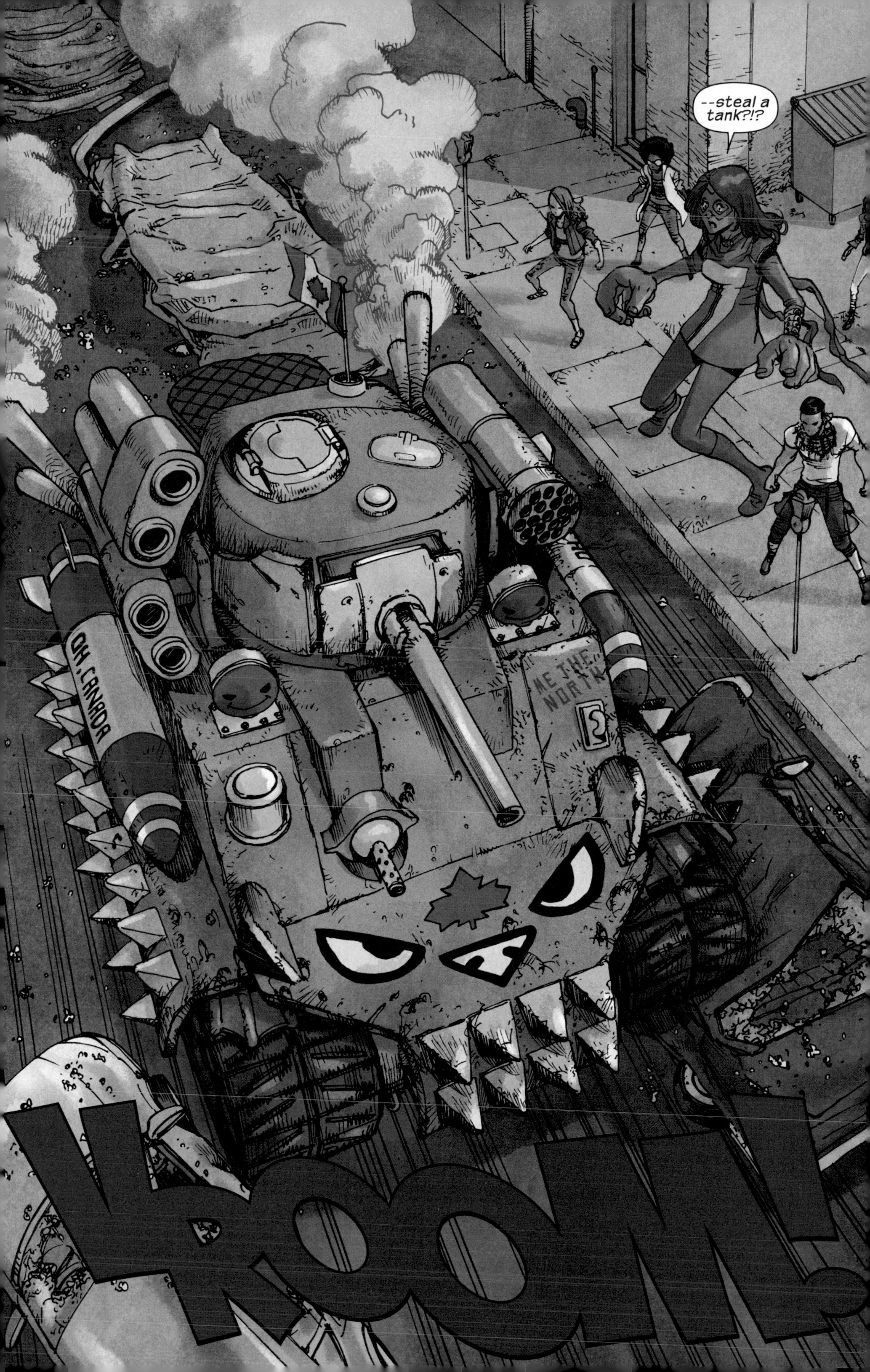
--steal a tank?!?
OH, CANADA
ME THE NORTH
KOOM!

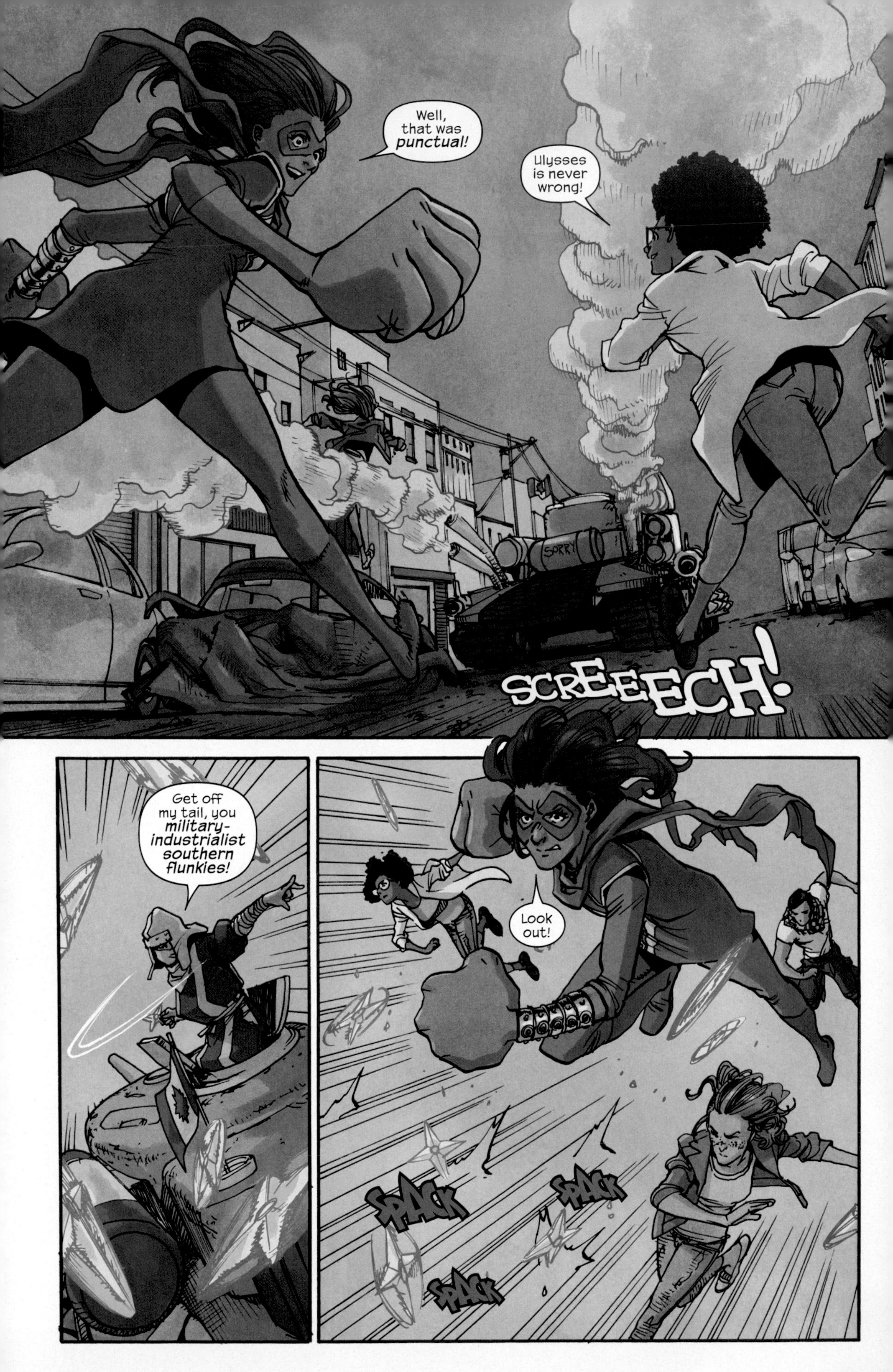
Well, that was punctual!
Ulysses is never wrong!
SORRY
SCREEECH!
Get off my tail, you military-industrialist southern flunkies!
Look out!
SPACK
SPACK
SPACK

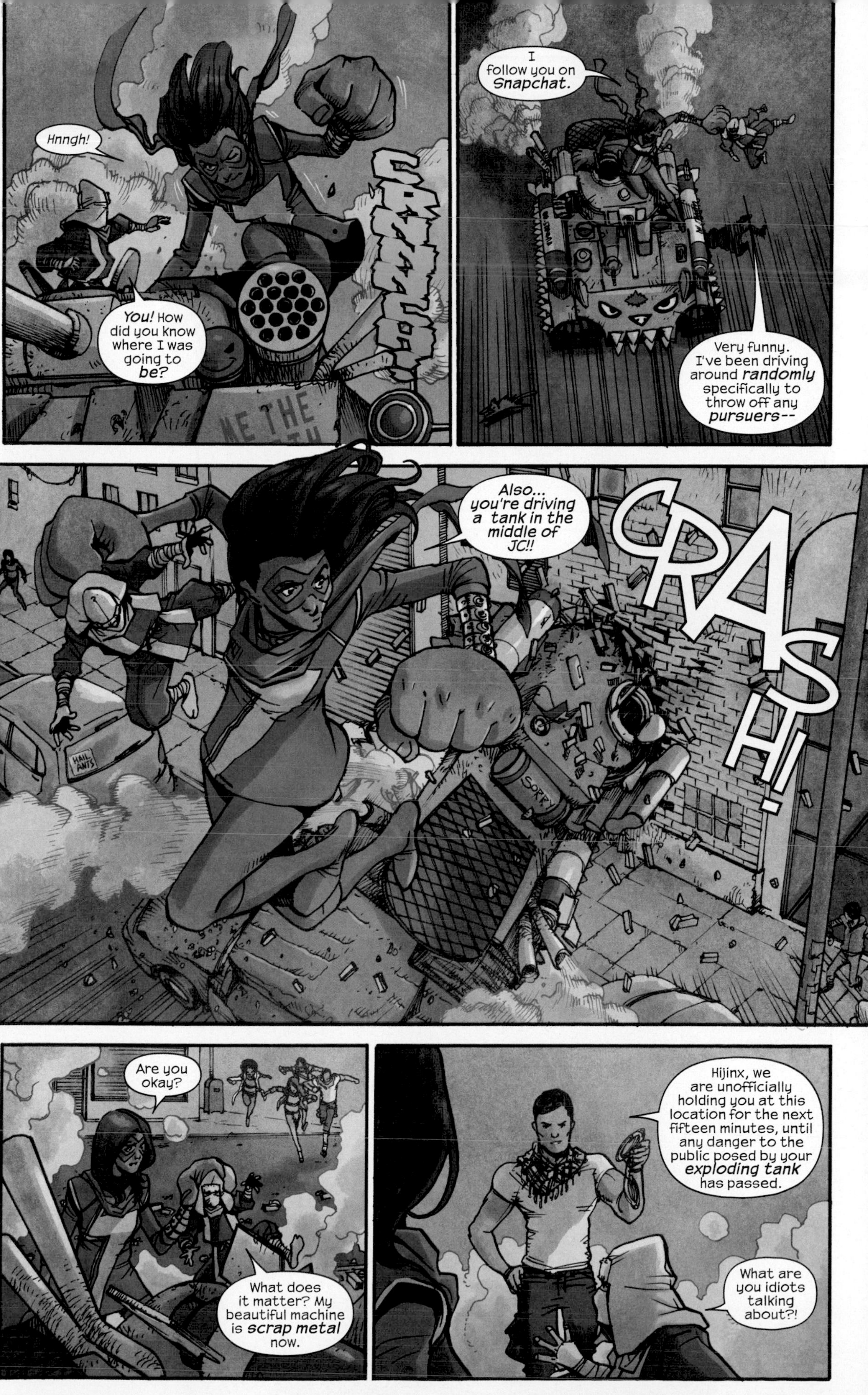
Hnngh!
CRRAAACK!
You! How did you know where I was going to be?
I follow you on Snapchat.
Very funny. I've been driving around randomly specifically to throw off any pursuers--
Also... you're driving a tank in the middle of JC!!
CRASH!
HAIL ANTS
SORRY
Are you okay?
What does it matter? My beautiful machine is scrap metal now.
Hijinx, we are unofficially holding you at this location for the next fifteen minutes, until any danger to the public posed by your exploding tank has passed.
What are you idiots talking about?!

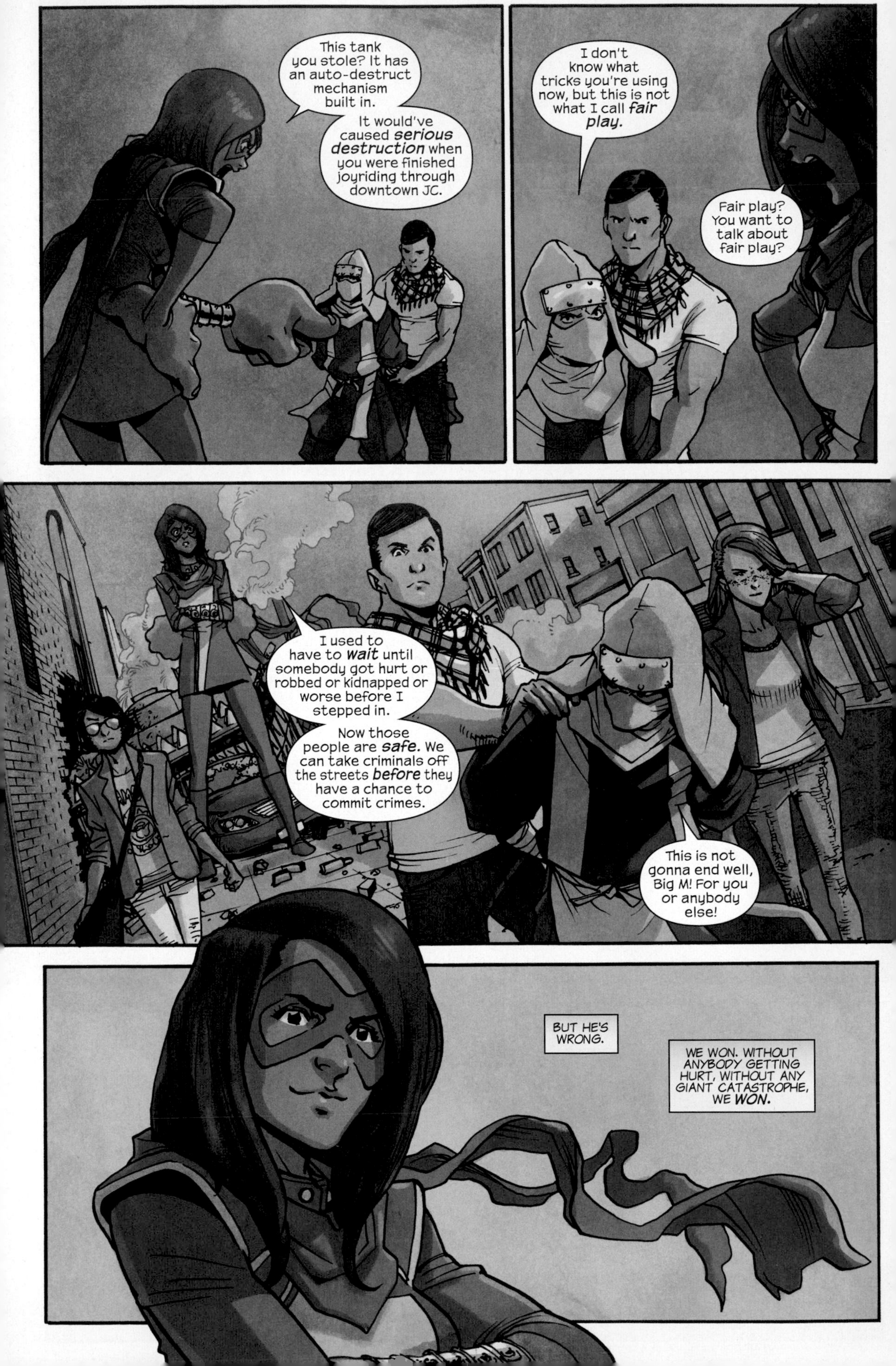

This tank you stole? It has an auto-destruct mechanism built in.
It would've caused *serious destruction* when you were finished joyriding through downtown JC.
I don't know what tricks you're using now, but this is not what I call *fair play.*
Fair play? You want to talk about fair play?
I used to have to *wait* until somebody got hurt or robbed or kidnapped or worse before I stepped in.
Now those people are *safe.* We can take criminals off the streets *before* they have a chance to commit crimes.
This is not gonna end well, Big M! For you or anybody else!
BUT HE'S WRONG.
WE WON. WITHOUT ANYBODY GETTING HURT, WITHOUT ANY GIANT CATASTROPHE, WE *WON.*

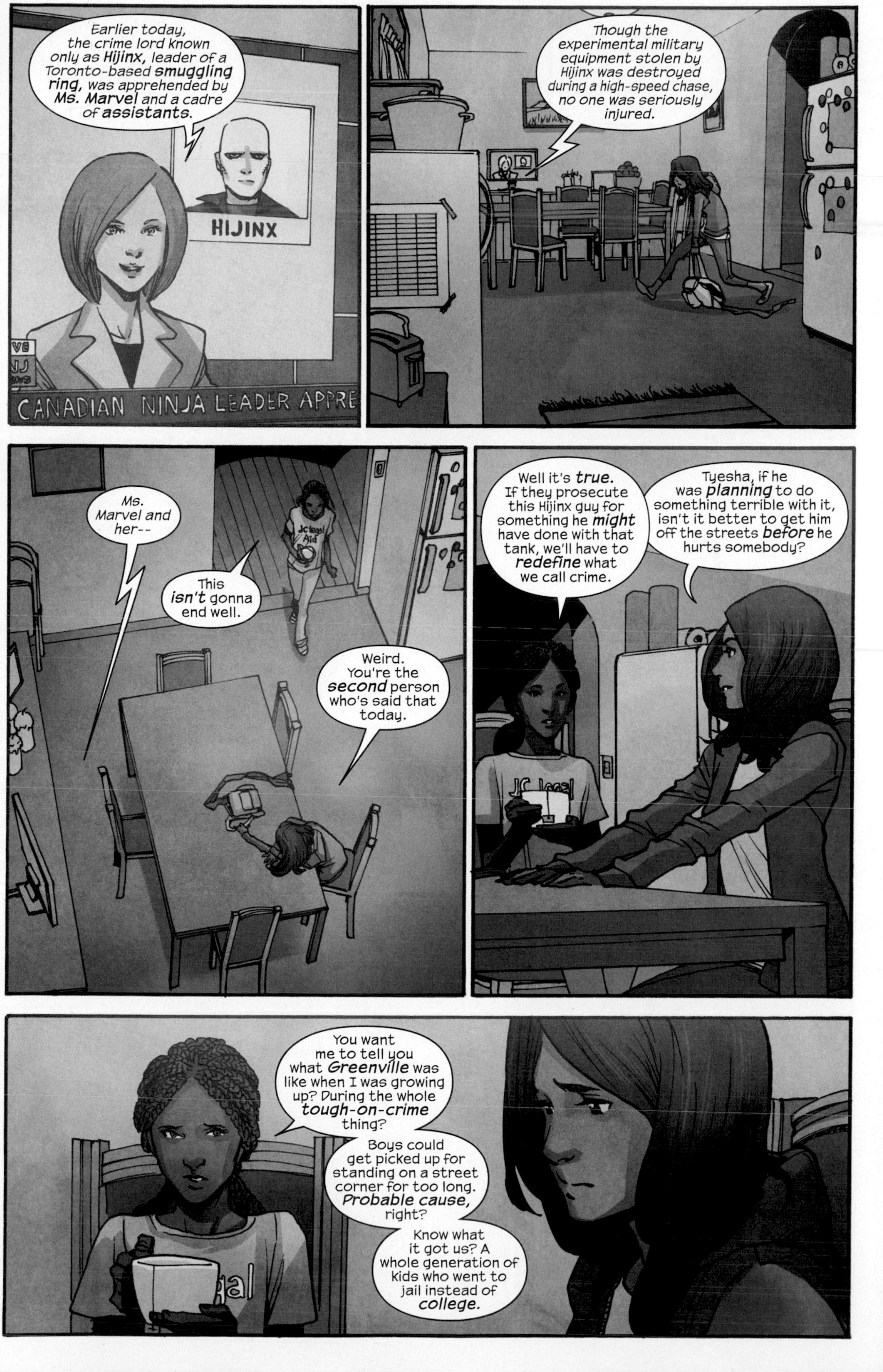
Earlier today, the crime lord known only as Hijinx, leader of a Toronto-based smuggling ring, was apprehended by Ms. Marvel and a cadre of assistants.
HIJINX
CANADIAN NINJA LEADER APPRE
Though the experimental military equipment stolen by Hijinx was destroyed during a high-speed chase, no one was seriously injured.
Ms. Marvel and her--
This isn't gonna end well.
Weird. You're the second person who's said that today.
Well it's true. If they prosecute this Hijinx guy for something he might have done with that tank, we'll have to redefine what we call crime.
Tyesha, if he was planning to do something terrible with it, isn't it better to get him off the streets before he hurts somebody?
You want me to tell you what Greenville was like when I was growing up? During the whole tough-on-crime thing?
Boys could get picked up for standing on a street corner for too long. Probable cause, right?
Know what it got us? A whole generation of kids who went to jail instead of college.

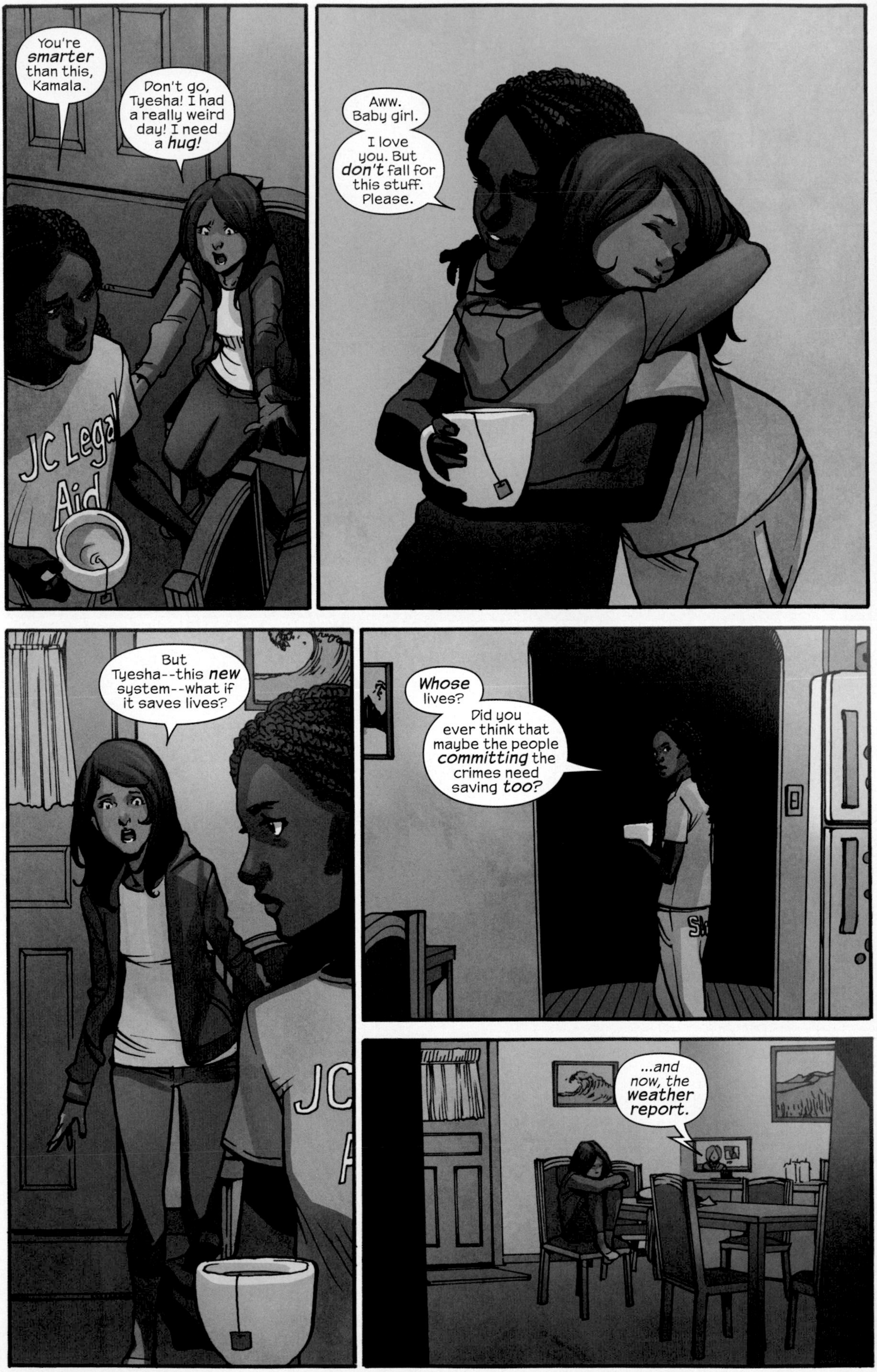
You're smarter than this, Kamala.
Don't go, Tyesha! I had a really weird day! I need a hug!
JC Legal Aid
Aww. Baby girl.
I love you. But don't fall for this stuff. Please.
But Tyesha--this new system--what if it saves lives?
JC
Whose lives?
Did you ever think that maybe the people committing the crimes need saving too?
...and now, the weather report.

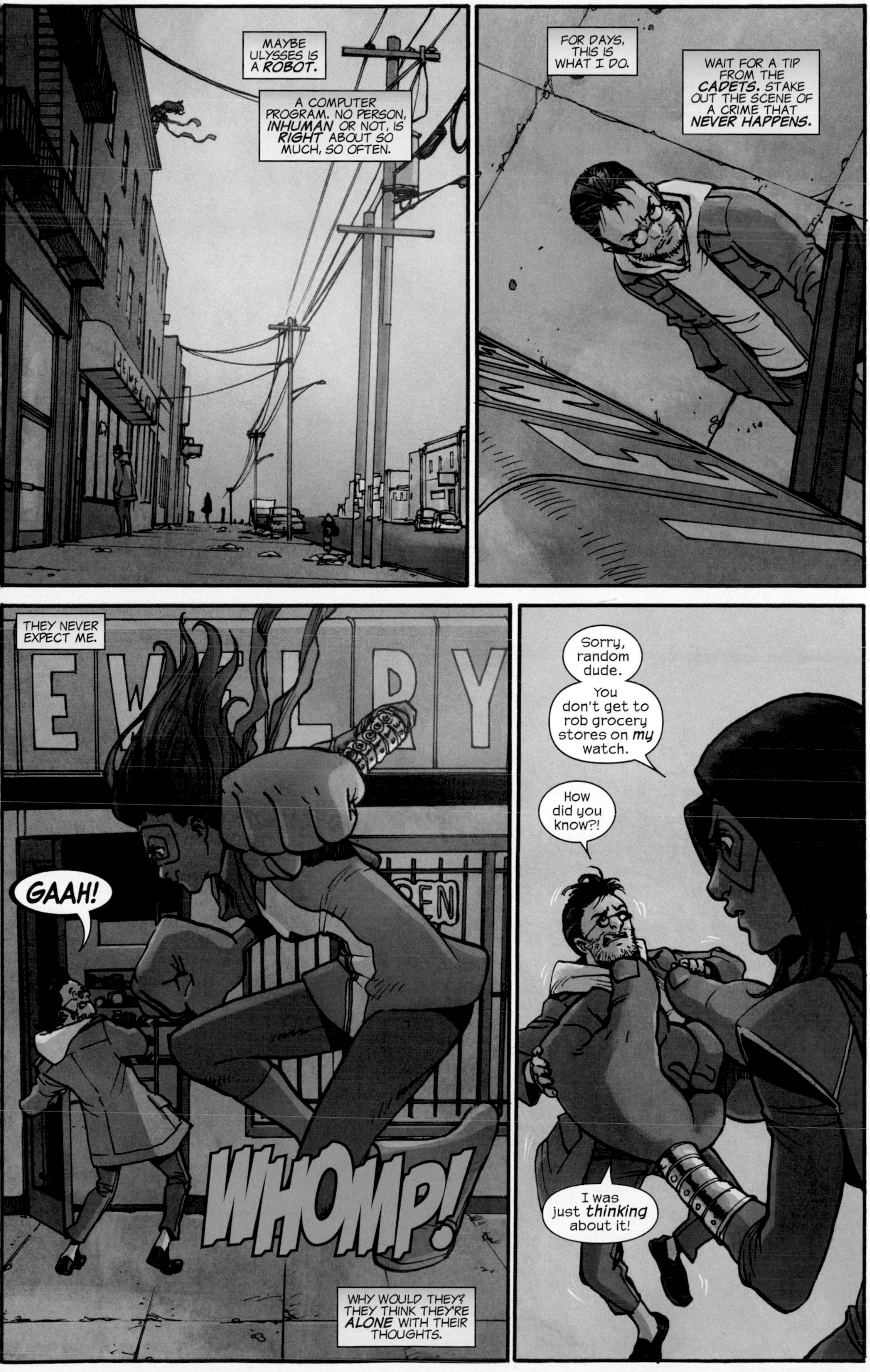
MAYBE ULYSSES IS A ROBOT.
A COMPUTER PROGRAM. NO PERSON, INHUMAN OR NOT, IS RIGHT ABOUT SO MUCH, SO OFTEN.
FOR DAYS, THIS IS WHAT I DO.
WAIT FOR A TIP FROM THE CADETS. STAKE OUT THE SCENE OF A CRIME THAT NEVER HAPPENS.
THEY NEVER EXPECT ME.
GAAH!
WHOMP!
WHY WOULD THEY? THEY THINK THEY'RE ALONE WITH THEIR THOUGHTS.
Sorry, random dude.
You don't get to rob grocery stores on my watch.
How did you know?!
I was just thinking about it!

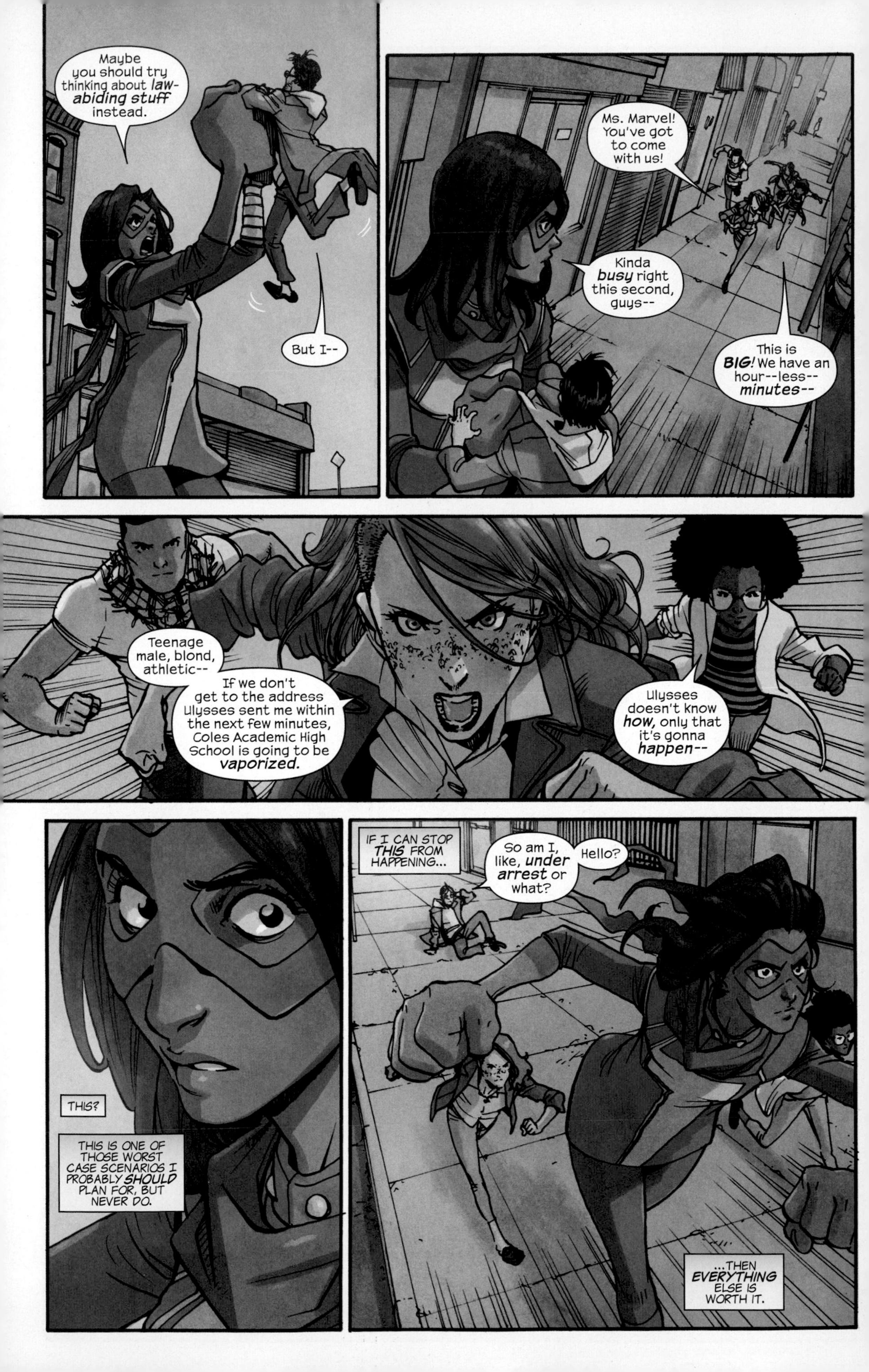
Maybe you should try thinking about law-abiding stuff instead.
But I--
Ms. Marvel! You've got to come with us!
Kinda busy right this second, guys--
This is BIG! We have an hour--less--minutes--
Teenage male, blond, athletic--
If we don't get to the address Ulysses sent me within the next few minutes, Coles Academic High School is going to be vaporized.
Ulysses doesn't know how, only that it's gonna happen--
THIS?
THIS IS ONE OF THOSE WORST CASE SCENARIOS I PROBABLY SHOULD PLAN FOR, BUT NEVER DO.
IF I CAN STOP THIS FROM HAPPENING...
So am I, like, under arrest or what?
Hello?
...THEN EVERYTHING ELSE IS WORTH IT.

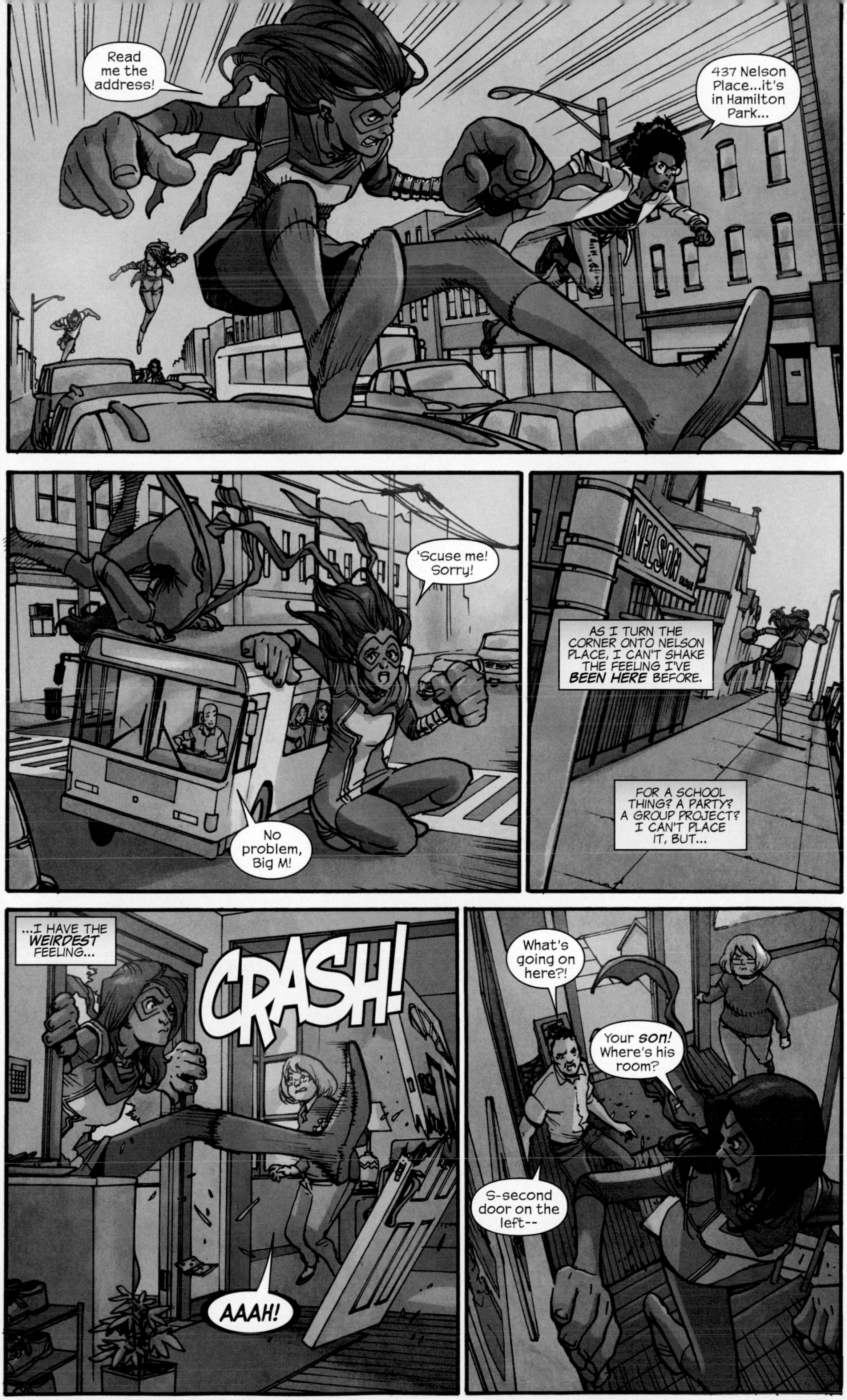

Read me the address!
437 Nelson Place...it's in Hamilton Park...
'Scuse me! Sorry!
No problem, Big M!
NELSON
AS I TURN THE CORNER ONTO NELSON PLACE, I CAN'T SHAKE THE FEELING I'VE BEEN HERE BEFORE.
FOR A SCHOOL THING? A PARTY? A GROUP PROJECT? I CAN'T PLACE IT, BUT...
...I HAVE THE WEIRDEST FEELING...
CRASH!
AAAH!
What's going on here?!
Your son! Where's his room?
S-second door on the left--

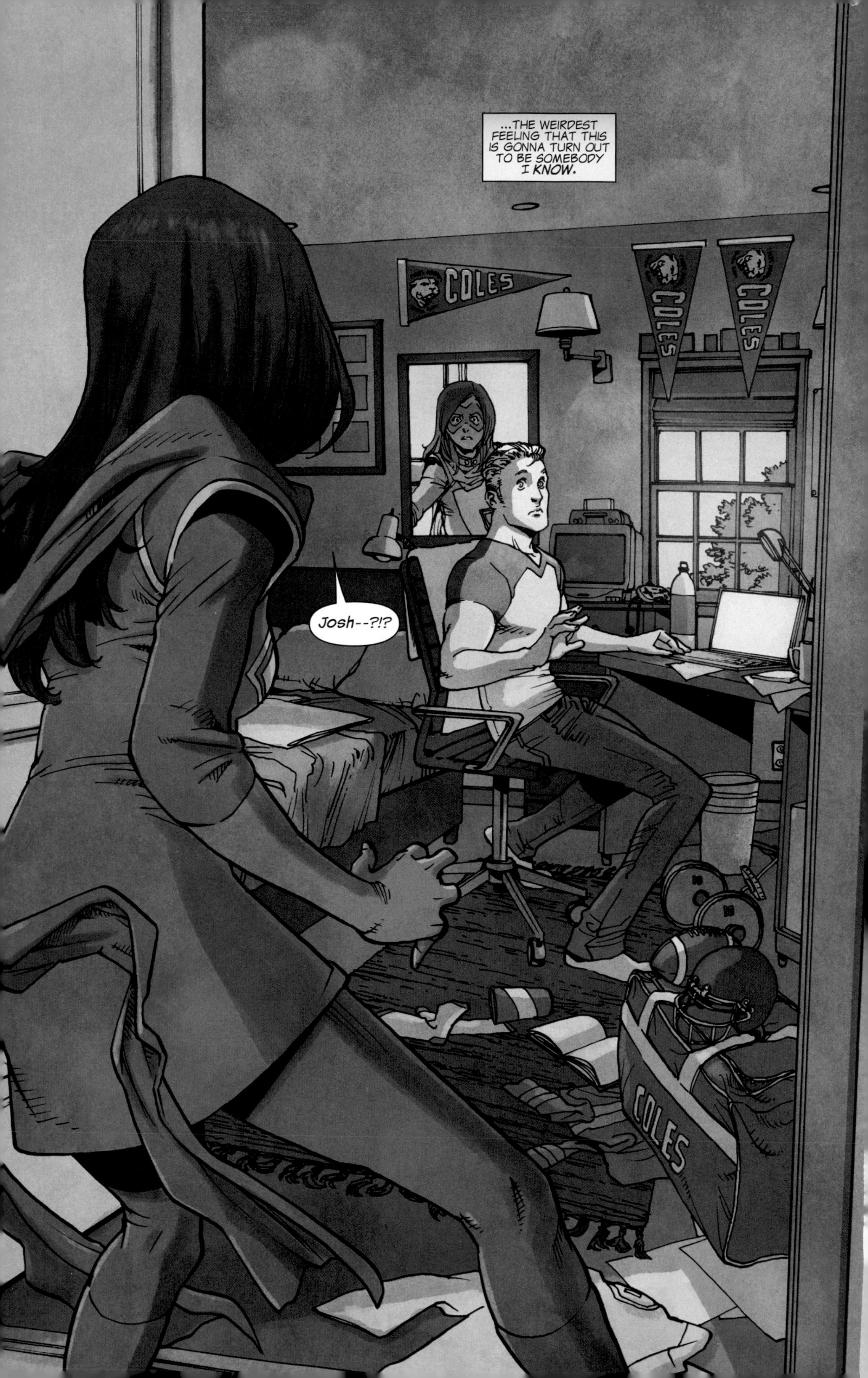
...THE WEIRDEST FEELING THAT THIS IS GONNA TURN OUT TO BE SOMEBODY I KNOW.
COLES
COLES
COLES
Josh--?!?
COLES

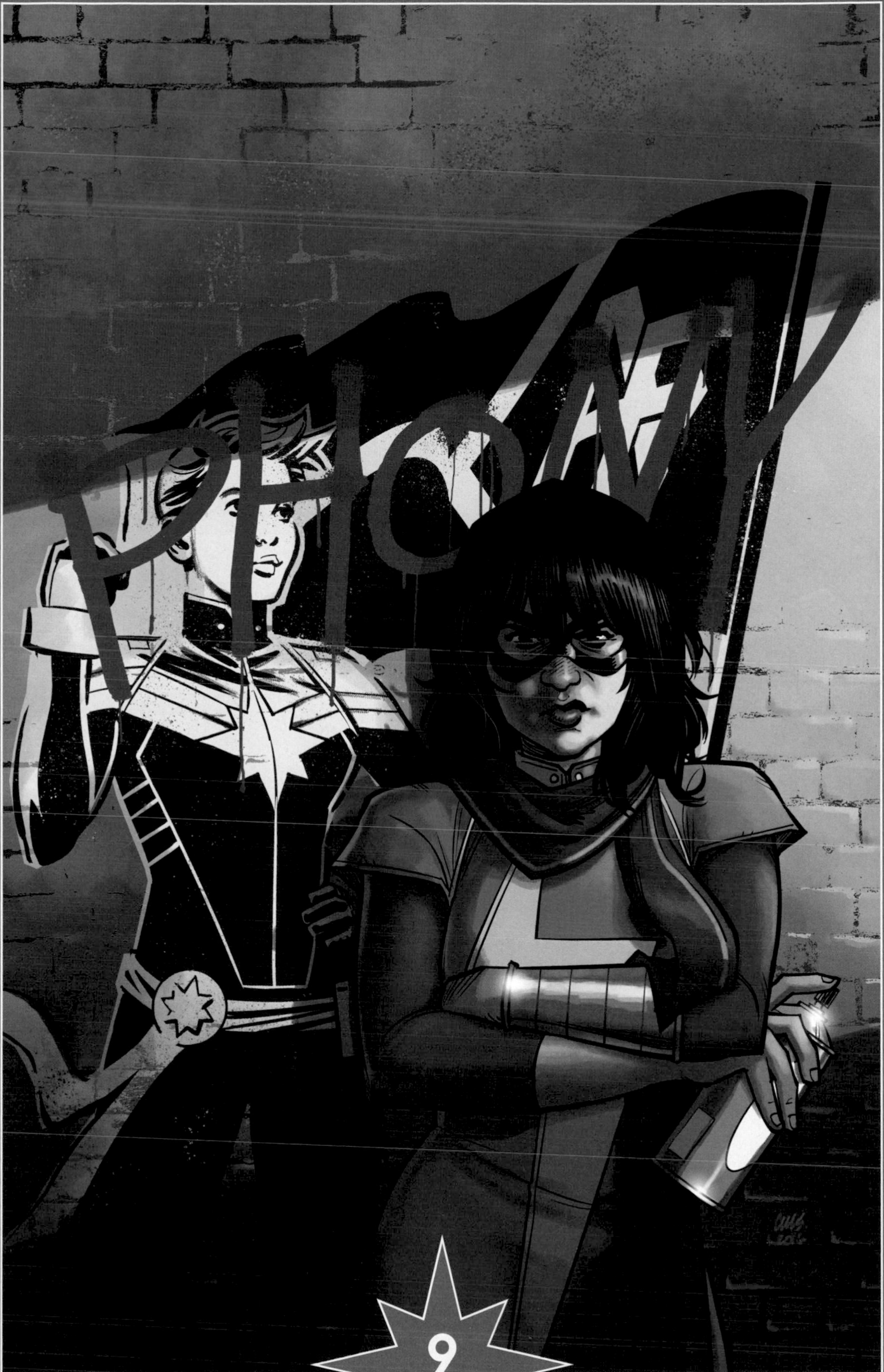
PHONY
9

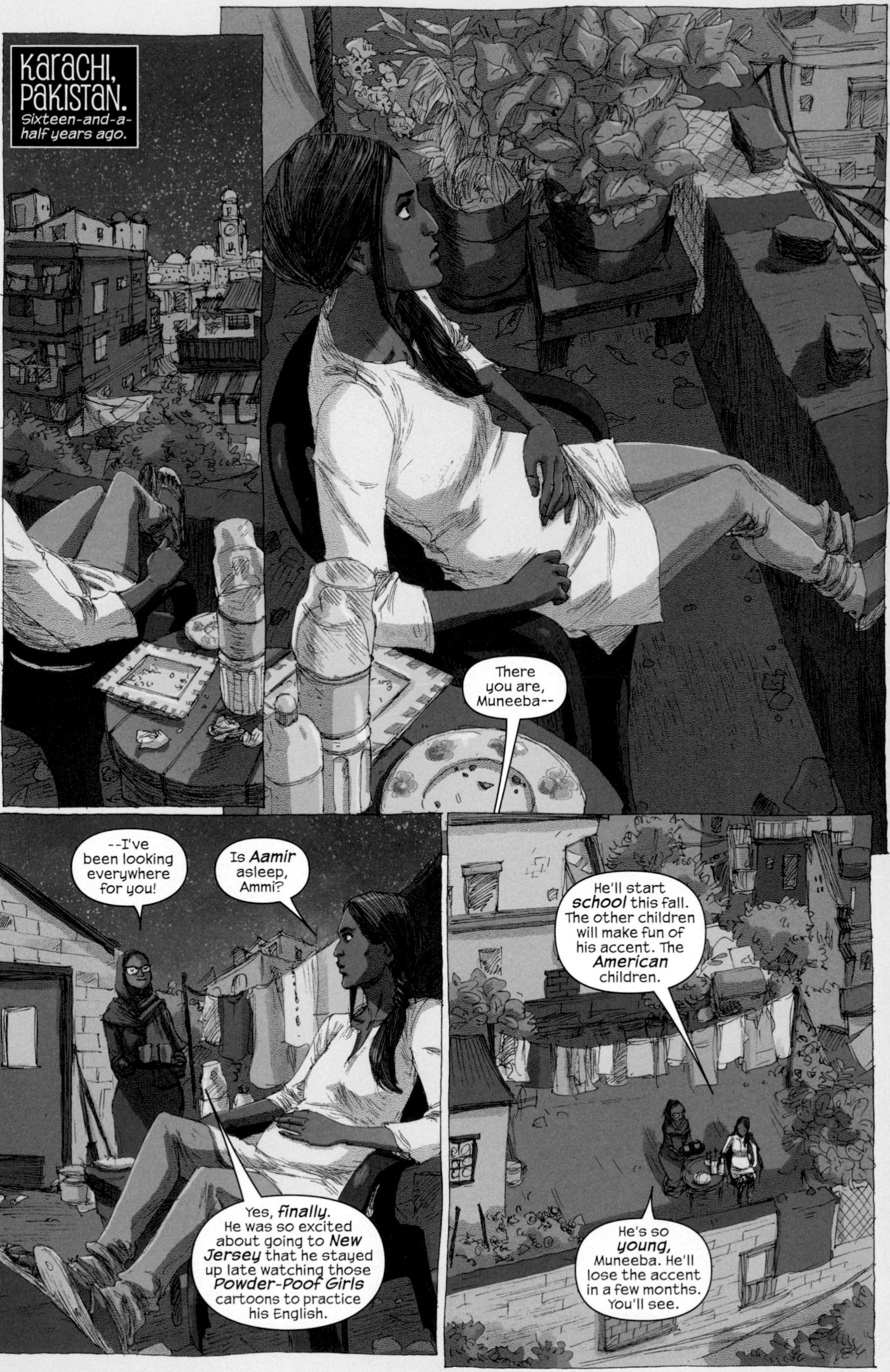
KARACHI, PAKISTAN.
Sixteen-and-a-half years ago.
There you are, Muneeba--
--I've been looking everywhere for you!
Is Aamir asleep, Ammi?
Yes, finally. He was so excited about going to New Jersey that he stayed up late watching those Powder-Poof Girls cartoons to practice his English.
He'll start school this fall. The other children will make fun of his accent. The American children.
He's so young, Muneeba. He'll lose the accent in a few months. You'll see.

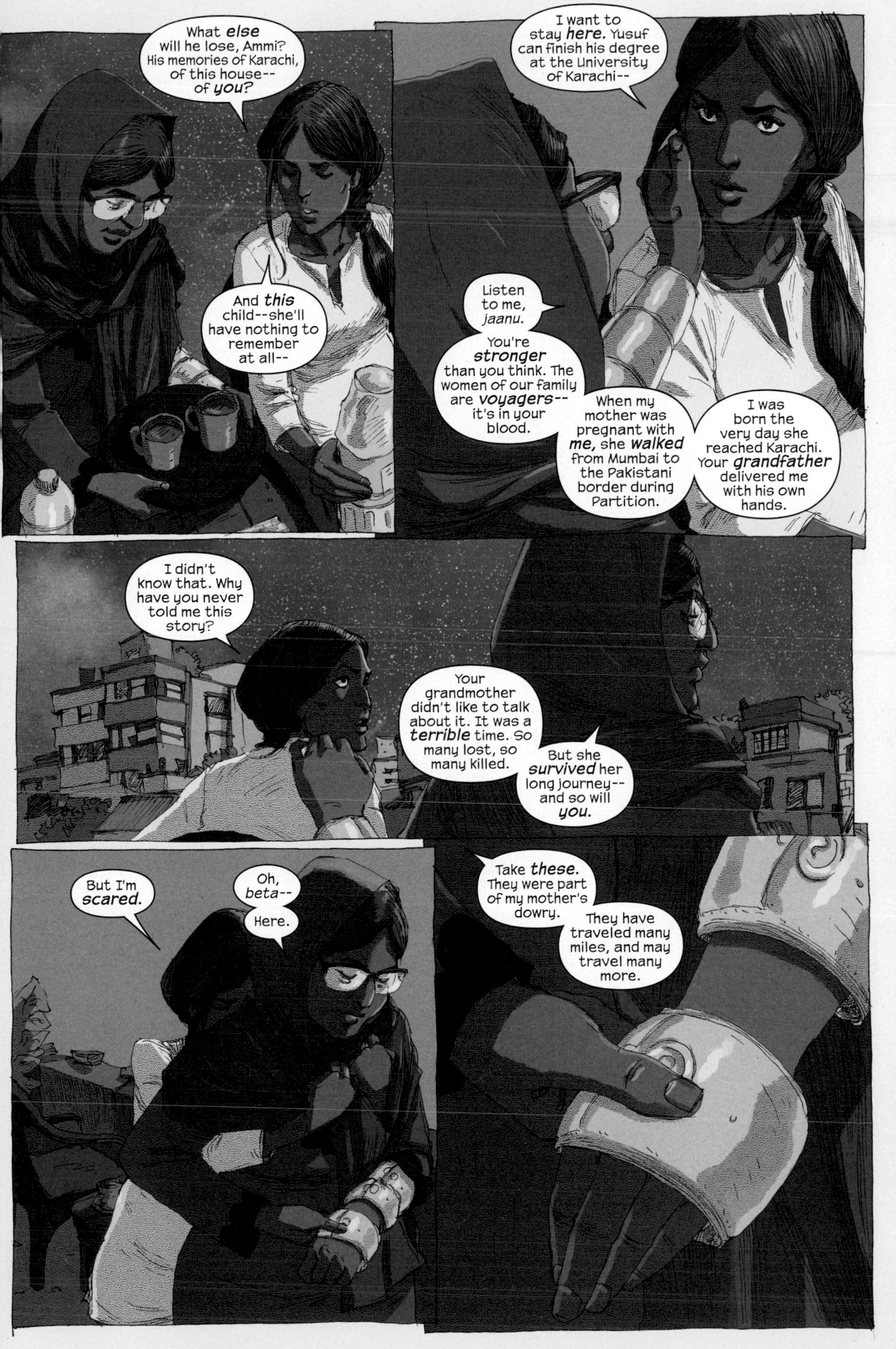

What *else* will he lose, Ammi? His memories of Karachi, of this house-- of *you?*
And *this* child--she'll have nothing to remember at all--
I want to stay *here.* Yusuf can finish his degree at the University of Karachi--
Listen to me, *jaanu.*
You're *stronger* than you think. The women of our family are *voyagers*-- it's in your blood.
When my mother was pregnant with *me,* she *walked* from Mumbai to the Pakistani border during Partition.
I was born the very day she reached Karachi. Your *grandfather* delivered me with his own hands.
I didn't know that. Why have you never told me this story?
Your grandmother didn't like to talk about it. It was a *terrible* time. So many lost, so many killed.
But she *survived* her long journey-- and so will *you.*
But I'm *scared.*
Oh, *beta*--
Here.
Take *these.* They were part of my mother's dowry.
They have traveled many miles, and may travel many more.

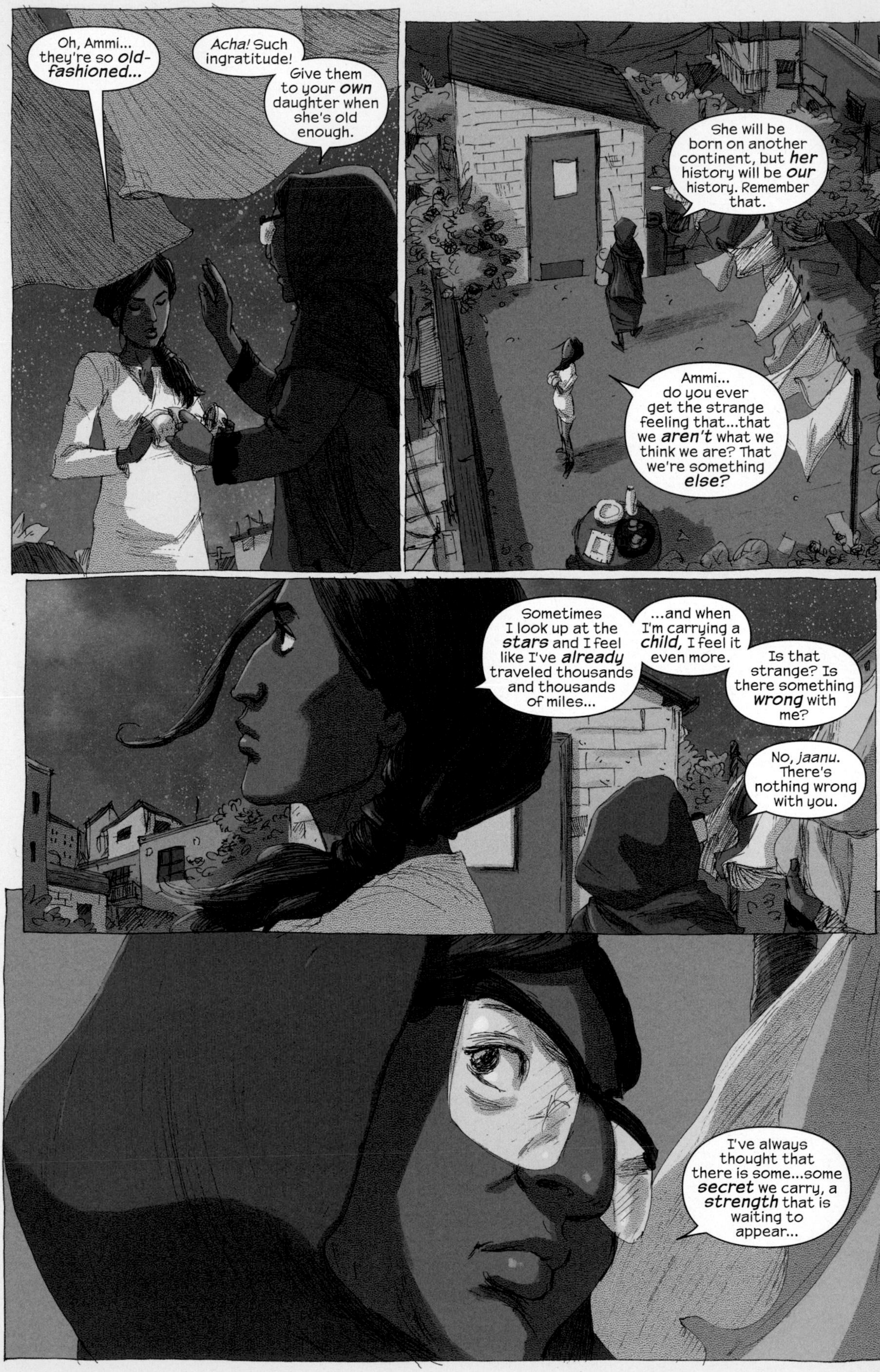
Oh, Ammi... they're so old-fashioned...
Acha! Such ingratitude!
Give them to your own daughter when she's old enough.
She will be born on another continent, but her history will be our history. Remember that.
Ammi... do you ever get the strange feeling that...that we aren't what we think we are? That we're something else?
Sometimes I look up at the stars and I feel like I've already traveled thousands and thousands of miles...
...and when I'm carrying a child, I feel it even more.
Is that strange? Is there something wrong with me?
No, jaanu. There's nothing wrong with you.
I've always thought that there is some...some secret we carry, a strength that is waiting to appear...

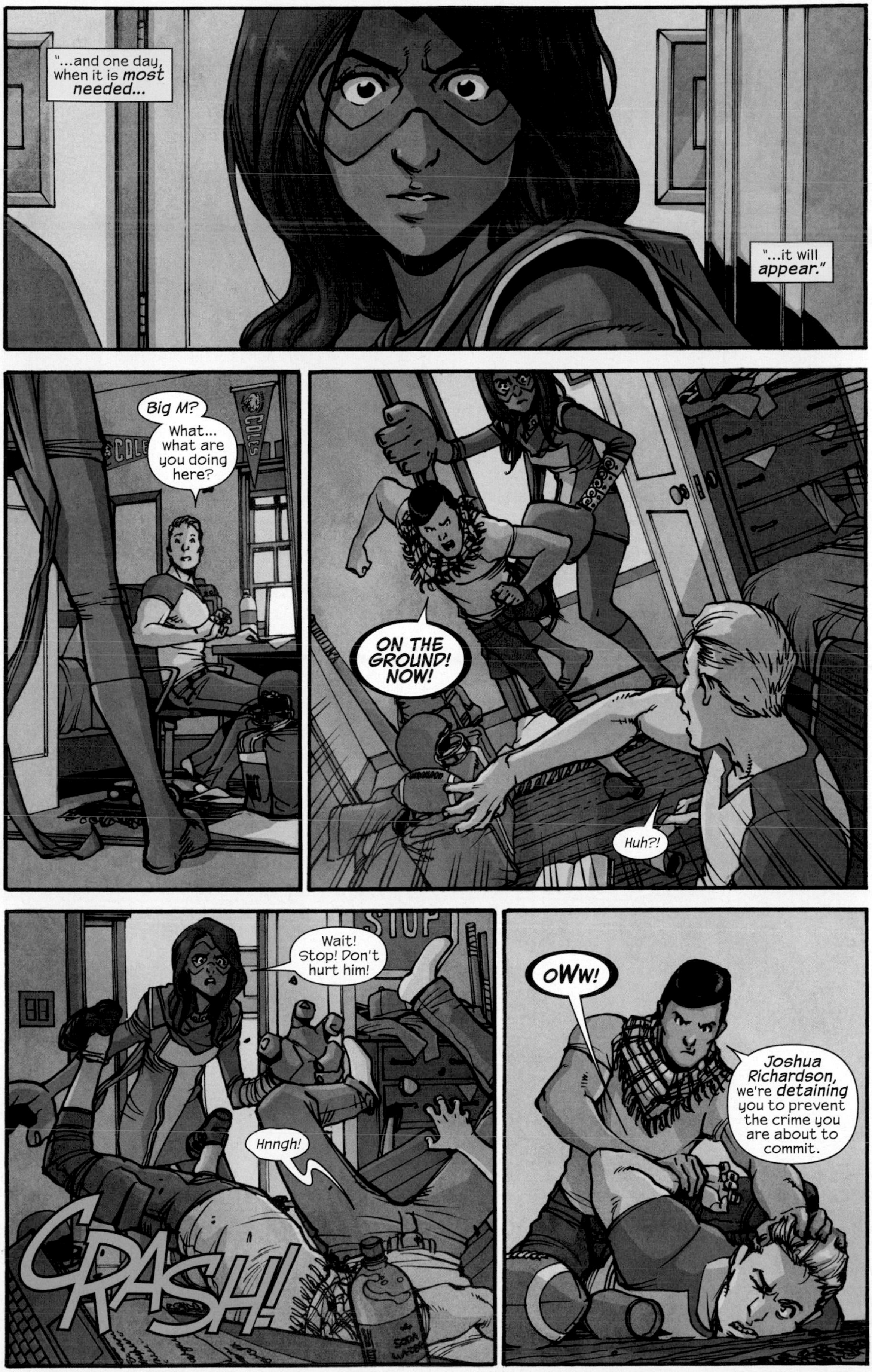
"...and one day, when it is *most needed*...
"...it will *appear*."
Big M?
What... what are you doing here?
COLES
ON THE GROUND! NOW!
Huh?!
Wait! Stop! Don't hurt him!
Hnngh!
CRASH!
OWW!
Joshua Richardson, we're *detaining* you to prevent the crime you are about to commit.

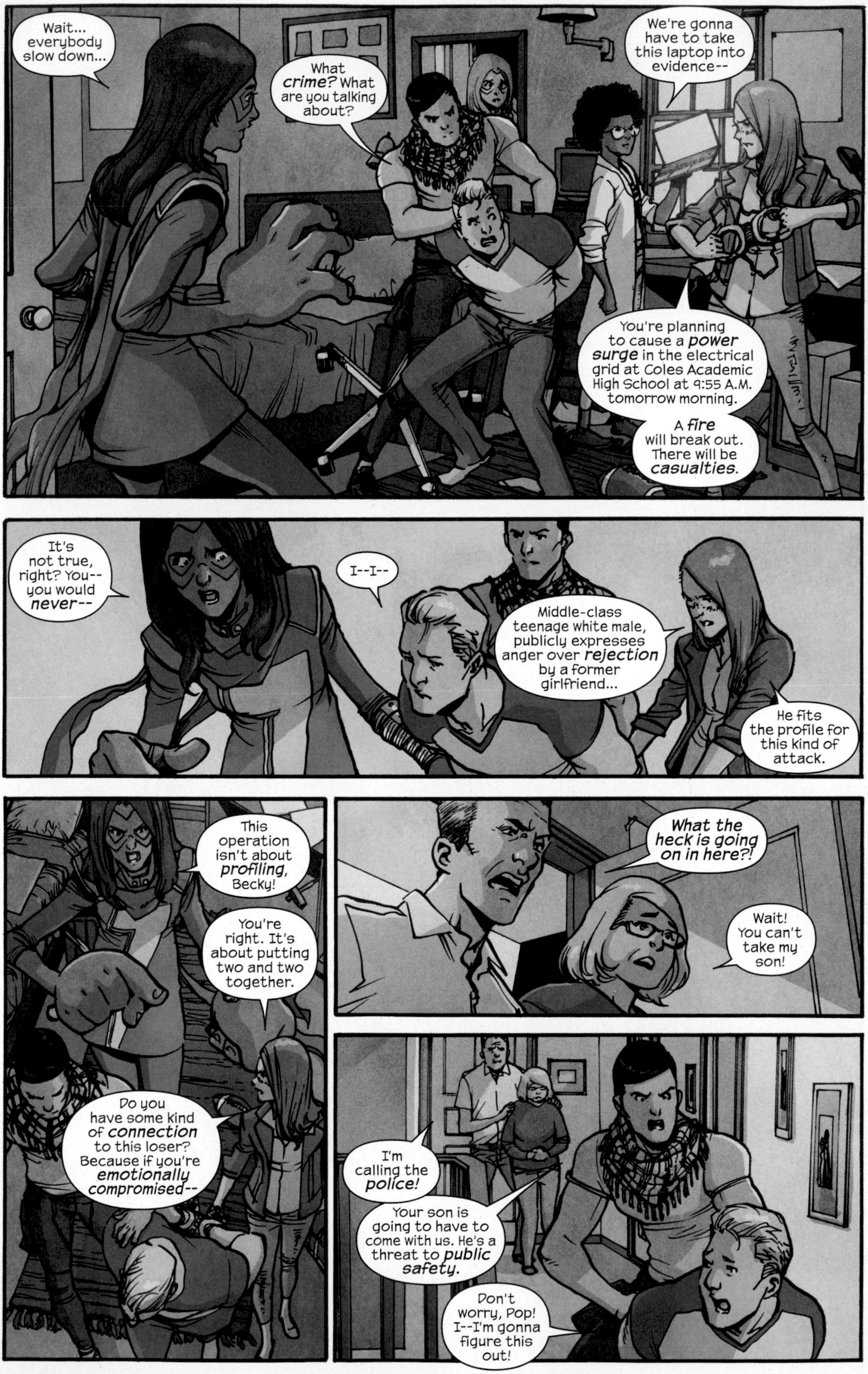
Wait... everybody slow down...
What crime? What are you talking about?
We're gonna have to take this laptop into evidence--
You're planning to cause a power surge in the electrical grid at Coles Academic High School at 9:55 A.M. tomorrow morning.
A fire will break out. There will be casualties.
It's not true, right? You-- you would never--
I--I--
Middle-class teenage white male, publicly expresses anger over rejection by a former girlfriend...
He fits the profile for this kind of attack.
This operation isn't about profiling, Becky!
You're right. It's about putting two and two together.
Do you have some kind of connection to this loser? Because if you're emotionally compromised--
What the heck is going on in here?!
Wait! You can't take my son!
I'm calling the police!
Your son is going to have to come with us. He's a threat to public safety.
Don't worry, Pop! I--I'm gonna figure this out!

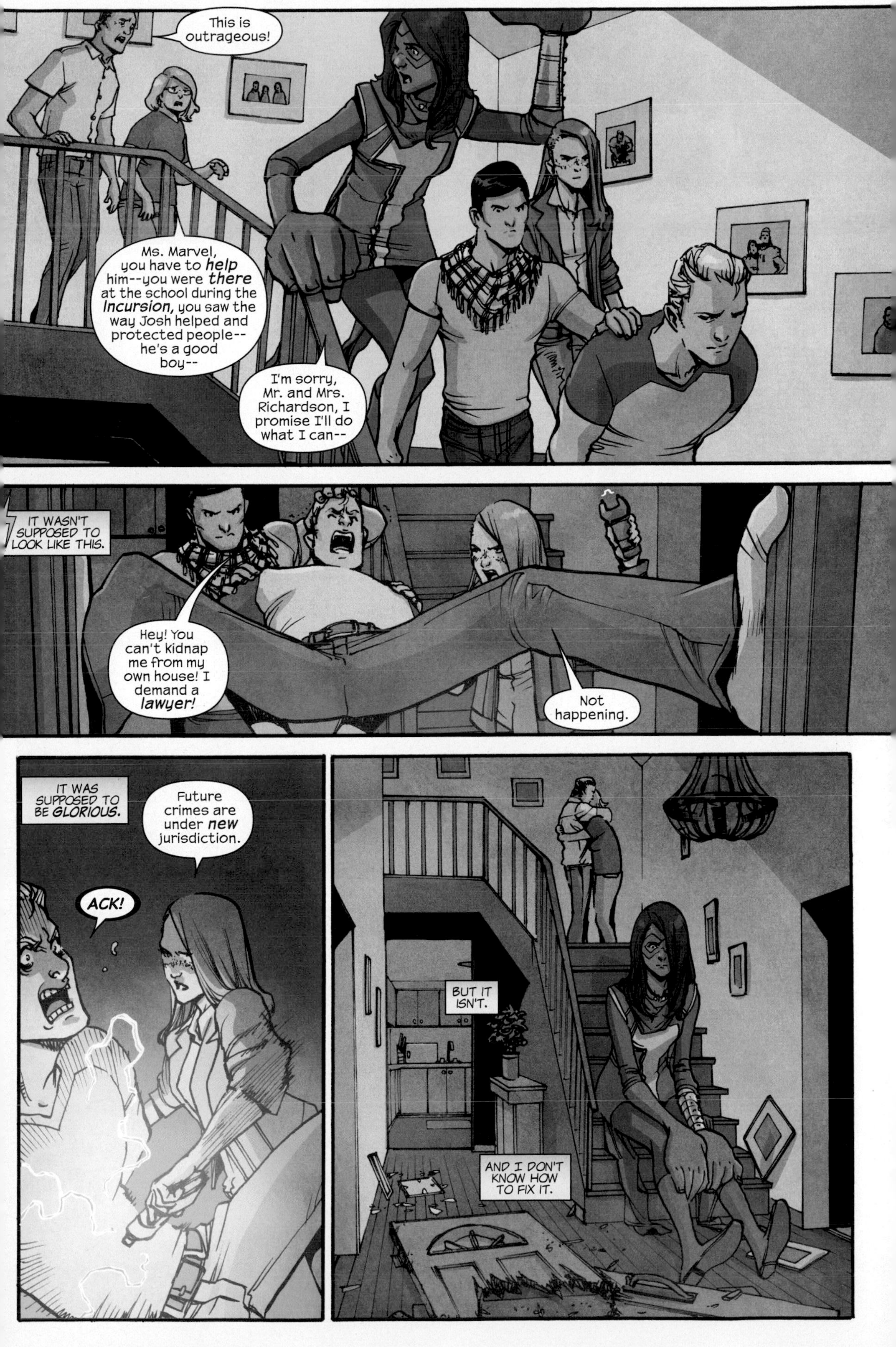
This is outrageous!
Ms. Marvel, you have to help him--you were there at the school during the Incursion, you saw the way Josh helped and protected people--he's a good boy--
I'm sorry, Mr. and Mrs. Richardson, I promise I'll do what I can--
IT WASN'T SUPPOSED TO LOOK LIKE THIS.
Hey! You can't kidnap me from my own house! I demand a lawyer!
Not happening.
IT WAS SUPPOSED TO BE GLORIOUS.
Future crimes are under new jurisdiction.
ACK!
BUT IT ISN'T.
AND I DON'T KNOW HOW TO FIX IT.

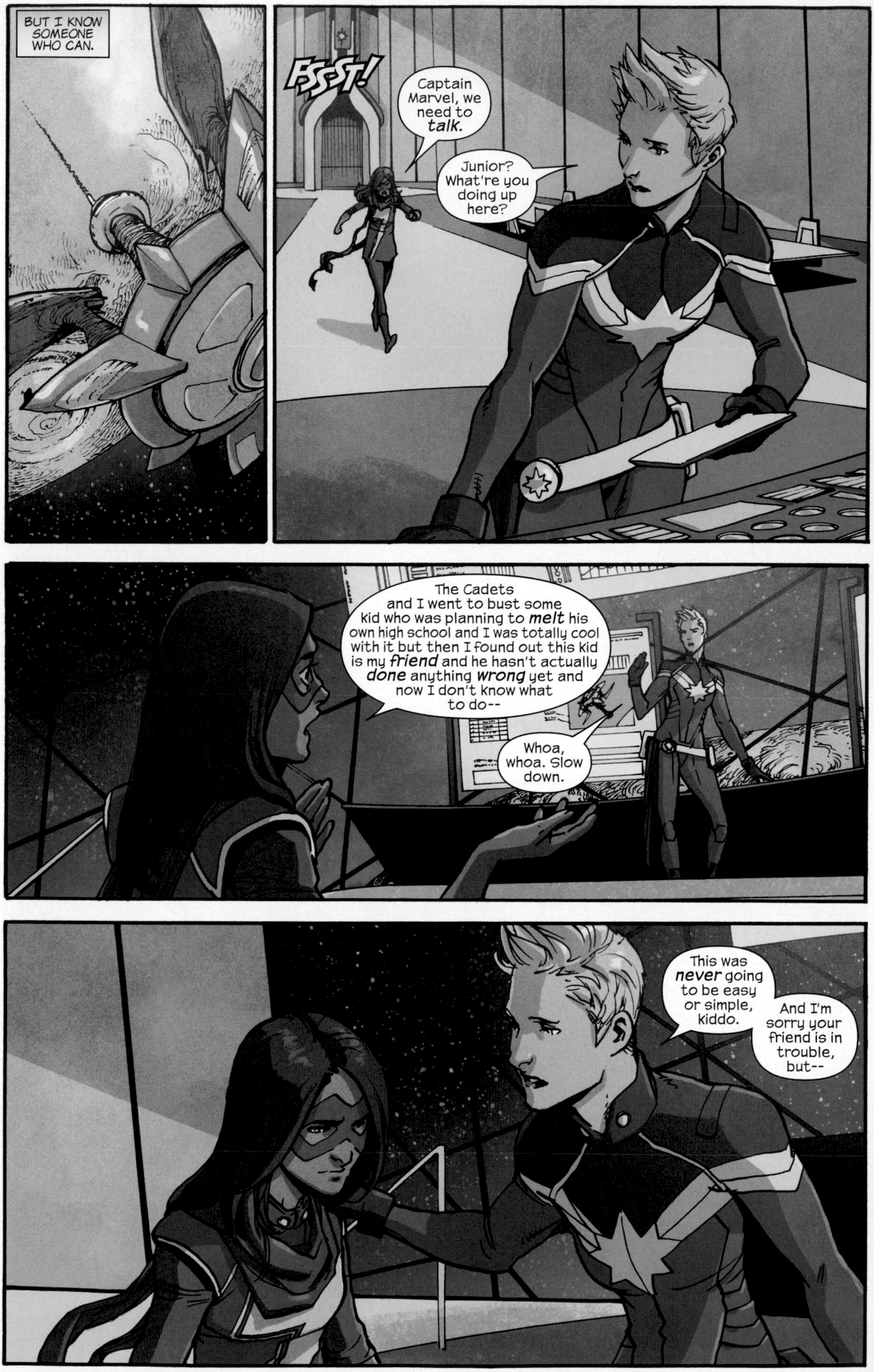
BUT I KNOW SOMEONE WHO CAN.
FSSST!
Captain Marvel, we need to talk.
Junior? What're you doing up here?
The Cadets and I went to bust some kid who was planning to melt his own high school and I was totally cool with it but then I found out this kid is my friend and he hasn't actually done anything wrong yet and now I don't know what to do--
Whoa, whoa. Slow down.
This was never going to be easy or simple, kiddo.
And I'm sorry your friend is in trouble, but--

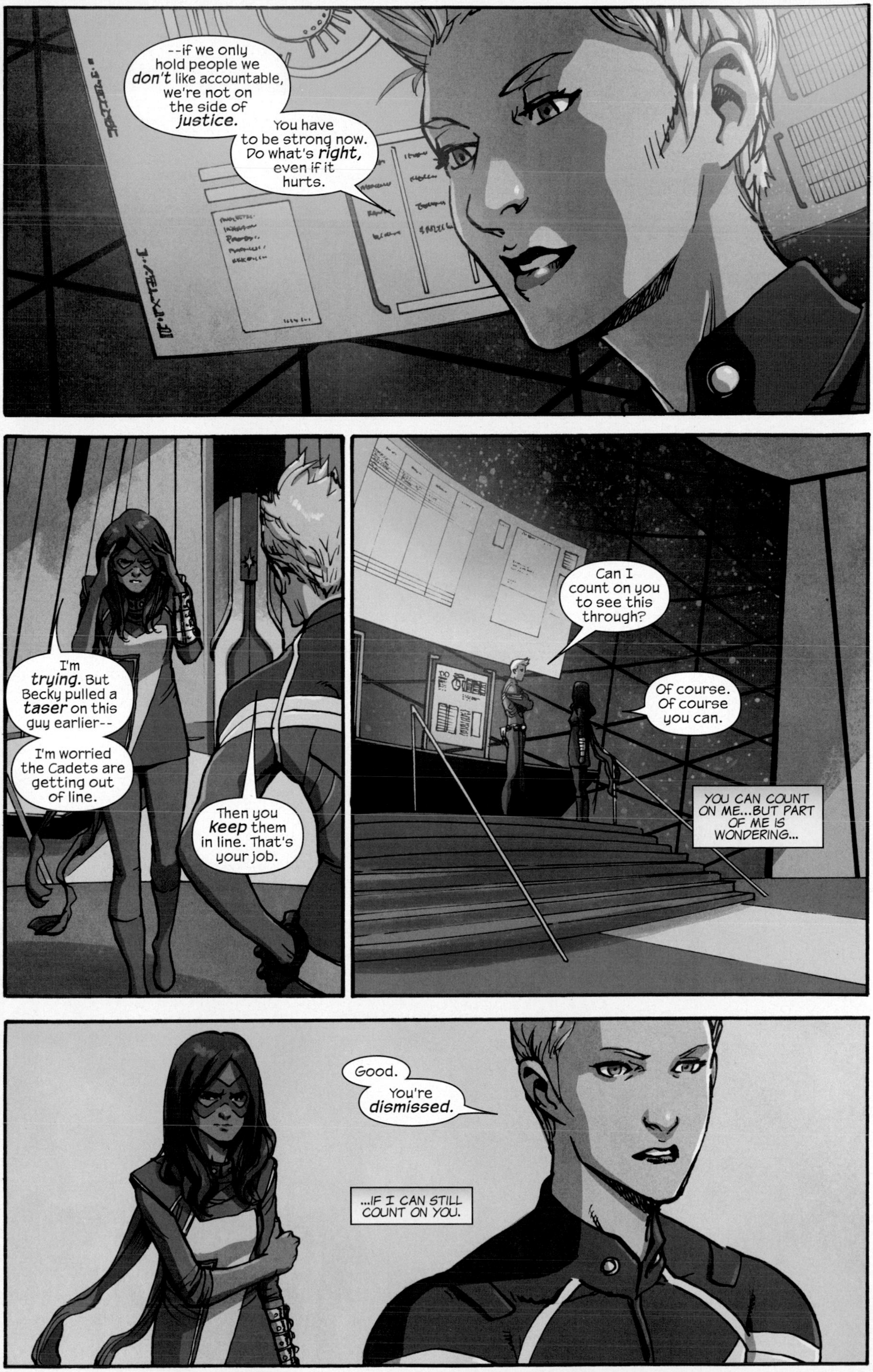
--if we only hold people we don't like accountable, we're not on the side of justice.
You have to be strong now. Do what's right, even if it hurts.
I'm trying. But Becky pulled a taser on this guy earlier--
I'm worried the Cadets are getting out of line.
Then you keep them in line. That's your job.
Can I count on you to see this through?
Of course. Of course you can.
YOU CAN COUNT ON ME...BUT PART OF ME IS WONDERING...
Good.
You're dismissed.
...IF I CAN STILL COUNT ON YOU.

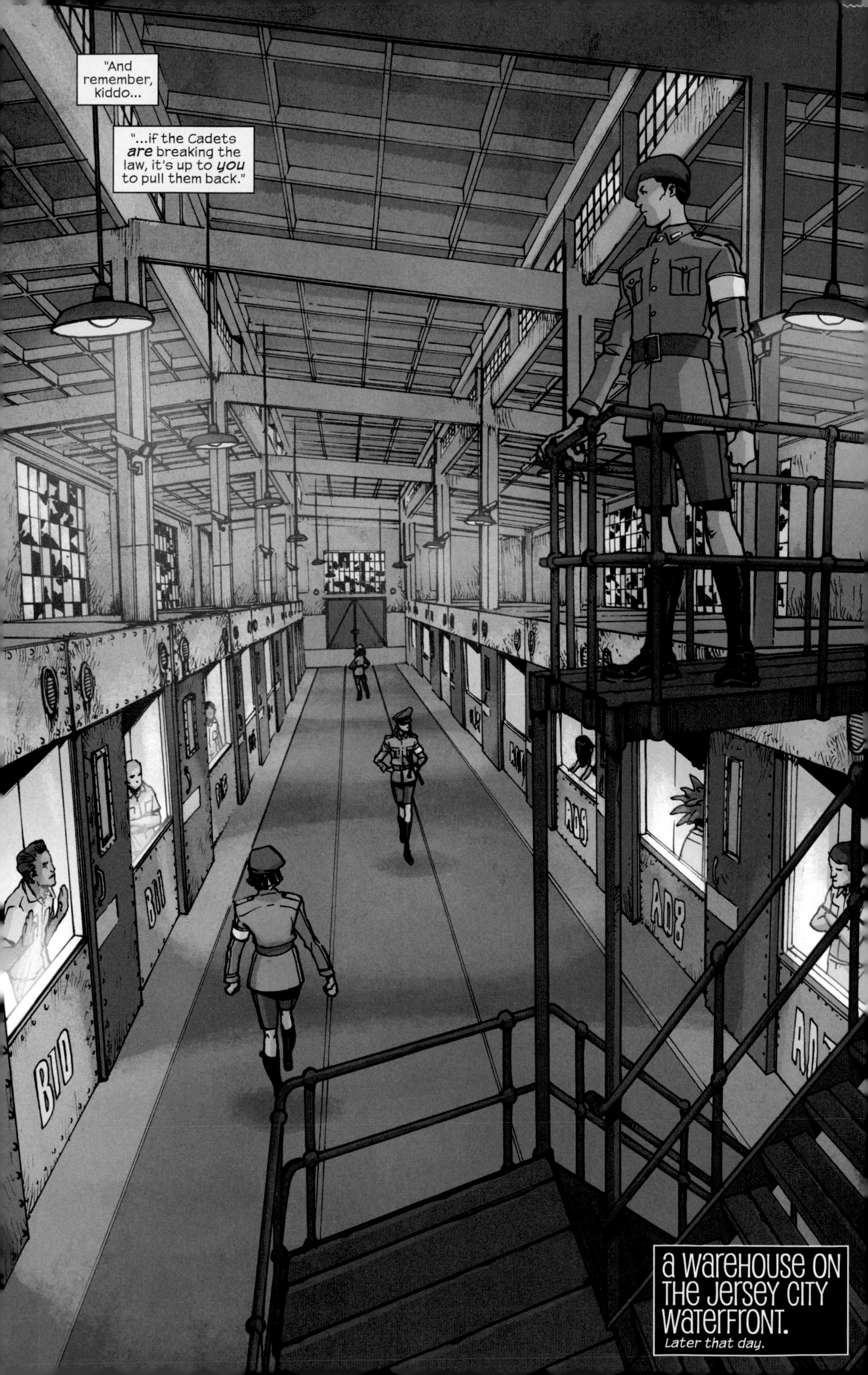

"And remember, kiddo...
"...if the Cadets *are* breaking the law, it's up to *you* to pull them back."
A WAREHOUSE ON THE JERSEY CITY WATERFRONT.
Later that day.

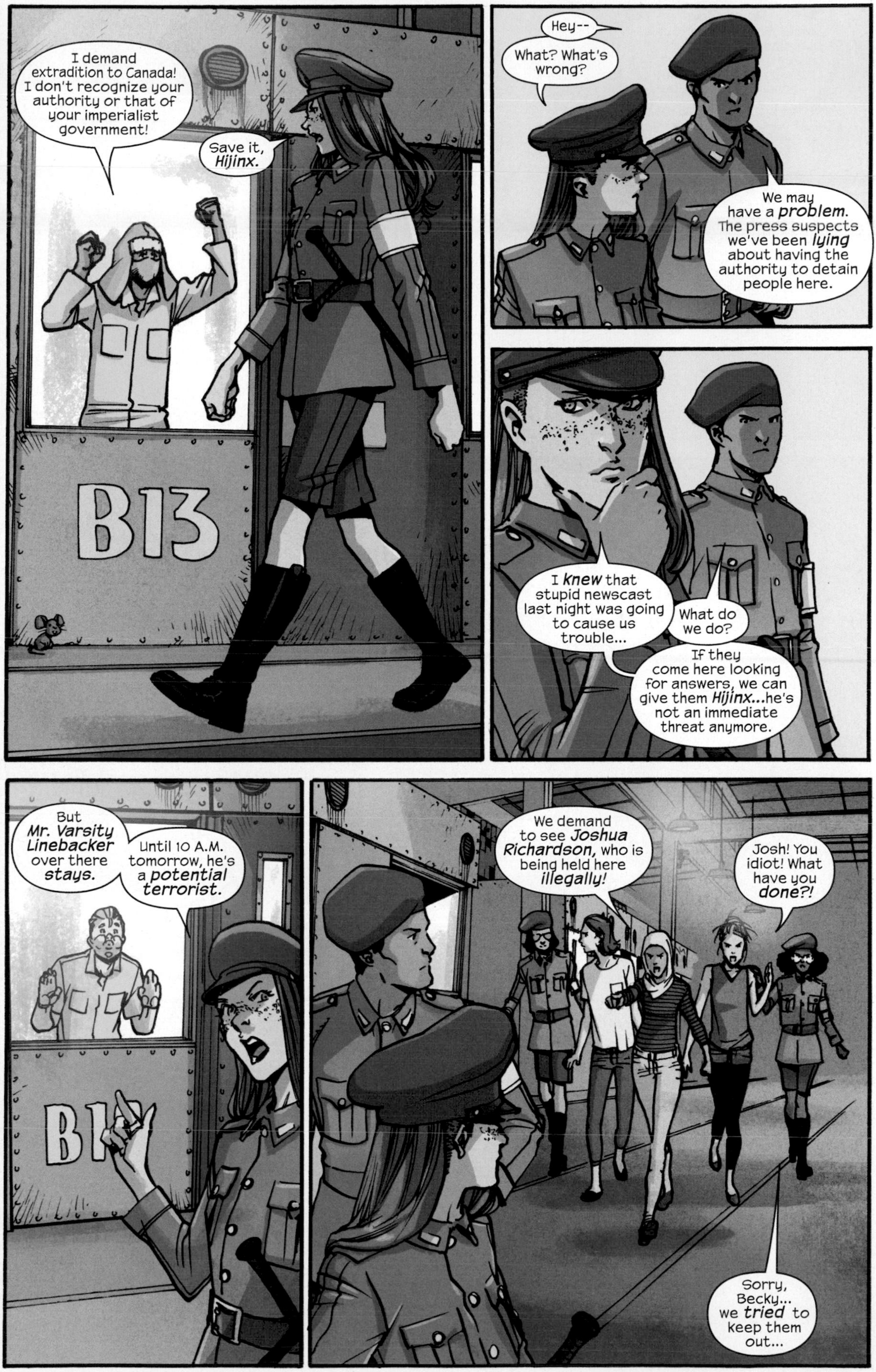
I demand extradition to Canada! I don't recognize your authority or that of your imperialist government!
Save it, Hijinx.
B13
Hey--
What? What's wrong?
We may have a problem. The press suspects we've been lying about having the authority to detain people here.
I knew that stupid newscast last night was going to cause us trouble...
What do we do?
If they come here looking for answers, we can give them Hijinx...he's not an immediate threat anymore.
But Mr. Varsity Linebacker over there stays.
Until 10 A.M. tomorrow, he's a potential terrorist.
We demand to see Joshua Richardson, who is being held here illegally!
Josh! You idiot! What have you done?!
Sorry, Becky... we tried to keep them out...

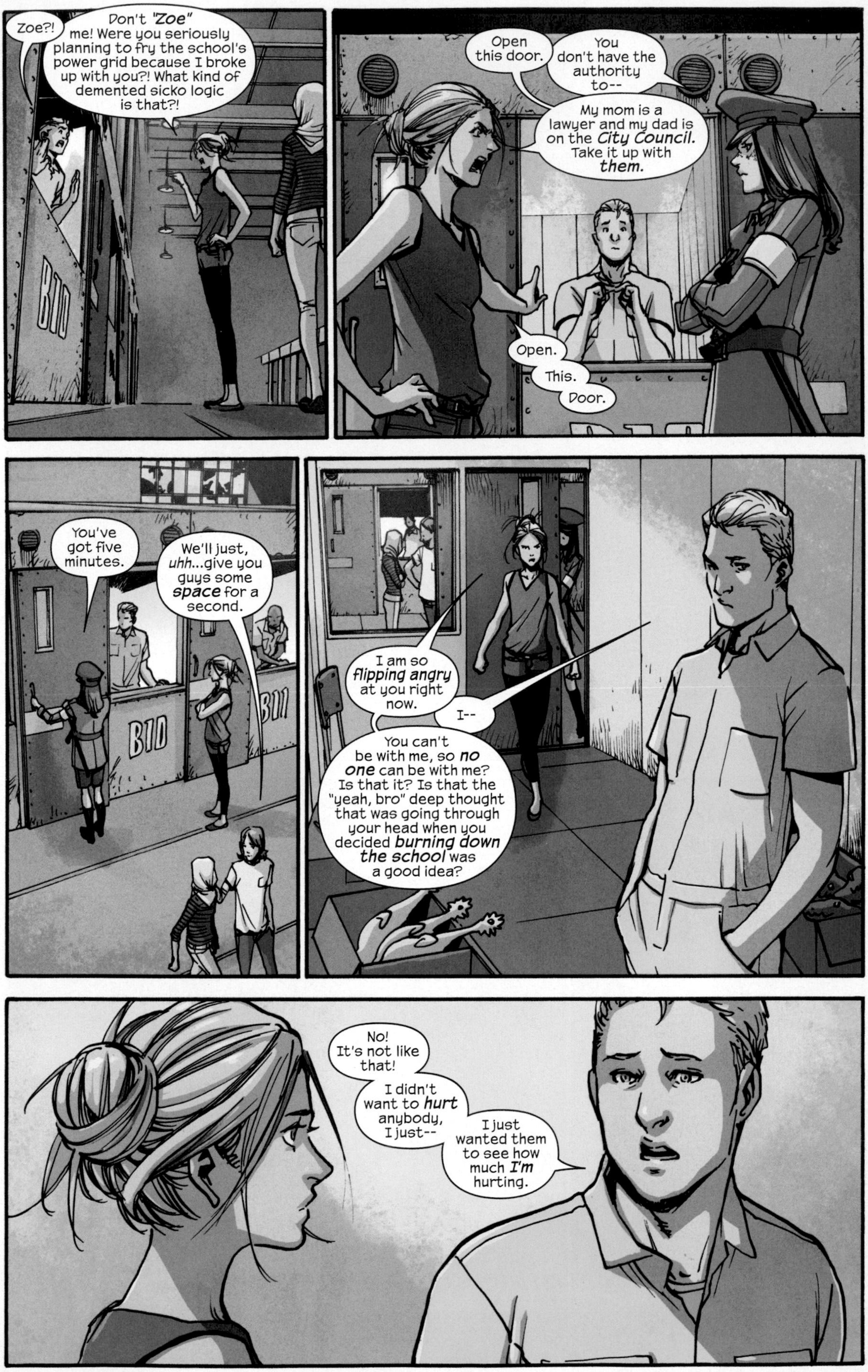

Zoe?!
Don't "Zoe" me! Were you seriously planning to fry the school's power grid because I broke up with you?! What kind of demented sicko logic is that?!
B10
Open this door.
You don't have the authority to--
My mom is a lawyer and my dad is on the City Council. Take it up with them.
Open.
This.
Door.
You've got five minutes.
We'll just, uhh...give you guys some space for a second.
B10
B11
I am so flipping angry at you right now.
I--
You can't be with me, so no one can be with me? Is that it? Is that the "yeah, bro" deep thought that was going through your head when you decided burning down the school was a good idea?
No! It's not like that!
I didn't want to hurt anybody, I just--
I just wanted them to see how much I'm hurting.

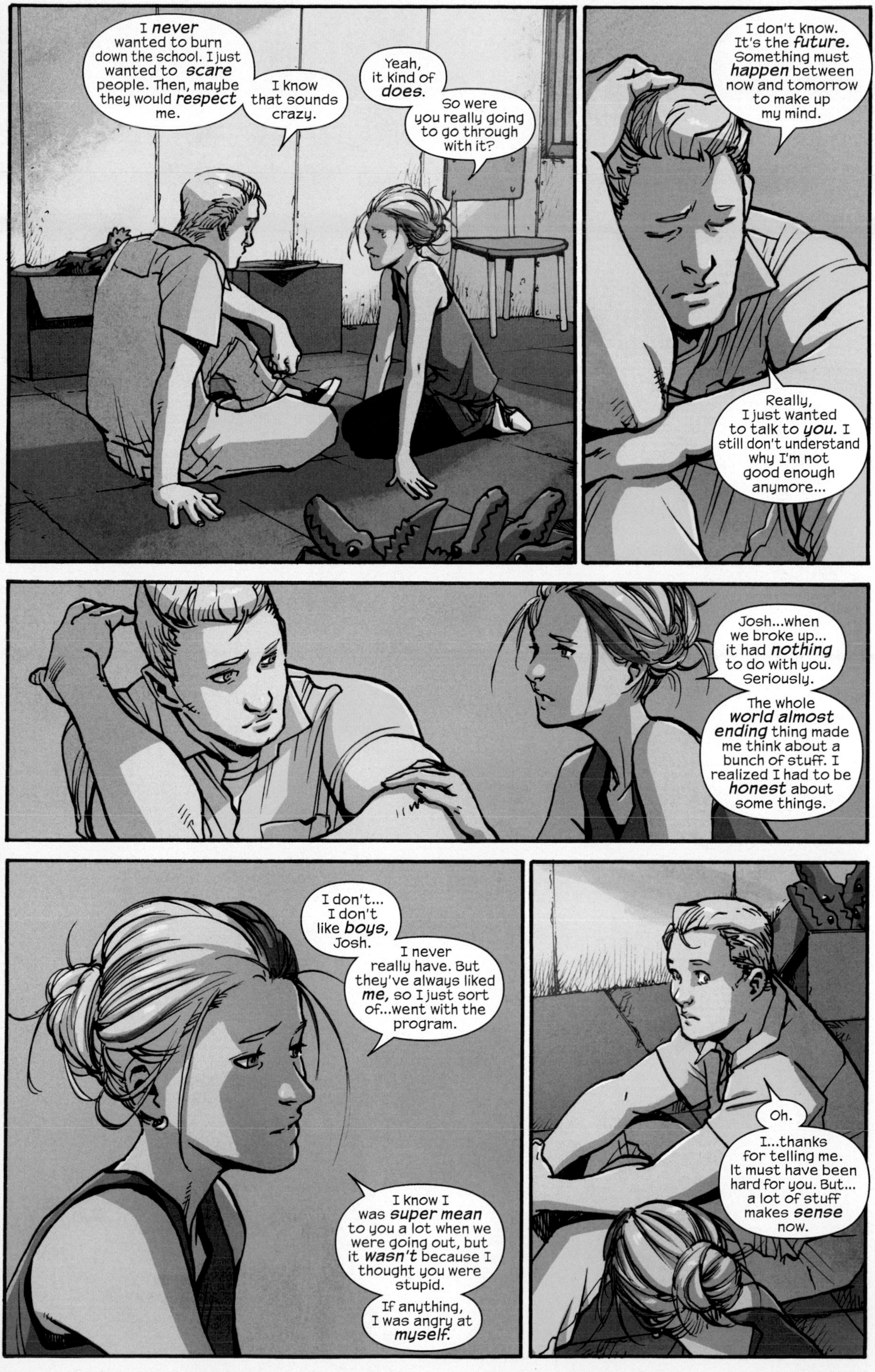
I never wanted to burn down the school. I just wanted to scare people. Then, maybe they would respect me.
I know that sounds crazy.
Yeah, it kind of does.
So were you really going to go through with it?
I don't know. It's the future. Something must happen between now and tomorrow to make up my mind.
Really, I just wanted to talk to you. I still don't understand why I'm not good enough anymore...
Josh...when we broke up... it had nothing to do with you. Seriously.
The whole world almost ending thing made me think about a bunch of stuff. I realized I had to be honest about some things.
I don't... I don't like boys, Josh.
I never really have. But they've always liked me, so I just sort of...went with the program.
I know I was super mean to you a lot when we were going out, but it wasn't because I thought you were stupid.
If anything, I was angry at myself.
Oh.
I...thanks for telling me. It must have been hard for you. But... a lot of stuff makes sense now.

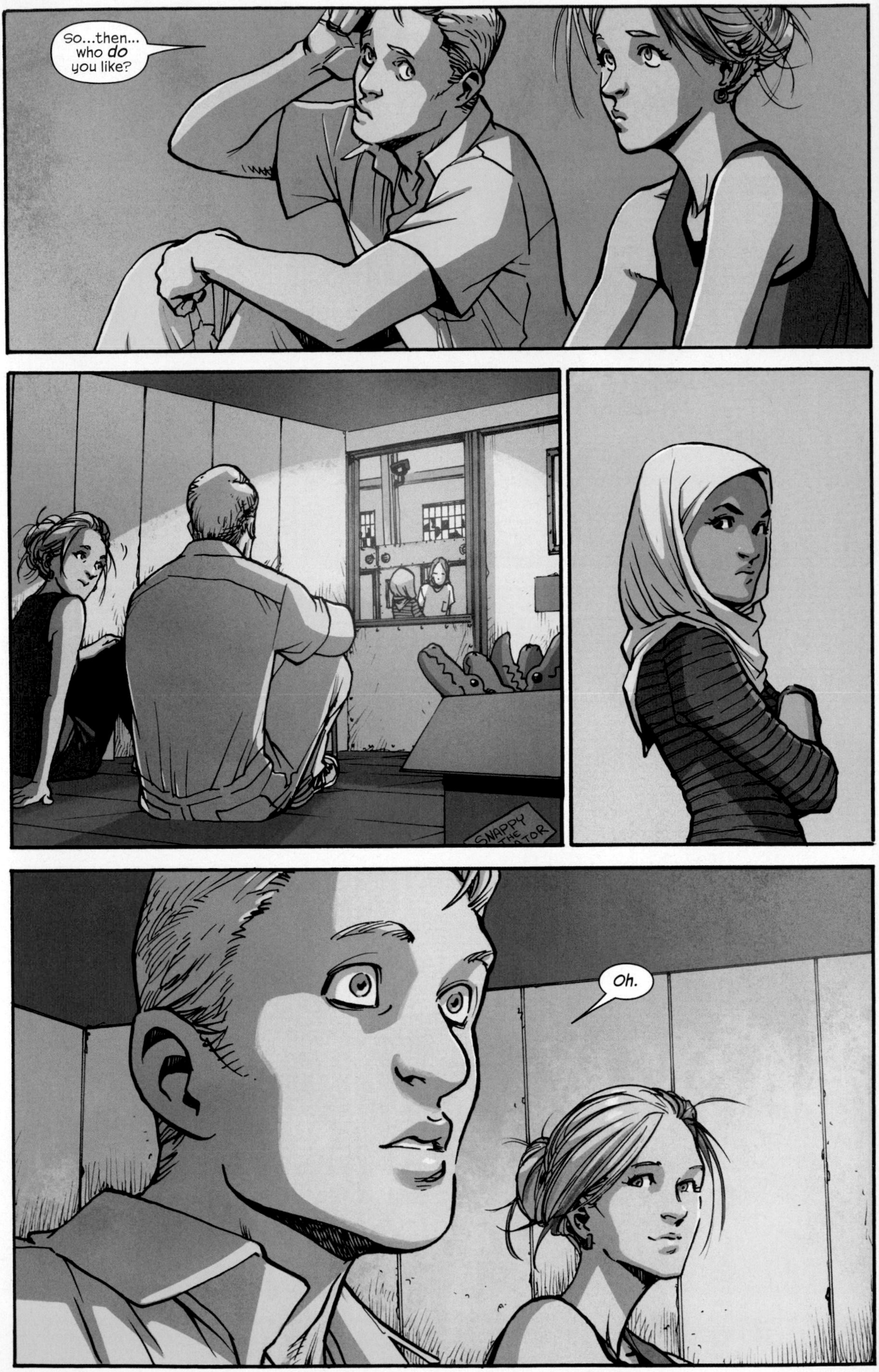
So...then... who **do** you like?
SNAPPY THE GATOR
Oh.

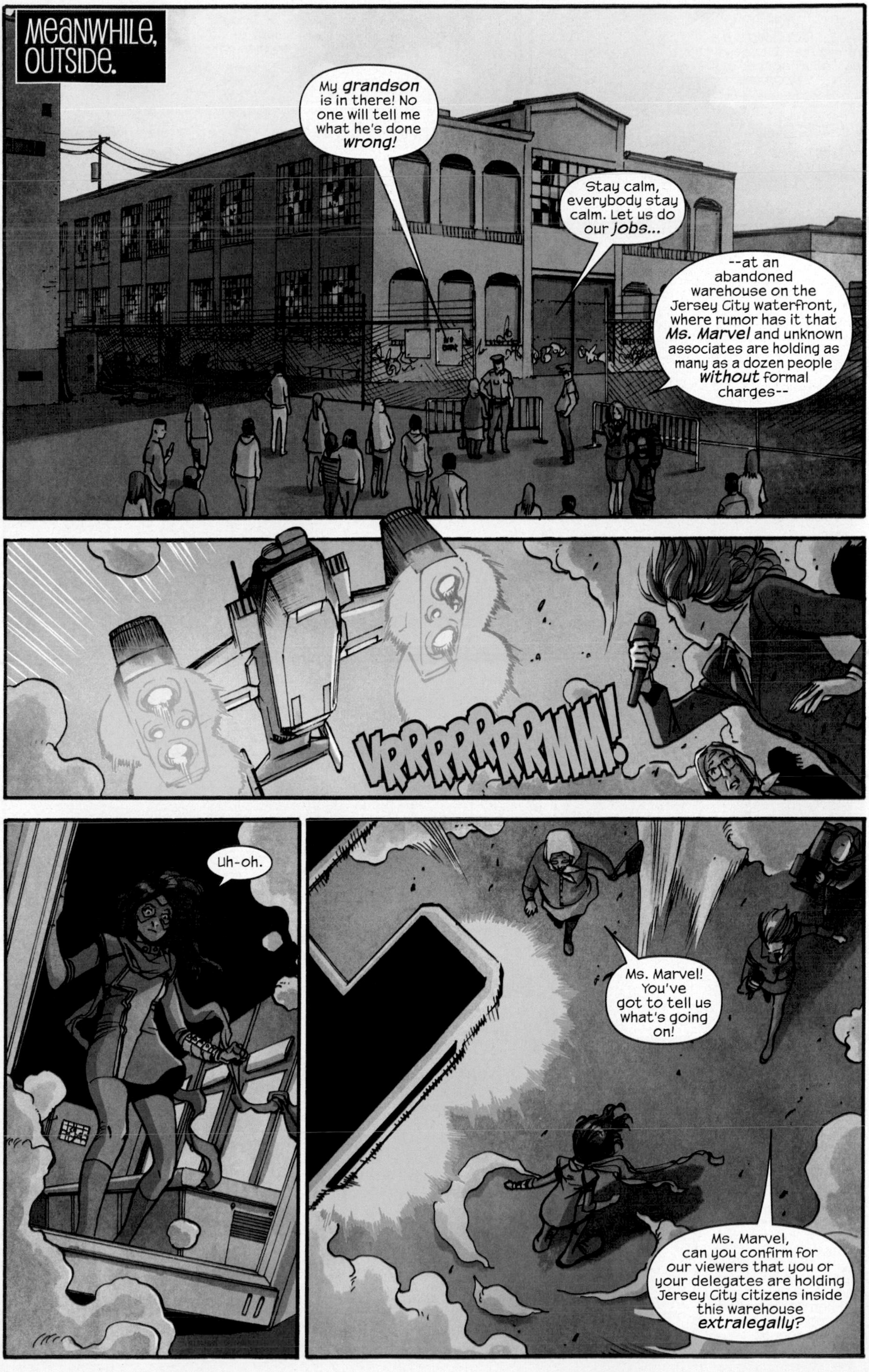
MEANWHILE, OUTSIDE.
My grandson is in there! No one will tell me what he's done wrong!
Stay calm, everybody stay calm. Let us do our jobs...
--at an abandoned warehouse on the Jersey City waterfront, where rumor has it that Ms. Marvel and unknown associates are holding as many as a dozen people without formal charges--
VRRRRRRRMM!
Uh-oh.
Ms. Marvel! You've got to tell us what's going on!
Ms. Marvel, can you confirm for our viewers that you or your delegates are holding Jersey City citizens inside this warehouse extralegally?

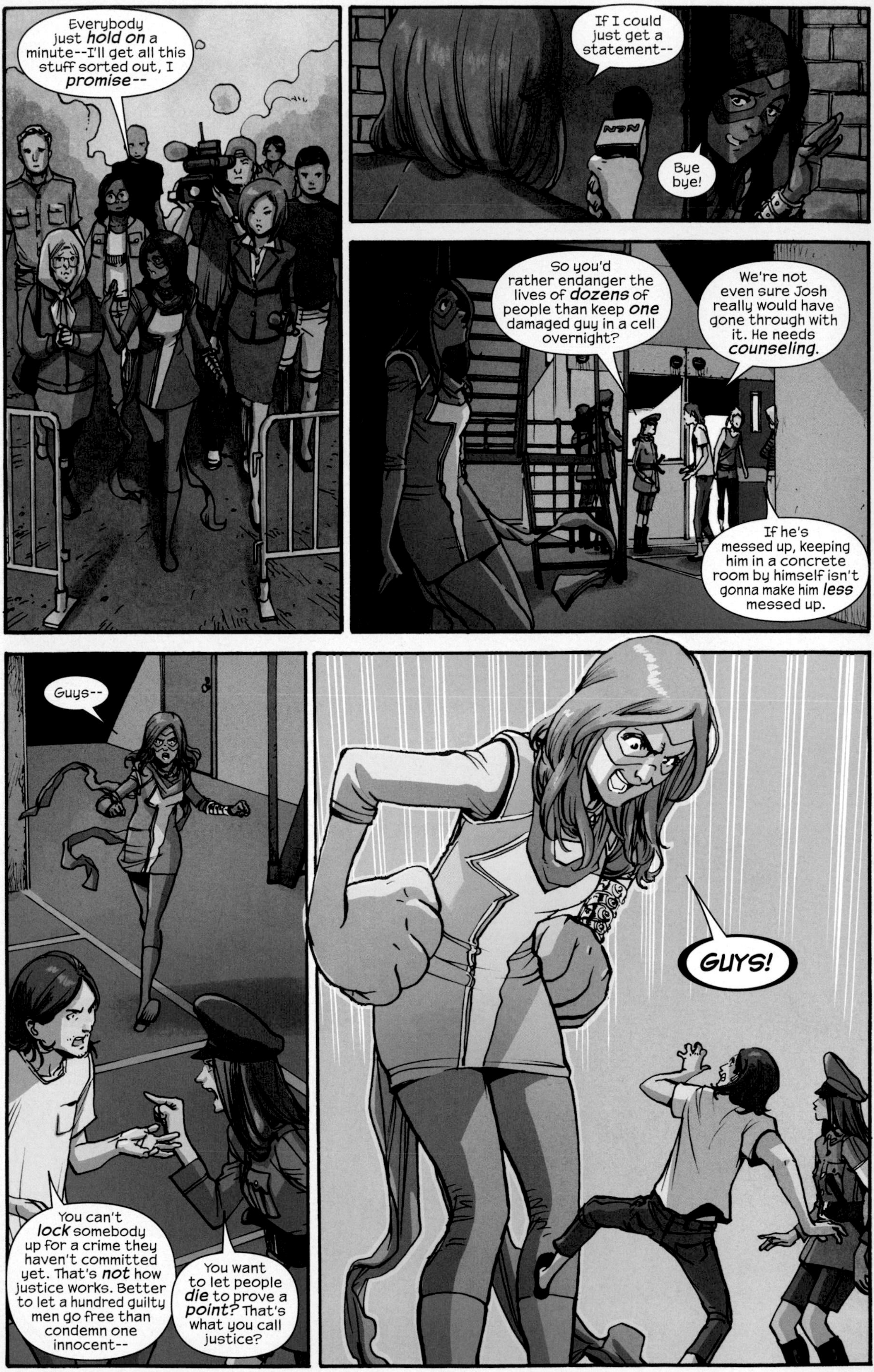
Everybody just hold on a minute--I'll get all this stuff sorted out, I promise--
If I could just get a statement--
NGN
Bye bye!
So you'd rather endanger the lives of dozens of people than keep one damaged guy in a cell overnight?
We're not even sure Josh really would have gone through with it. He needs counseling.
If he's messed up, keeping him in a concrete room by himself isn't gonna make him less messed up.
Guys--
You can't lock somebody up for a crime they haven't committed yet. That's not how justice works. Better to let a hundred guilty men go free than condemn one innocent--
You want to let people die to prove a point? That's what you call justice?
GUYS!

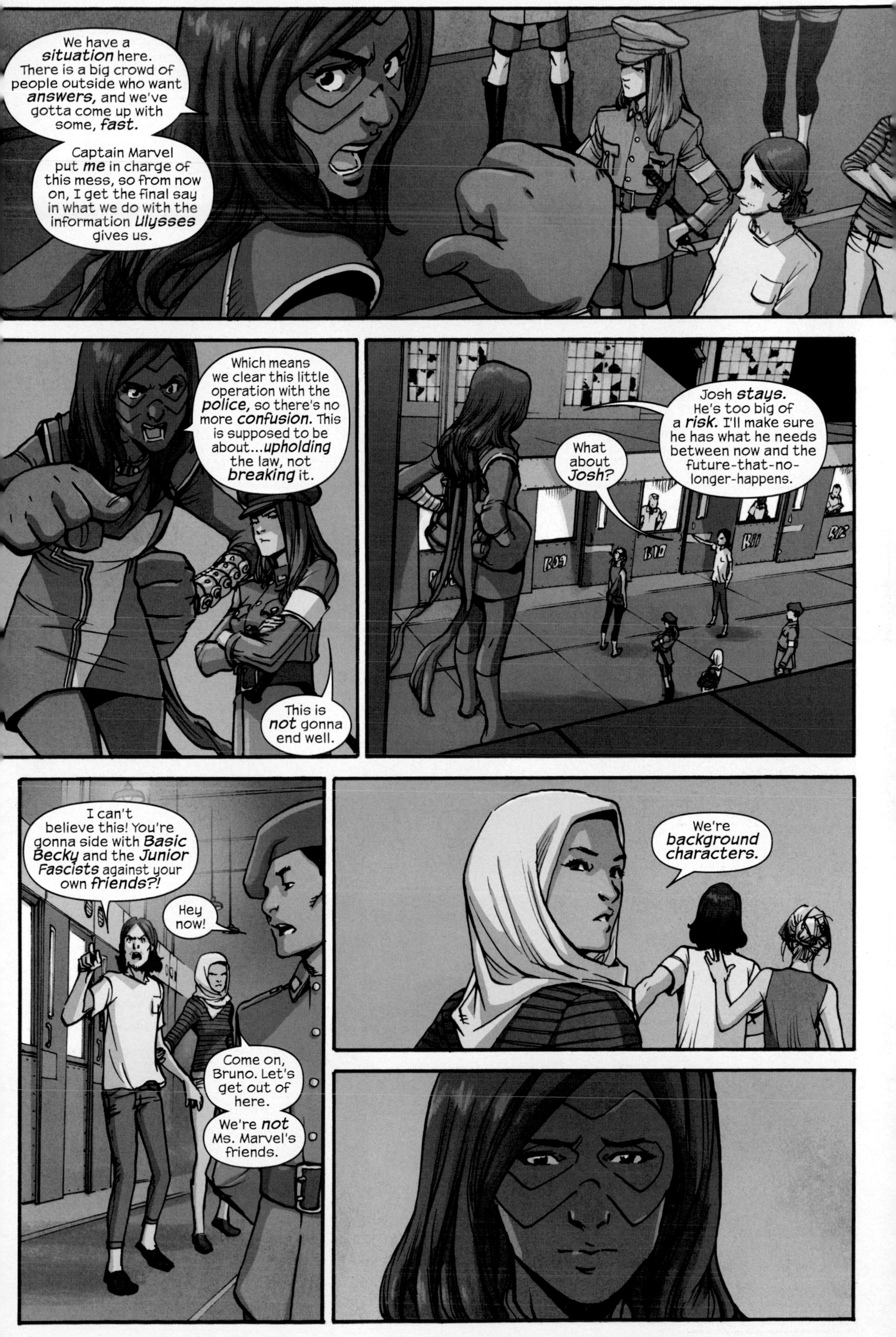
We have a situation here. There is a big crowd of people outside who want answers, and we've gotta come up with some, fast.
Captain Marvel put me in charge of this mess, so from now on, I get the final say in what we do with the information Ulysses gives us.
Which means we clear this little operation with the police, so there's no more confusion. This is supposed to be about...upholding the law, not breaking it.
This is not gonna end well.
What about Josh?
Josh stays. He's too big of a risk. I'll make sure he has what he needs between now and the future-that-no-longer-happens.
I can't believe this! You're gonna side with Basic Becky and the Junior Fascists against your own friends?!
Hey now!
Come on, Bruno. Let's get out of here.
We're not Ms. Marvel's friends.
We're background characters.

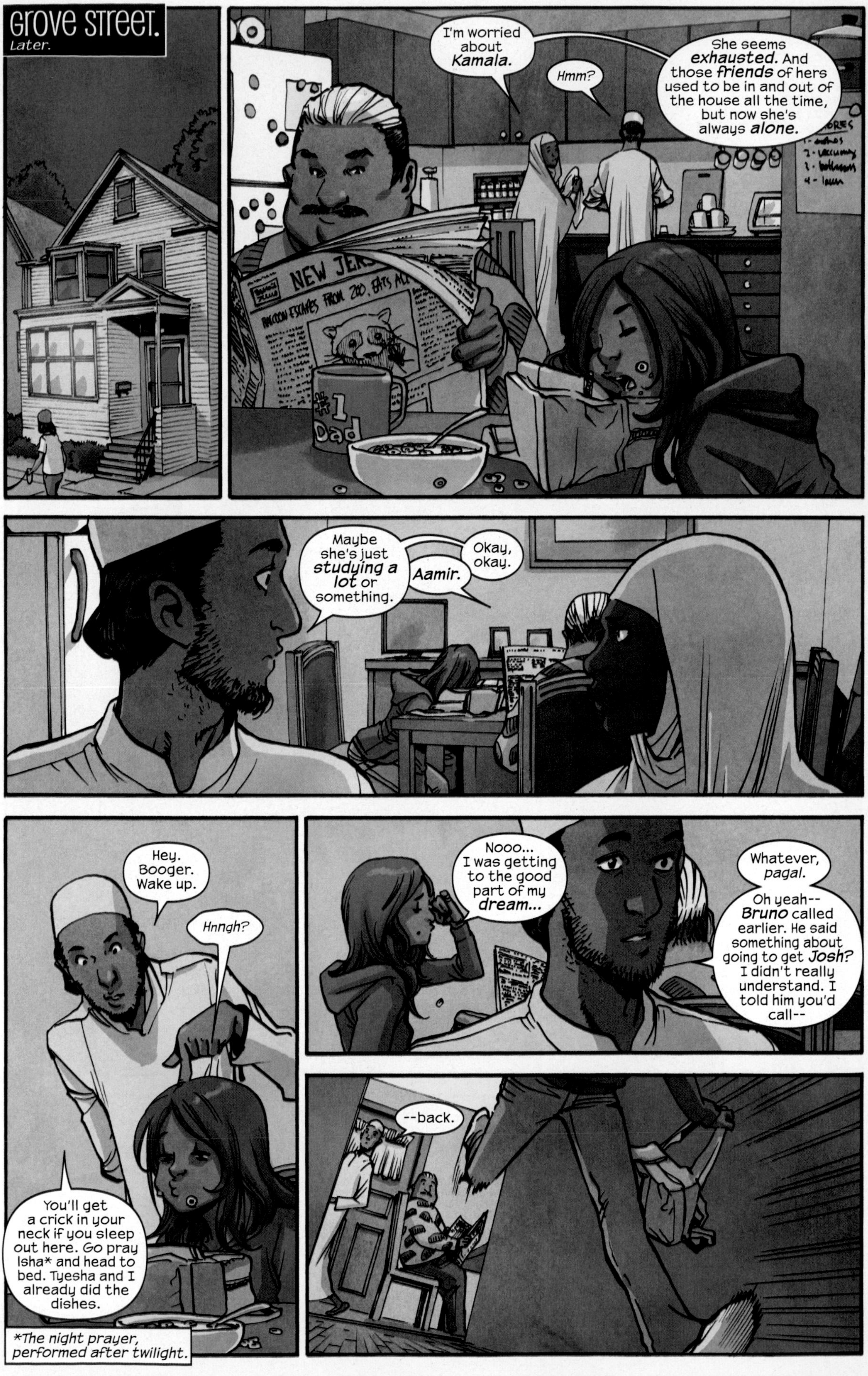
GROVE STREET.
Later.
I'm worried about Kamala.
Hmm?
She seems exhausted. And those friends of hers used to be in and out of the house all the time, but now she's always alone.
NEW JERS
RACCOON ESCAPES FROM ZOO, EATS ALL
#1 Dad
Maybe she's just studying a lot or something.
Aamir.
Okay, okay.
Hey. Booger. Wake up.
Hnngh?
You'll get a crick in your neck if you sleep out here. Go pray Isha* and head to bed. Tyesha and I already did the dishes.
Nooo... I was getting to the good part of my dream...
Whatever, pagal.
Oh yeah-- Bruno called earlier. He said something about going to get Josh? I didn't really understand. I told him you'd call--
--back.
*The night prayer, performed after twilight.

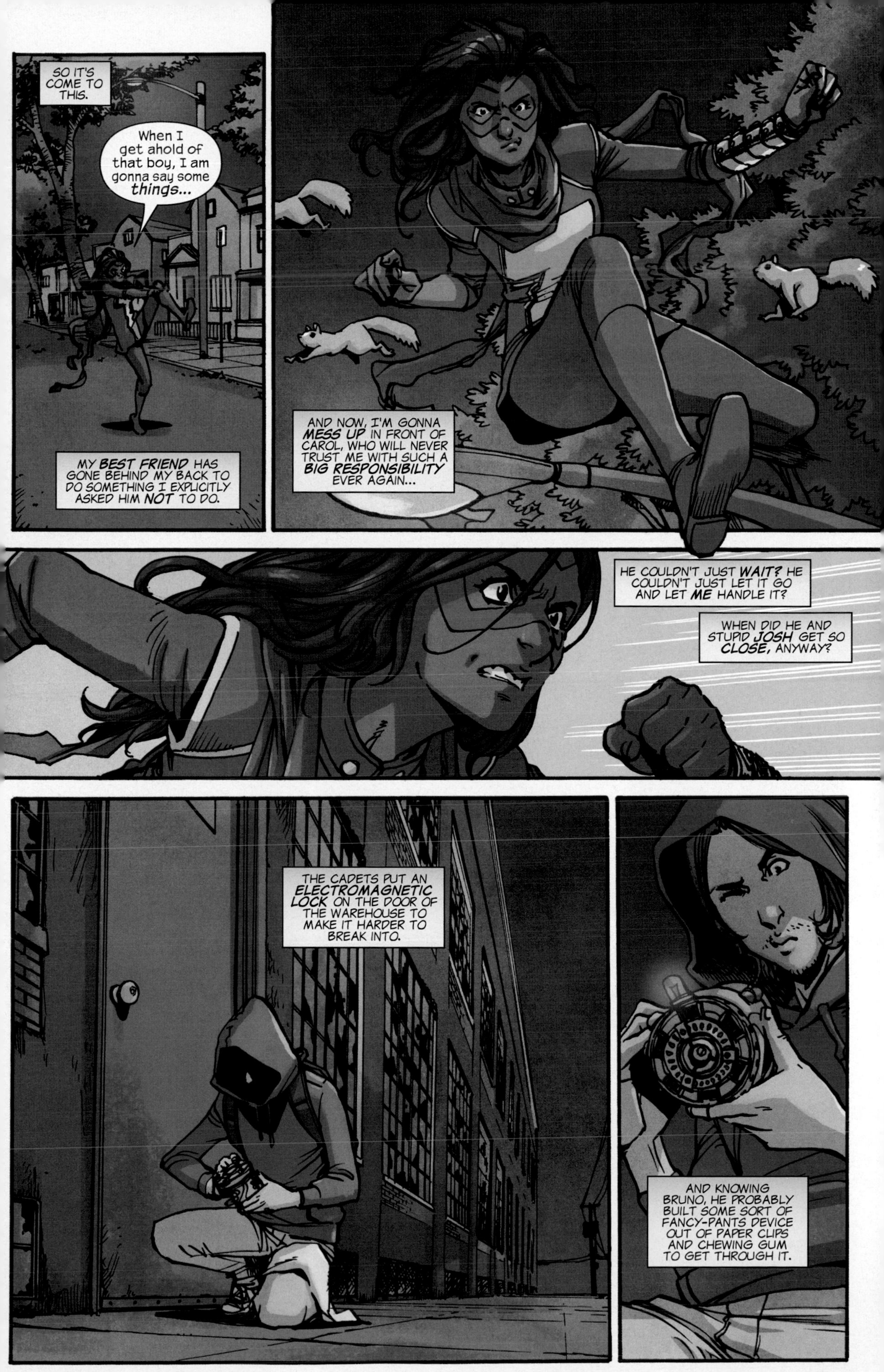
SO IT'S COME TO THIS.
When I get ahold of that boy, I am gonna say some *things...*
MY **BEST FRIEND** HAS GONE BEHIND MY BACK TO DO SOMETHING I EXPLICITLY ASKED HIM **NOT** TO DO.
AND NOW, I'M GONNA **MESS UP** IN FRONT OF CAROL, WHO WILL NEVER TRUST ME WITH SUCH A **BIG RESPONSIBILITY** EVER AGAIN...
HE COULDN'T JUST **WAIT?** HE COULDN'T JUST LET IT GO AND LET **ME** HANDLE IT?
WHEN DID HE AND STUPID **JOSH** GET SO **CLOSE,** ANYWAY?
THE CADETS PUT AN **ELECTROMAGNETIC LOCK** ON THE DOOR OF THE WAREHOUSE TO MAKE IT HARDER TO BREAK INTO.
AND KNOWING BRUNO, HE PROBABLY BUILT SOME SORT OF FANCY-PANTS DEVICE OUT OF PAPER CLIPS AND CHEWING GUM TO GET THROUGH IT.

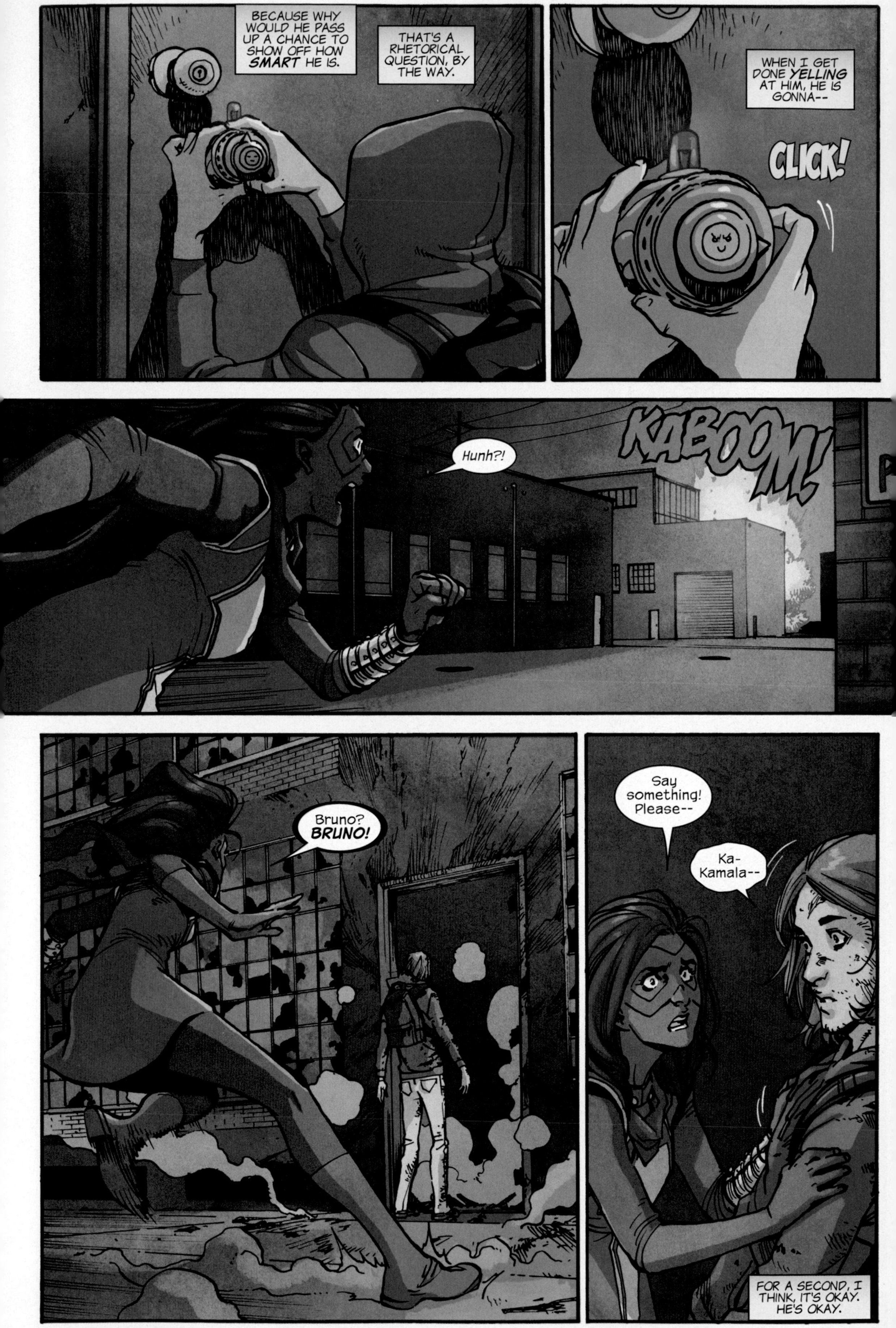
BECAUSE WHY WOULD HE PASS UP A CHANCE TO SHOW OFF HOW **SMART** HE IS.
THAT'S A RHETORICAL QUESTION, BY THE WAY.
WHEN I GET DONE **YELLING** AT HIM, HE IS GONNA--
CLICK!
Hunh?!
KABOOM!
Bruno? **BRUNO!**
Say something! Please--
Ka-Kamala--
FOR A SECOND, I THINK, IT'S OKAY. HE'S OKAY.

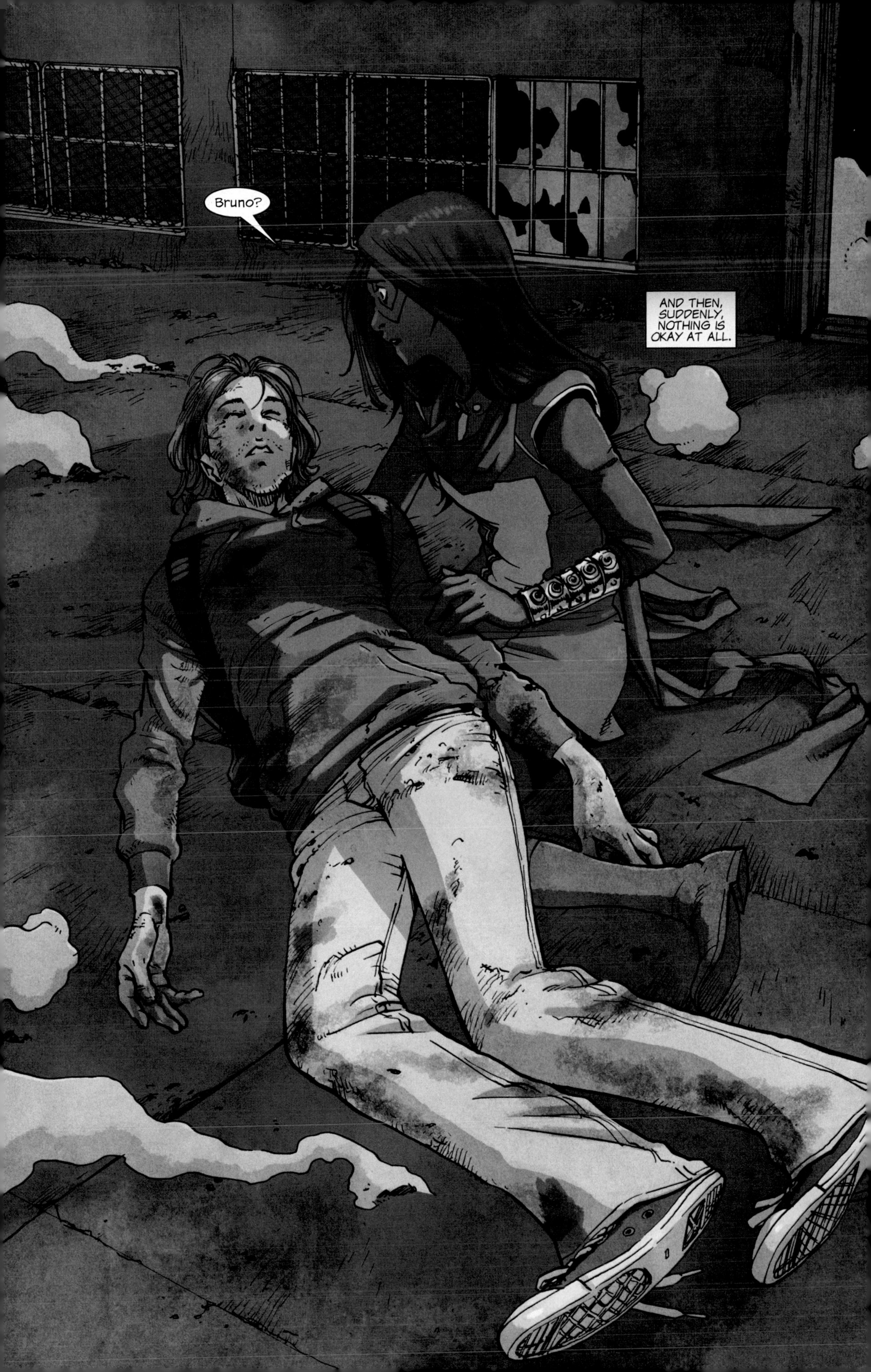
Bruno?
AND THEN, SUDDENLY, NOTHING IS OKAY AT ALL.

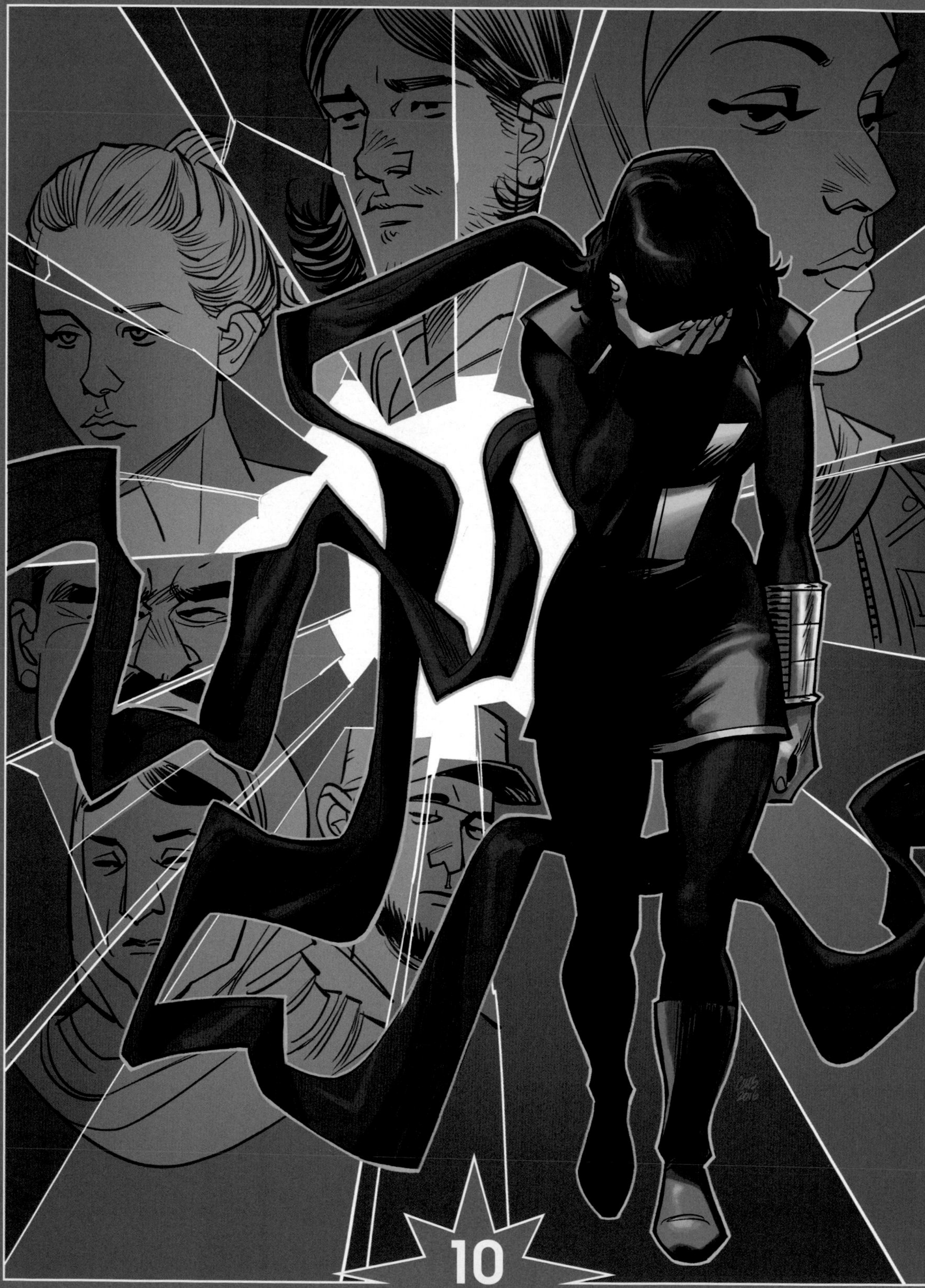
10

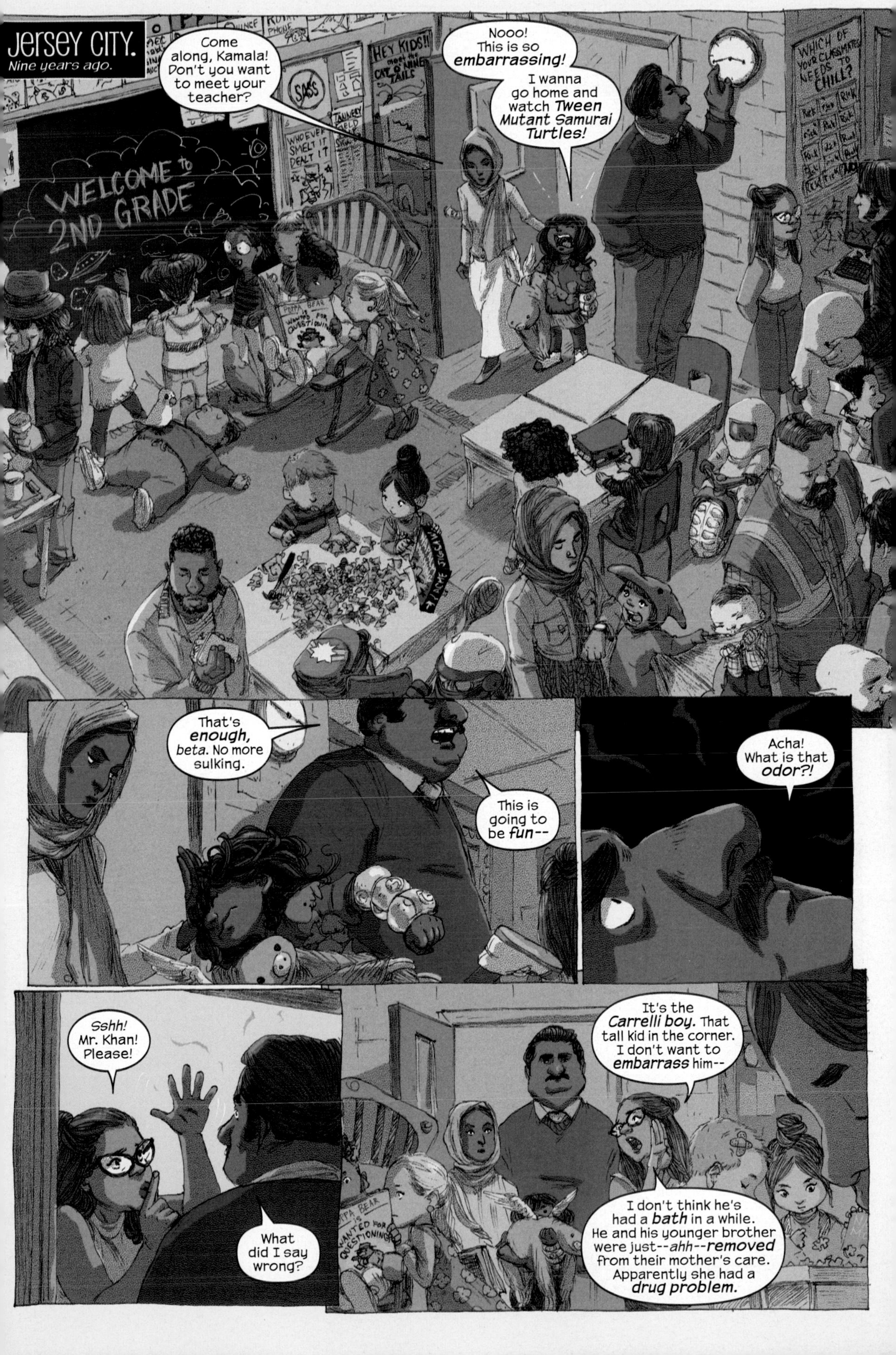
Jersey City.
Nine years ago.
Come along, Kamala! Don't you want to meet your teacher?
Nooo! This is so embarrassing!
I wanna go home and watch Tween Mutant Samurai Turtles!
WELCOME to 2ND GRADE
HEY KIDS!! meet the CAT O' NINE TAILS
SASS
WHOEVER SMELT IT DEALT IT
WHICH OF YOUR CLASSMATES NEEDS TO CHILL?
POPPA BEAR WANTED FOR QUESTIONING
That's enough, beta. No more sulking.
This is going to be fun--
Acha! What is that odor?!
Sshh! Mr. Khan! Please!
What did I say wrong?
It's the Carrelli boy. That tall kid in the corner. I don't want to embarrass him--
I don't think he's had a bath in a while. He and his younger brother were just--ahh--removed from their mother's care. Apparently she had a drug problem.

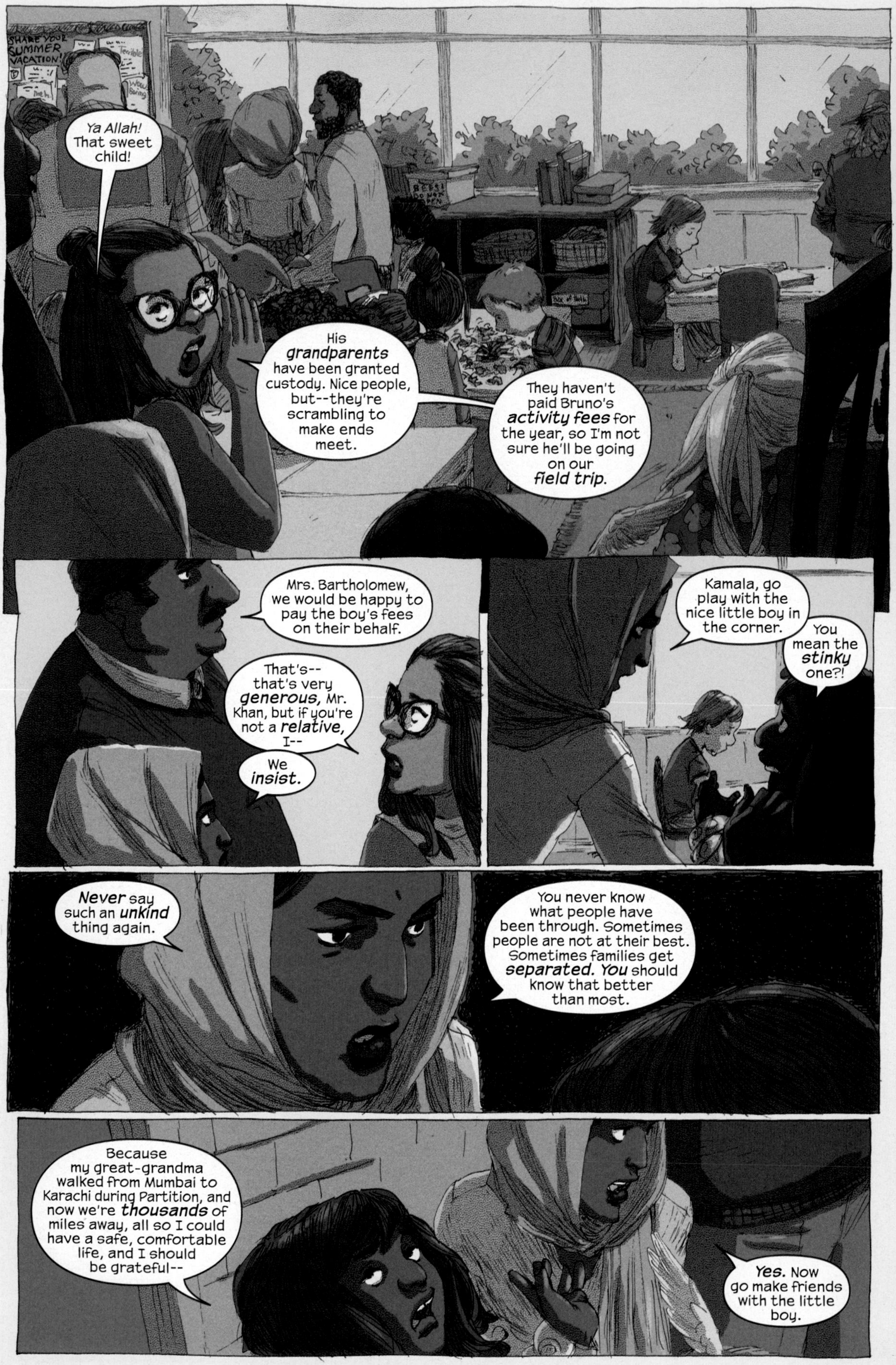
SHARE YOUR SUMMER VACATION!
Ya Allah! That sweet child!
His grandparents have been granted custody. Nice people, but--they're scrambling to make ends meet.
They haven't paid Bruno's activity fees for the year, so I'm not sure he'll be going on our field trip.
Mrs. Bartholomew, we would be happy to pay the boy's fees on their behalf.
That's-- that's very generous, Mr. Khan, but if you're not a relative, I--
We insist.
Kamala, go play with the nice little boy in the corner.
You mean the stinky one?!
Never say such an unkind thing again.
You never know what people have been through. Sometimes people are not at their best. Sometimes families get separated. You should know that better than most.
Because my great-grandma walked from Mumbai to Karachi during Partition, and now we're thousands of miles away, all so I could have a safe, comfortable life, and I should be grateful--
Yes. Now go make friends with the little boy.

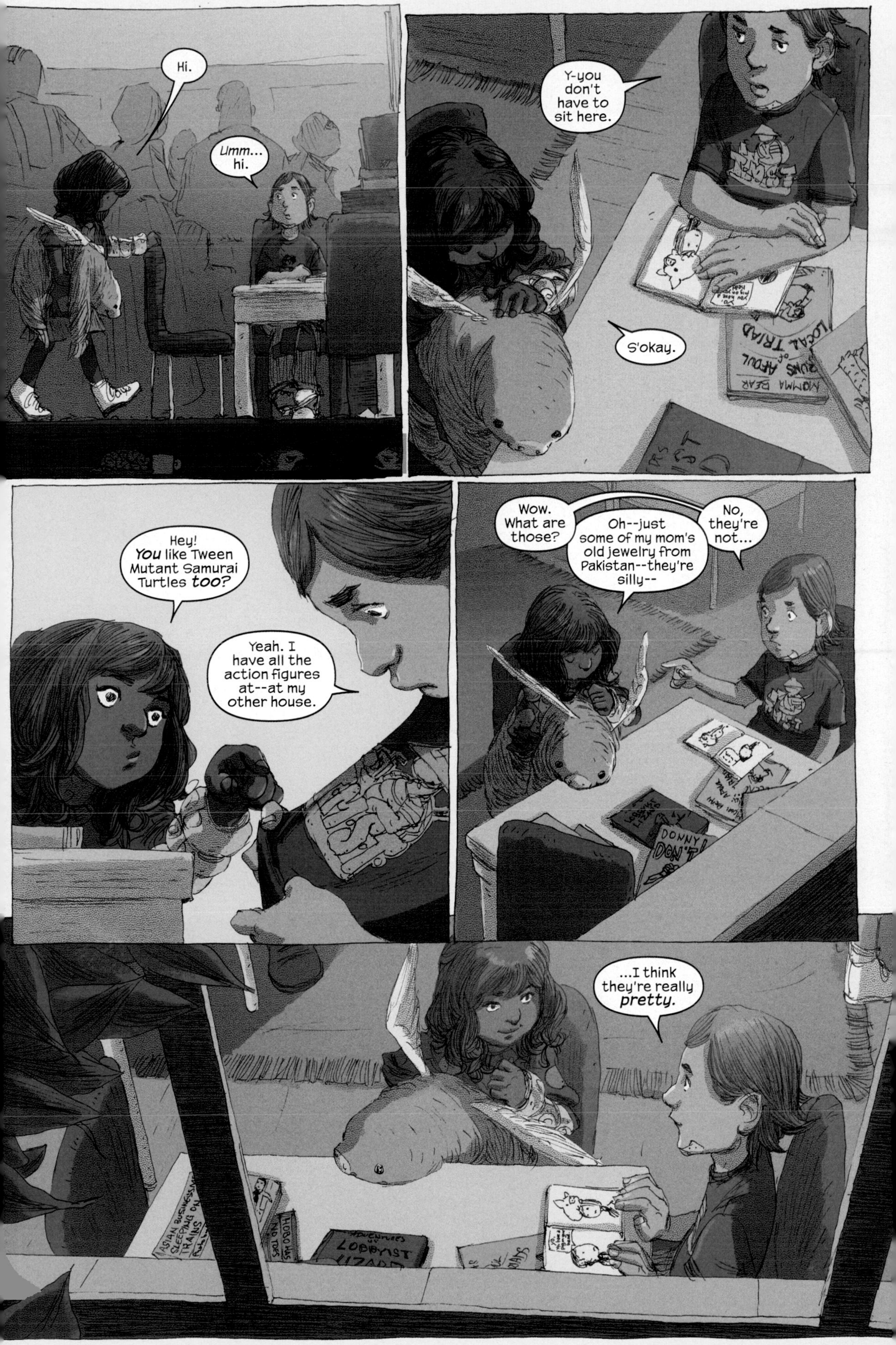
Hi.
Umm... hi.
Y-you don't have to sit here.
S'okay.
Hey! YOU like Tween Mutant Samurai Turtles too?
Yeah. I have all the action figures at--at my other house.
Wow. What are those?
Oh--just some of my mom's old jewelry from Pakistan--they're silly--
No, they're not...
...I think they're really pretty.

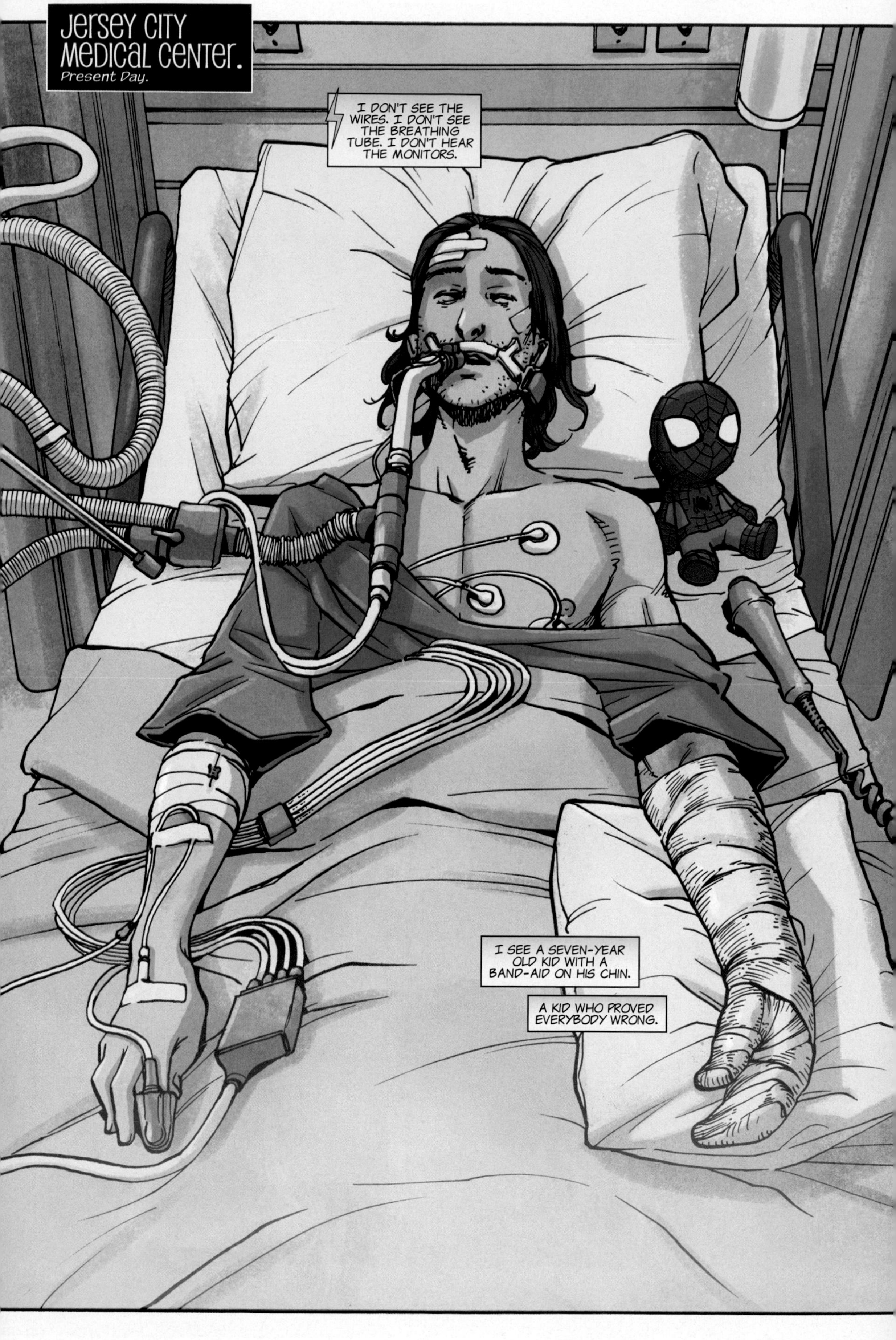

JERSEY CITY MEDICAL CENTER.
Present Day.
I DON'T SEE THE WIRES. I DON'T SEE THE BREATHING TUBE. I DON'T HEAR THE MONITORS.
I SEE A SEVEN-YEAR OLD KID WITH A BAND-AID ON HIS CHIN.
A KID WHO PROVED EVERYBODY WRONG.

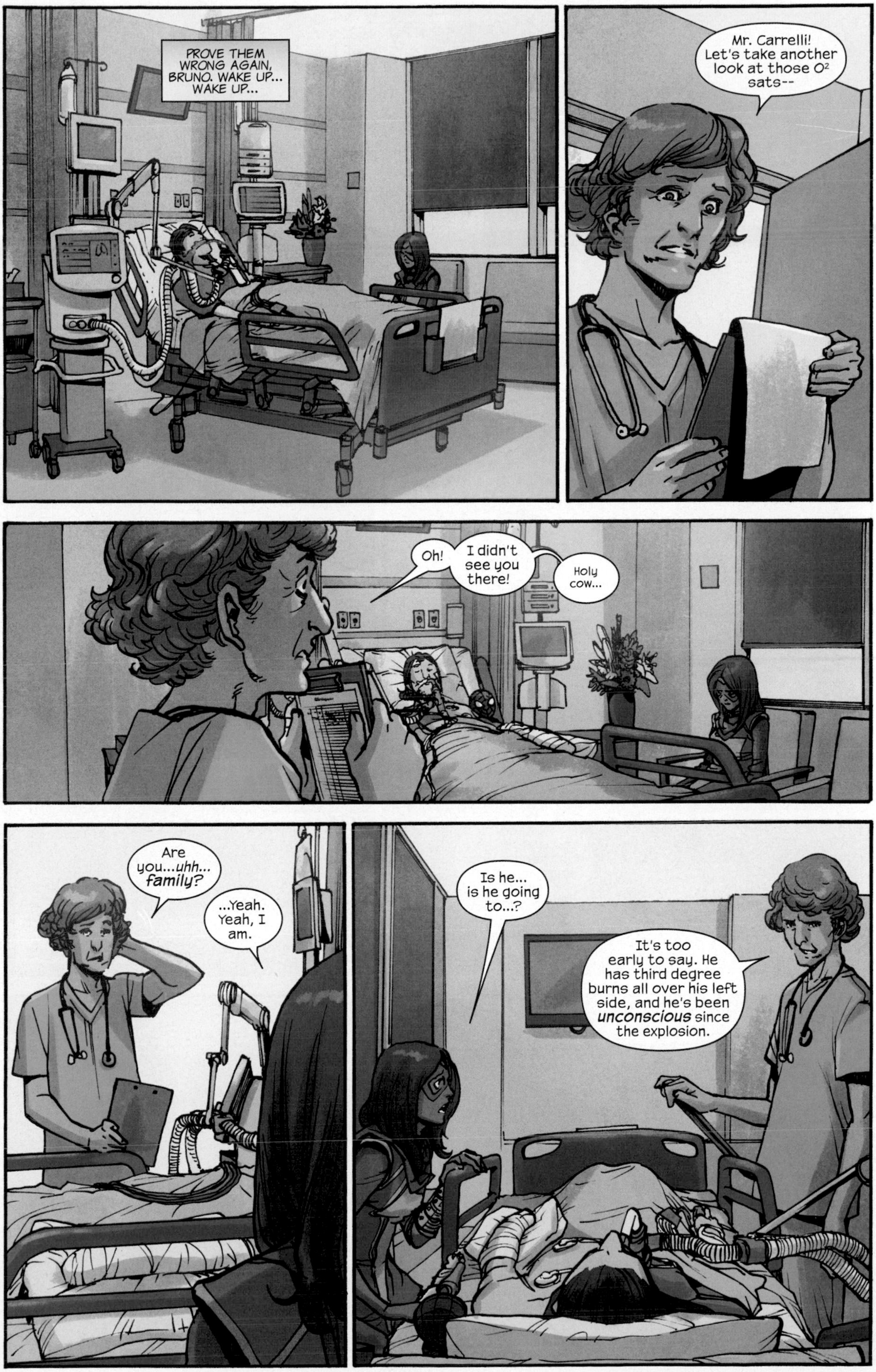
PROVE THEM WRONG AGAIN, BRUNO. WAKE UP... WAKE UP...
Mr. Carrelli! Let's take another look at those O² sats--
Oh!
I didn't see you there!
Holy cow...
Are you...uhh... family?
...Yeah. Yeah, I am.
Is he... is he going to...?
It's too early to say. He has third degree burns all over his left side, and he's been unconscious since the explosion.

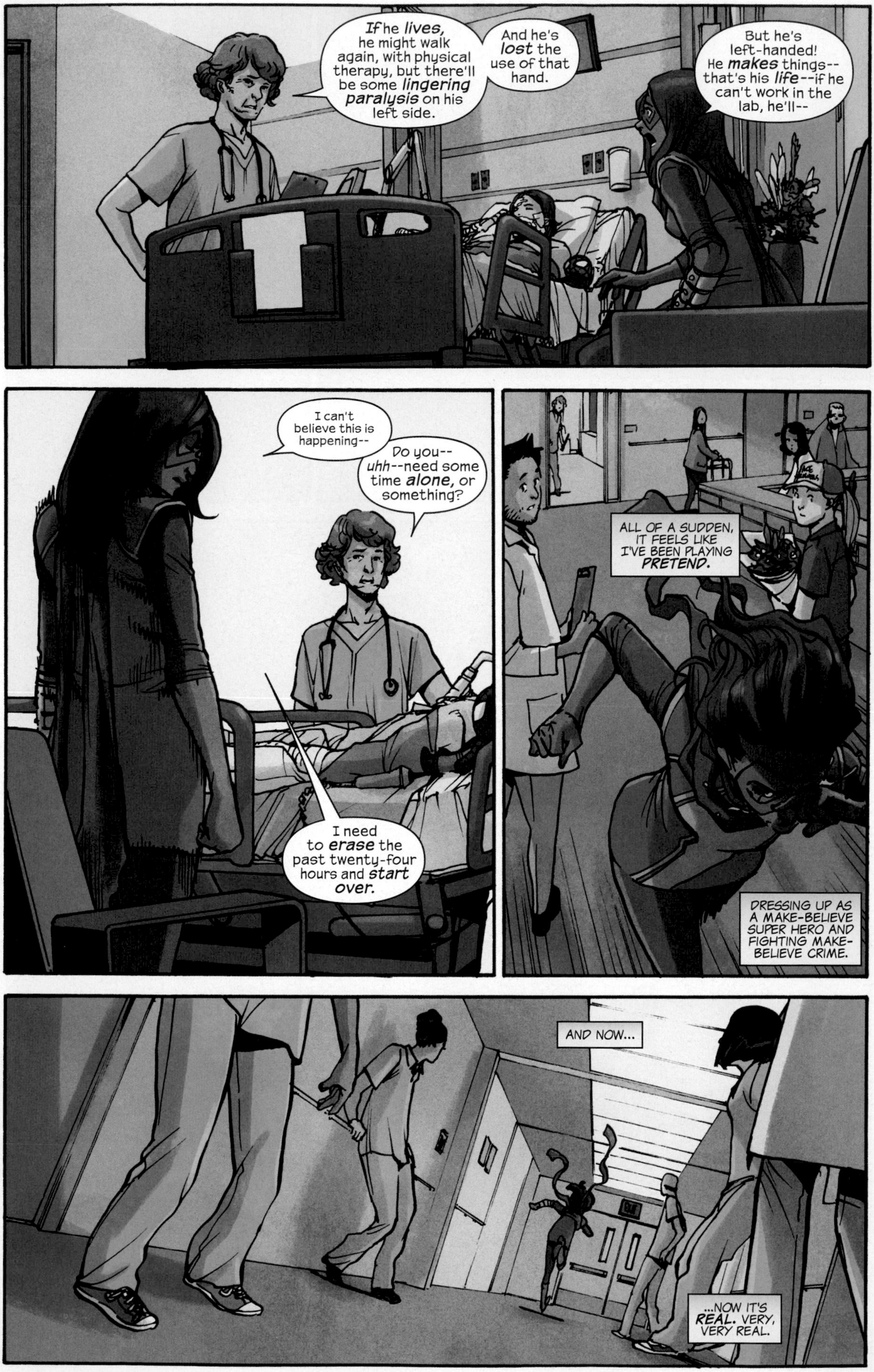
If he lives, he might walk again, with physical therapy, but there'll be some lingering paralysis on his left side.
And he's lost the use of that hand.
But he's left-handed! He makes things--that's his life--if he can't work in the lab, he'll--
I can't believe this is happening--
Do you--uhh--need some time alone, or something?
I need to erase the past twenty-four hours and start over.
ALL OF A SUDDEN, IT FEELS LIKE I'VE BEEN PLAYING PRETEND.
DRESSING UP AS A MAKE-BELIEVE SUPER HERO AND FIGHTING MAKE-BELIEVE CRIME.
AND NOW...
...NOW IT'S REAL. VERY, VERY REAL.

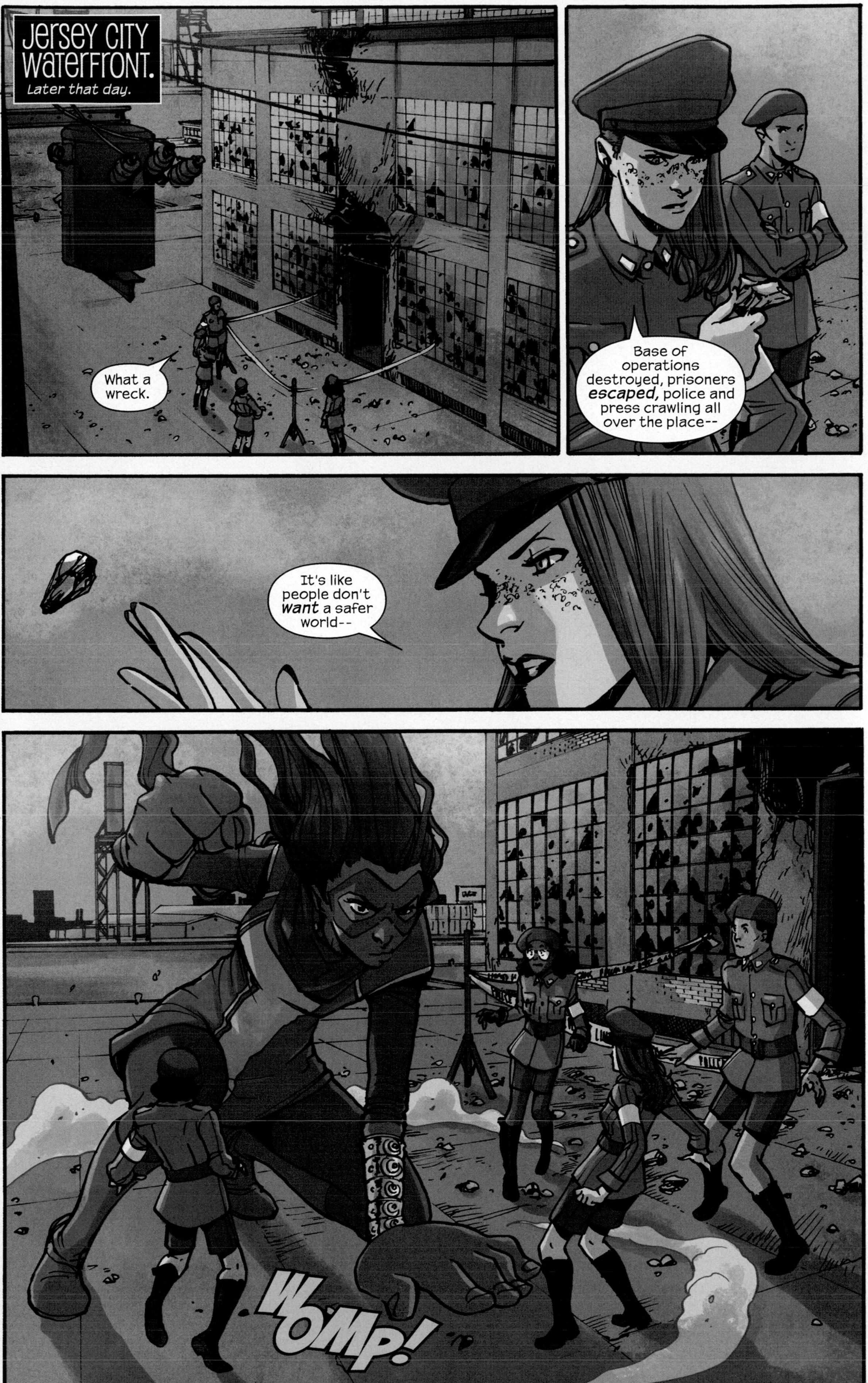
Jersey City Waterfront.
Later that day.
What a wreck.
Base of operations destroyed, prisoners *escaped,* police and press crawling all over the place--
It's like people don't *want* a safer world--
WOMP!

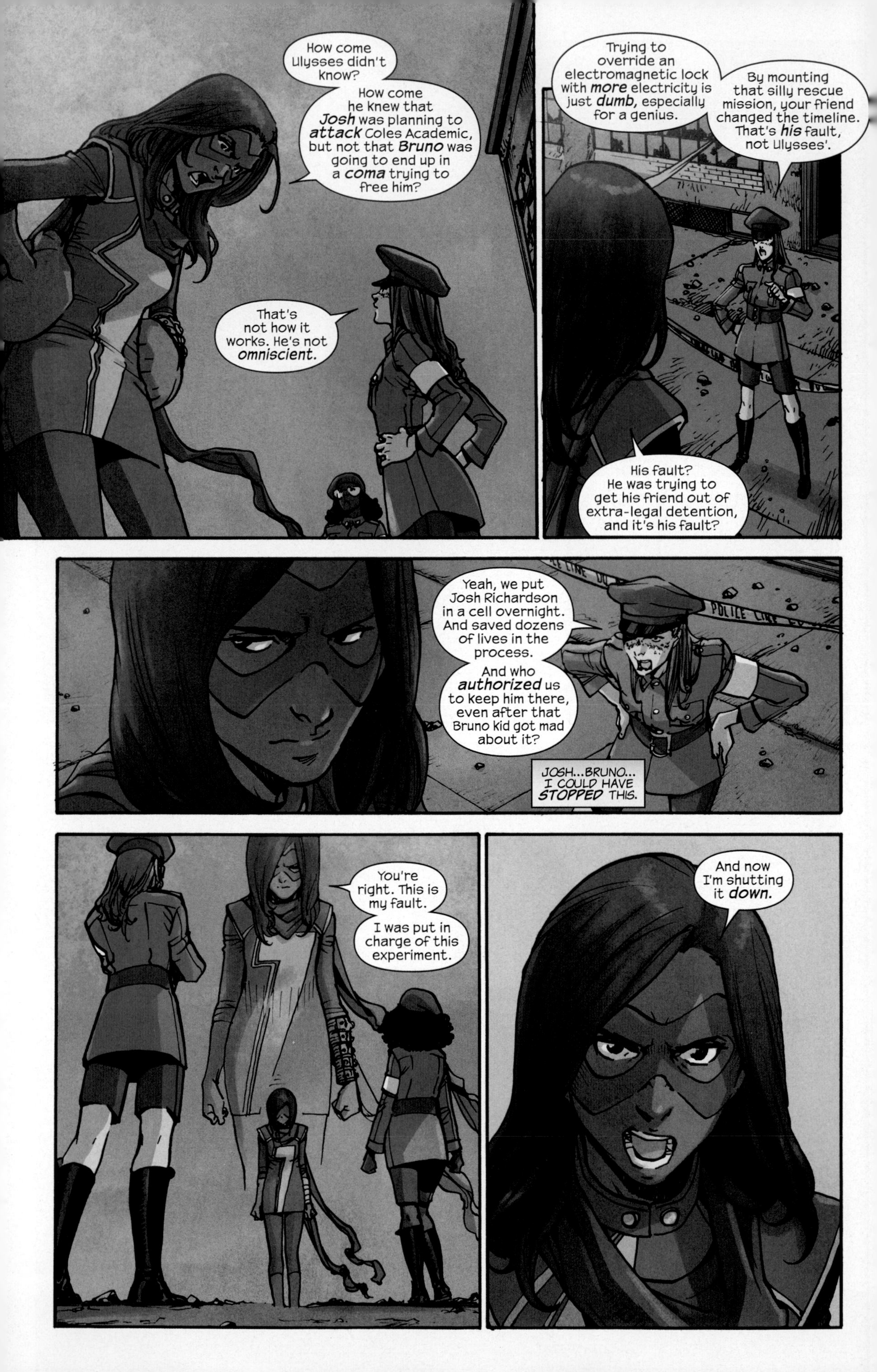
How come Ulysses didn't know?
How come he knew that Josh was planning to attack Coles Academic, but not that Bruno was going to end up in a coma trying to free him?
That's not how it works. He's not omniscient.
Trying to override an electromagnetic lock with more electricity is just dumb, especially for a genius.
By mounting that silly rescue mission, your friend changed the timeline. That's his fault, not Ulysses'.
His fault? He was trying to get his friend out of extra-legal detention, and it's his fault?
Yeah, we put Josh Richardson in a cell overnight. And saved dozens of lives in the process.
And who authorized us to keep him there, even after that Bruno kid got mad about it?
JOSH...BRUNO... I COULD HAVE STOPPED THIS.
You're right. This is my fault.
I was put in charge of this experiment.
And now I'm shutting it down.

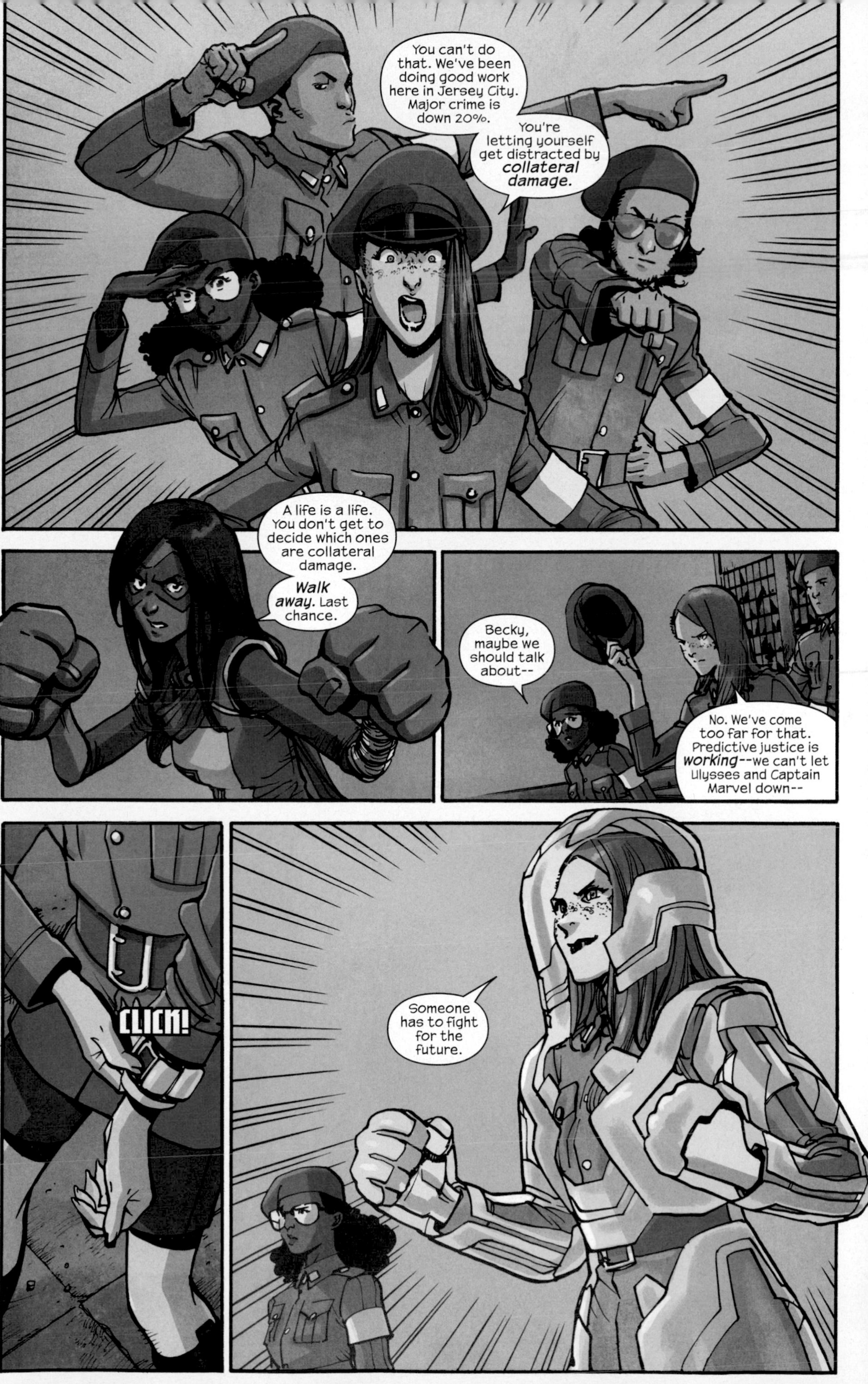
You can't do that. We've been doing good work here in Jersey City. Major crime is down 20%.
You're letting yourself get distracted by *collateral damage.*
A life is a life. You don't get to decide which ones are collateral damage.
Walk away. Last chance.
Becky, maybe we should talk about--
No. We've come too far for that. Predictive justice is *working*--we can't let Ulysses and Captain Marvel down--
CLICK!
Someone has to fight for the future.

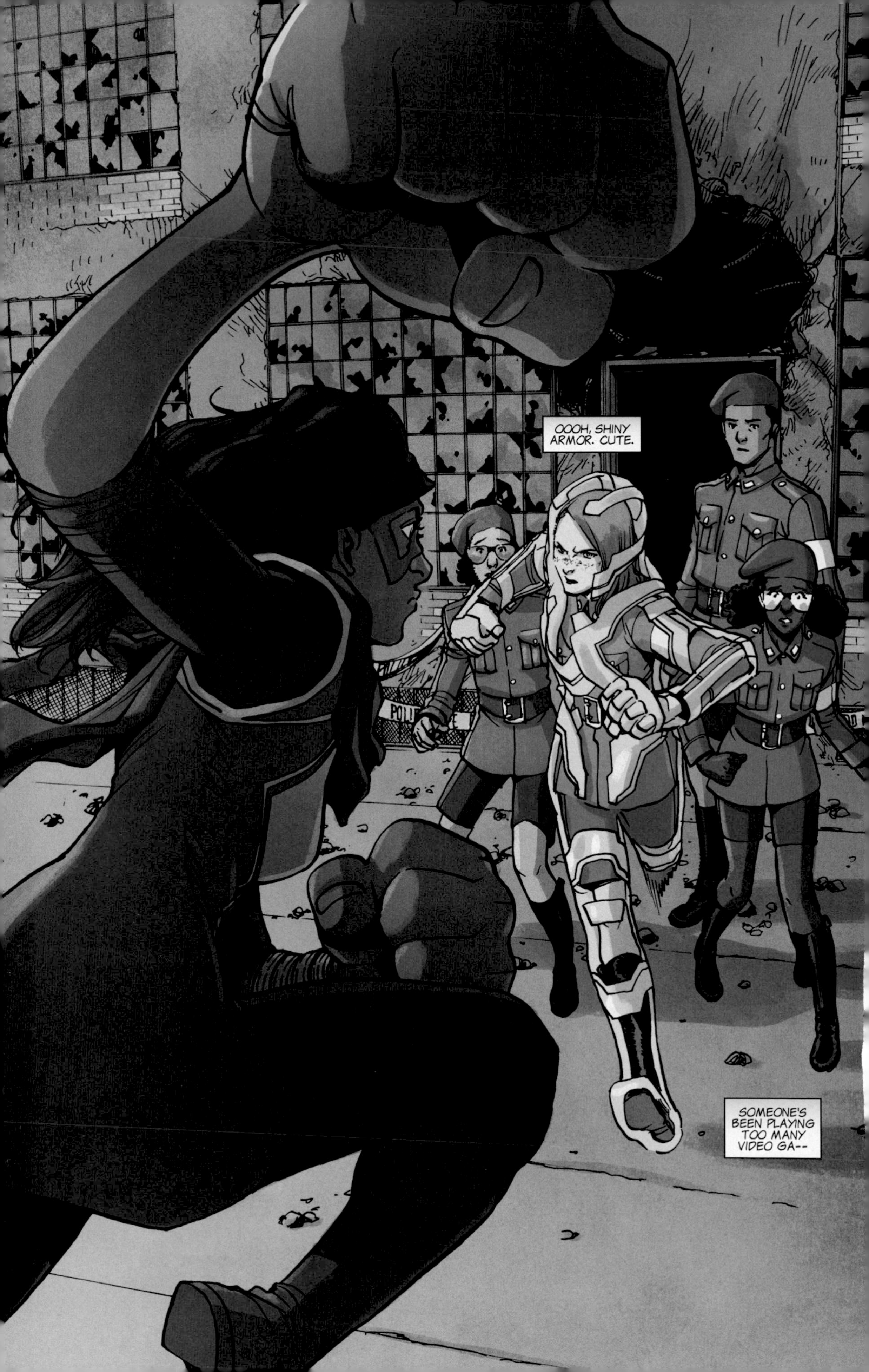

OOOH, SHINY ARMOR. CUTE.
SOMEONE'S BEEN PLAYING TOO MANY VIDEO GA--

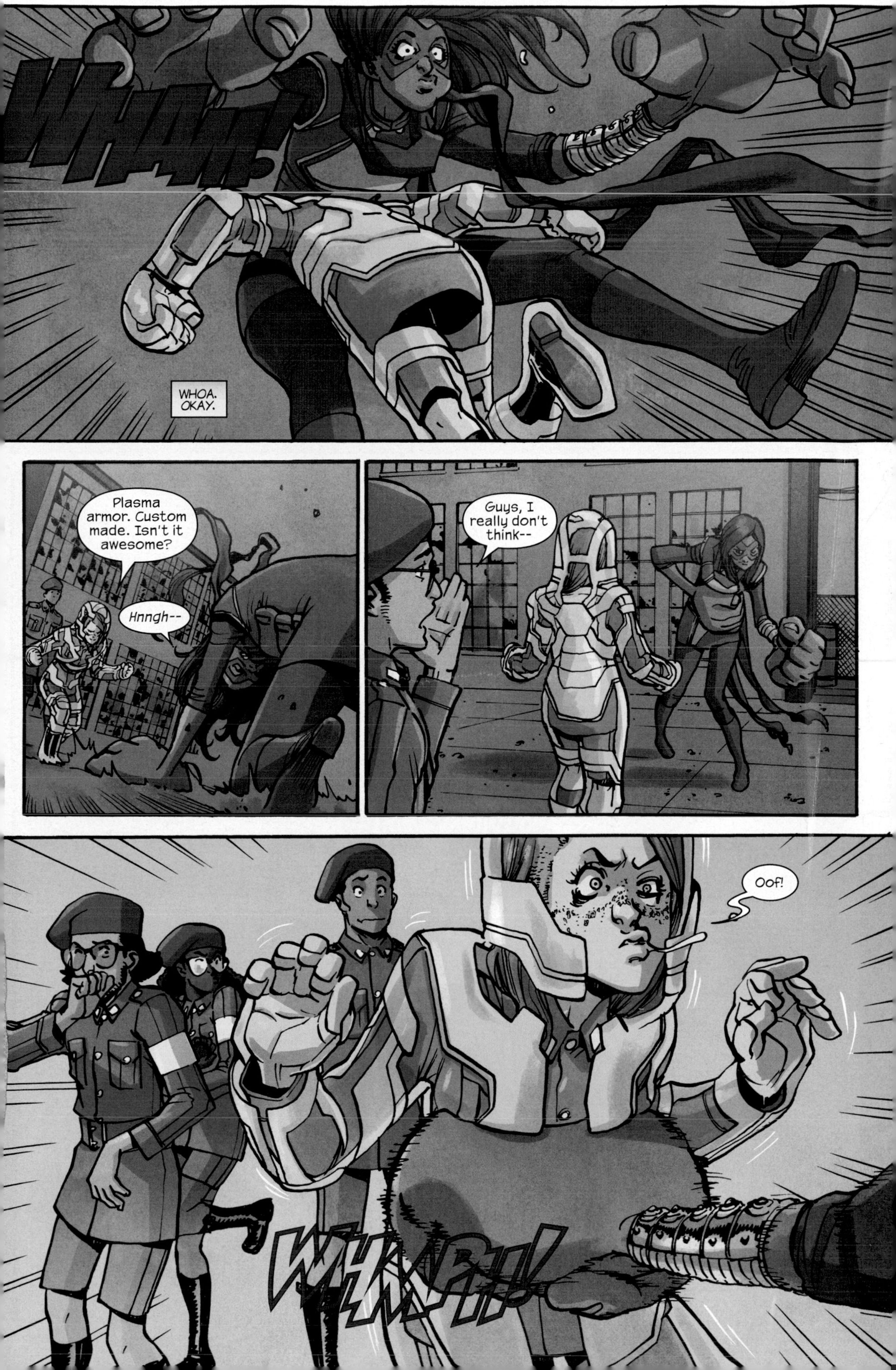
WHAM!
WHOA. OKAY.
Plasma armor. Custom made. Isn't it awesome?
Hnngh--
Guys, I really don't think--
Oof!
WHAAM!

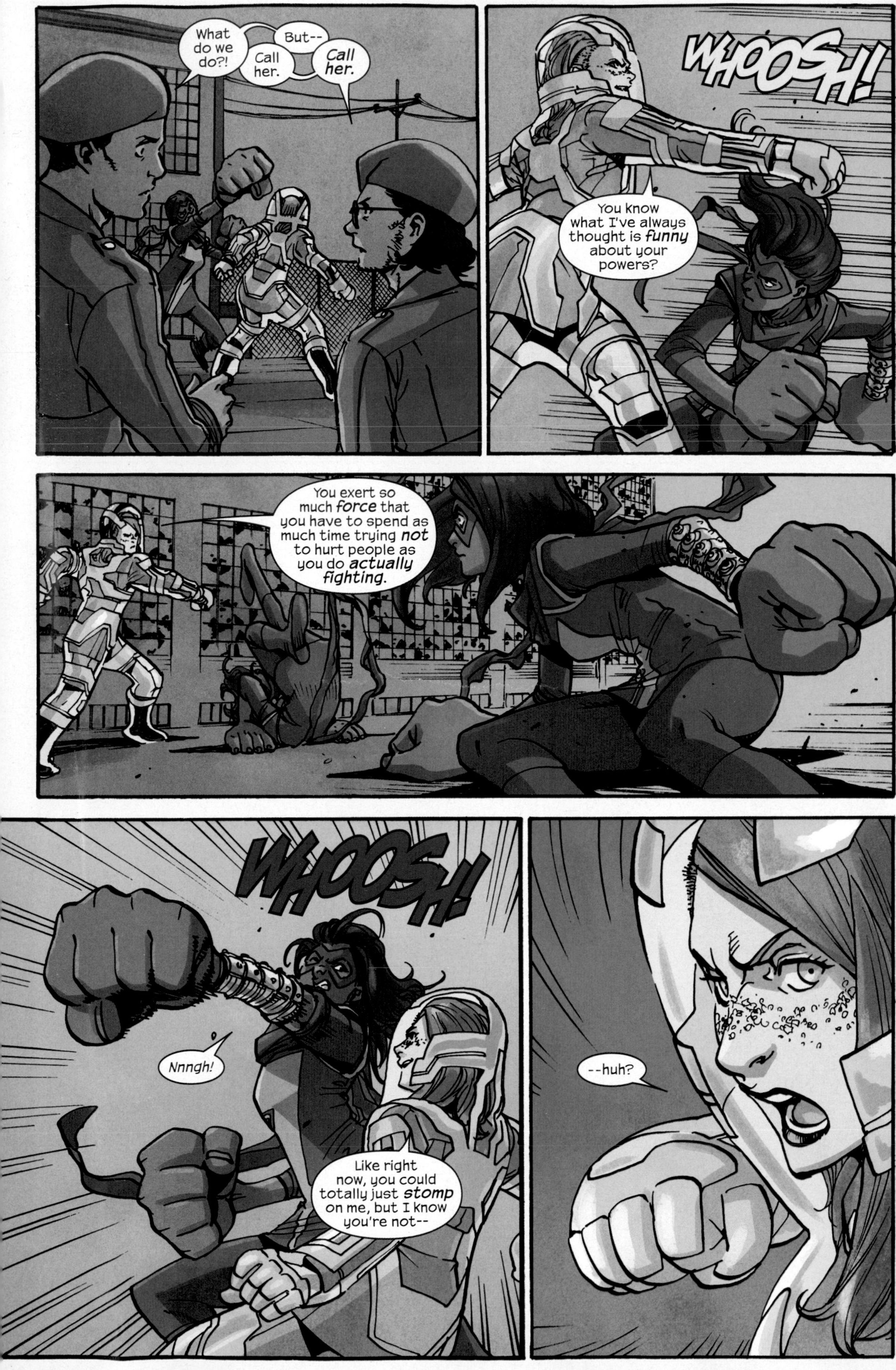
What do we do?!
But--
Call her.
Call her.
WHOOSH!
You know what I've always thought is funny about your powers?
You exert so much force that you have to spend as much time trying not to hurt people as you do actually fighting.
WHOOSH!
Nnngh!
Like right now, you could totally just stomp on me, but I know you're not--
--huh?

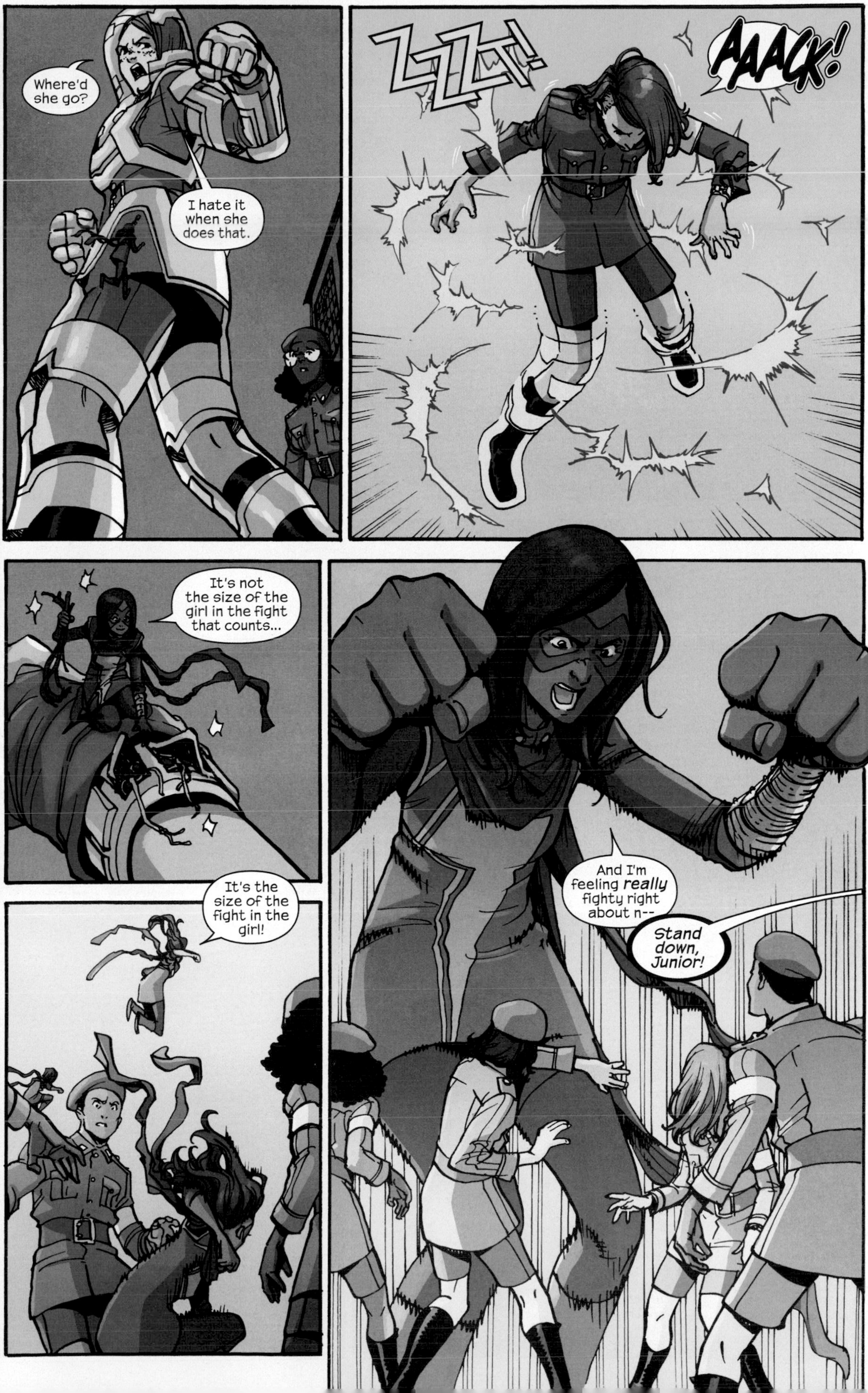

Where'd she go?
I hate it when she does that.
ZZZT!
AAACK!
It's not the size of the girl in the fight that counts...
It's the size of the fight in the girl!
And I'm feeling *really* fighty right about n--
Stand down, Junior!

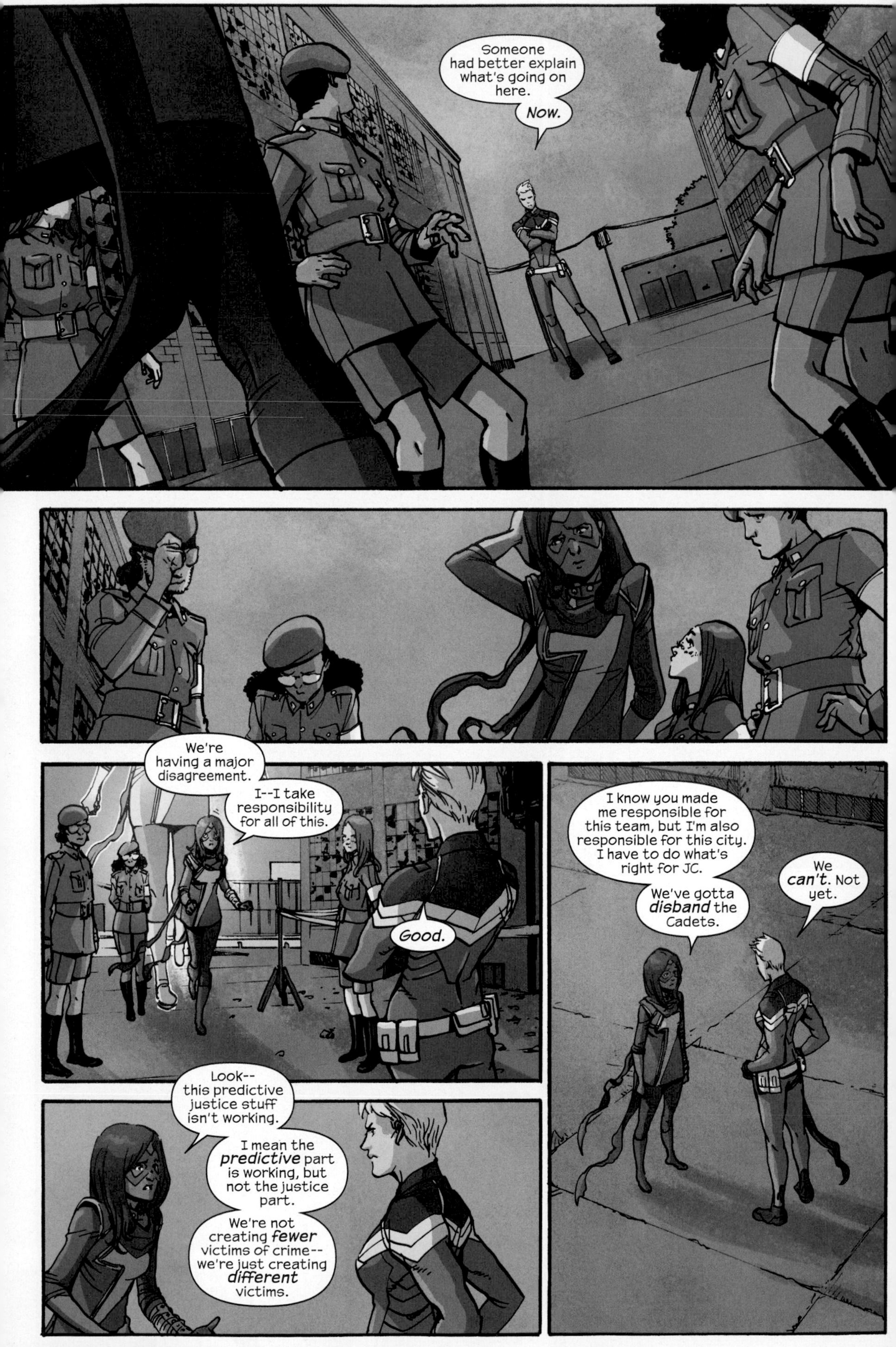
Someone had better explain what's going on here.
Now.
We're having a major disagreement.
I--I take responsibility for all of this.
Good.
I know you made me responsible for this team, but I'm also responsible for this city. I have to do what's right for JC.
We've gotta disband the Cadets.
We can't. Not yet.
Look-- this predictive justice stuff isn't working.
I mean the predictive part is working, but not the justice part.
We're not creating fewer victims of crime-- we're just creating different victims.

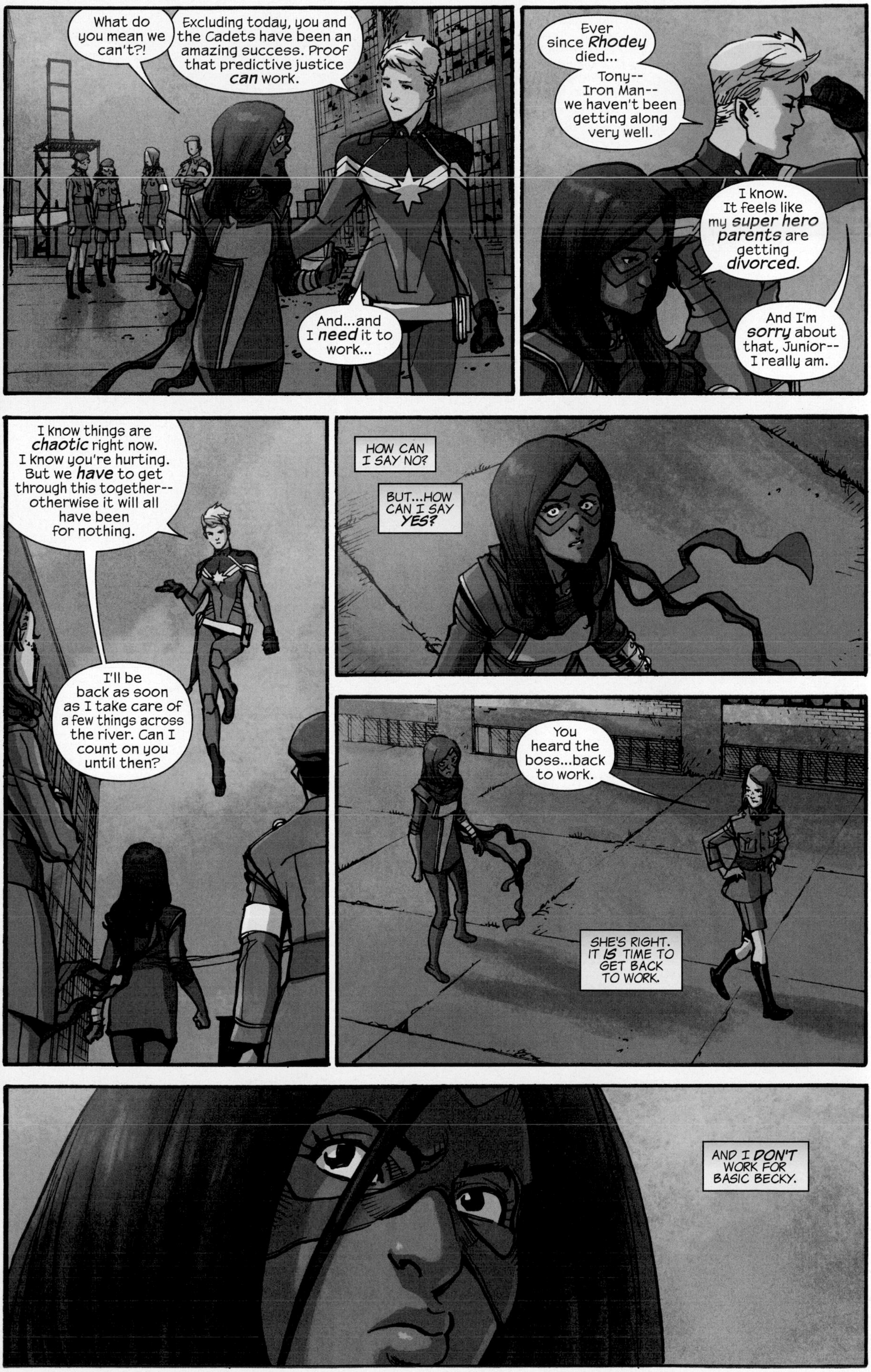
What do you mean we can't?!
Excluding today, you and the Cadets have been an amazing success. Proof that predictive justice *can* work.
And...and I *need* it to work...
Ever since *Rhodey* died...
Tony--Iron Man--we haven't been getting along very well.
I know. It feels like my *super hero parents* are getting *divorced*.
And I'm *sorry* about that, Junior--I really am.
I know things are *chaotic* right now. I know you're hurting. But we *have* to get through this together--otherwise it will all have been for nothing.
I'll be back as soon as I take care of a few things across the river. Can I count on you until then?
HOW CAN I SAY NO?
BUT...HOW CAN I SAY *YES?*
You heard the boss...back to work.
SHE'S RIGHT. IT *IS* TIME TO GET BACK TO WORK.
AND I *DON'T* WORK FOR BASIC BECKY.

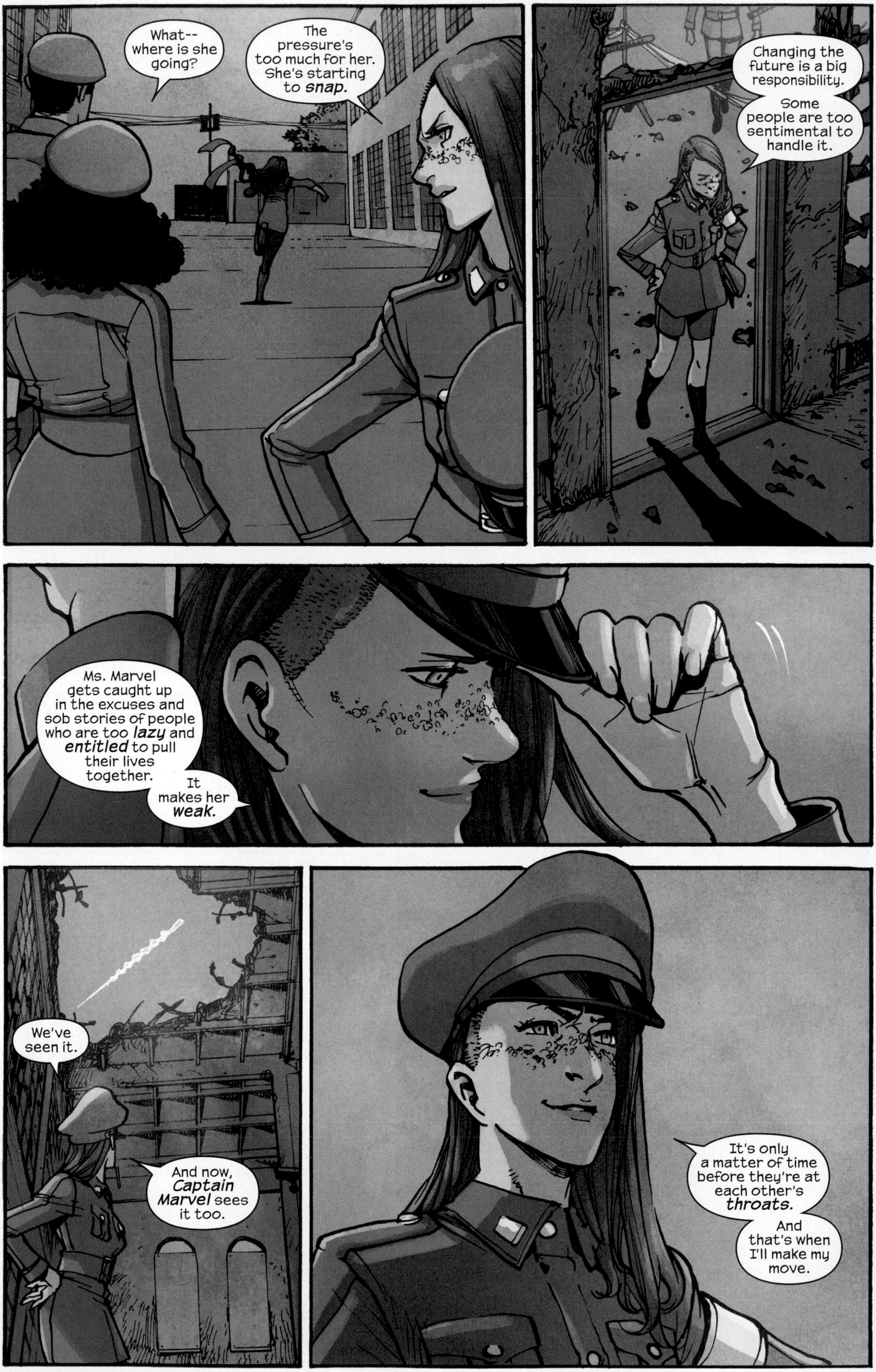
What-- where is she going?
The pressure's too much for her. She's starting to snap.
Changing the future is a big responsibility.
Some people are too sentimental to handle it.
Ms. Marvel gets caught up in the excuses and sob stories of people who are too lazy and entitled to pull their lives together.
It makes her weak.
We've seen it.
And now, Captain Marvel sees it too.
It's only a matter of time before they're at each other's throats.
And that's when I'll make my move.

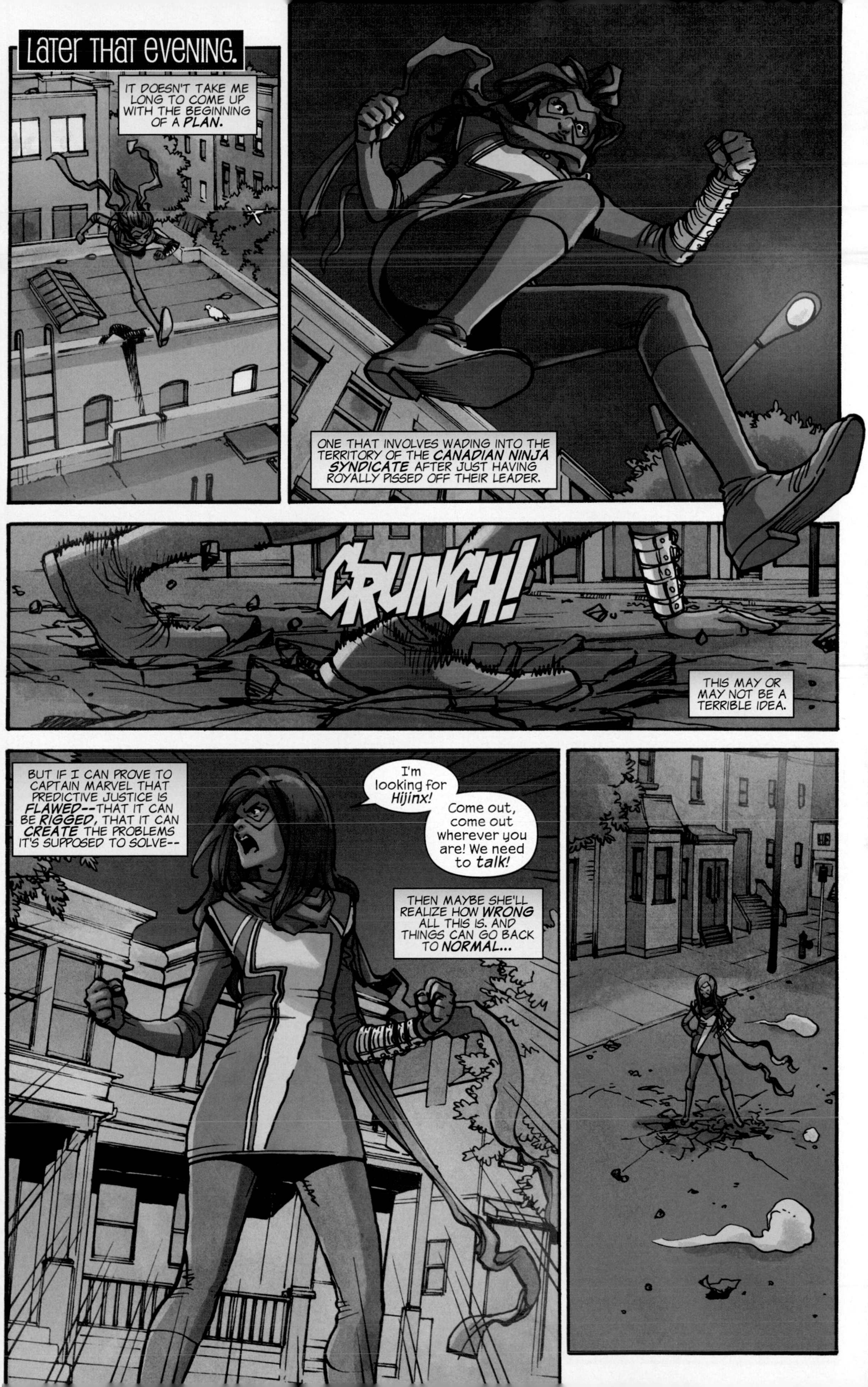

LATER THAT EVENING.
IT DOESN'T TAKE ME LONG TO COME UP WITH THE BEGINNING OF A PLAN.
ONE THAT INVOLVES WADING INTO THE TERRITORY OF THE CANADIAN NINJA SYNDICATE AFTER JUST HAVING ROYALLY PISSED OFF THEIR LEADER.
CRUNCH!
THIS MAY OR MAY NOT BE A TERRIBLE IDEA.
BUT IF I CAN PROVE TO CAPTAIN MARVEL THAT PREDICTIVE JUSTICE IS FLAWED--THAT IT CAN BE RIGGED, THAT IT CAN CREATE THE PROBLEMS IT'S SUPPOSED TO SOLVE--
I'm looking for Hijinx!
Come out, come out wherever you are! We need to talk!
THEN MAYBE SHE'LL REALIZE HOW WRONG ALL THIS IS. AND THINGS CAN GO BACK TO NORMAL...

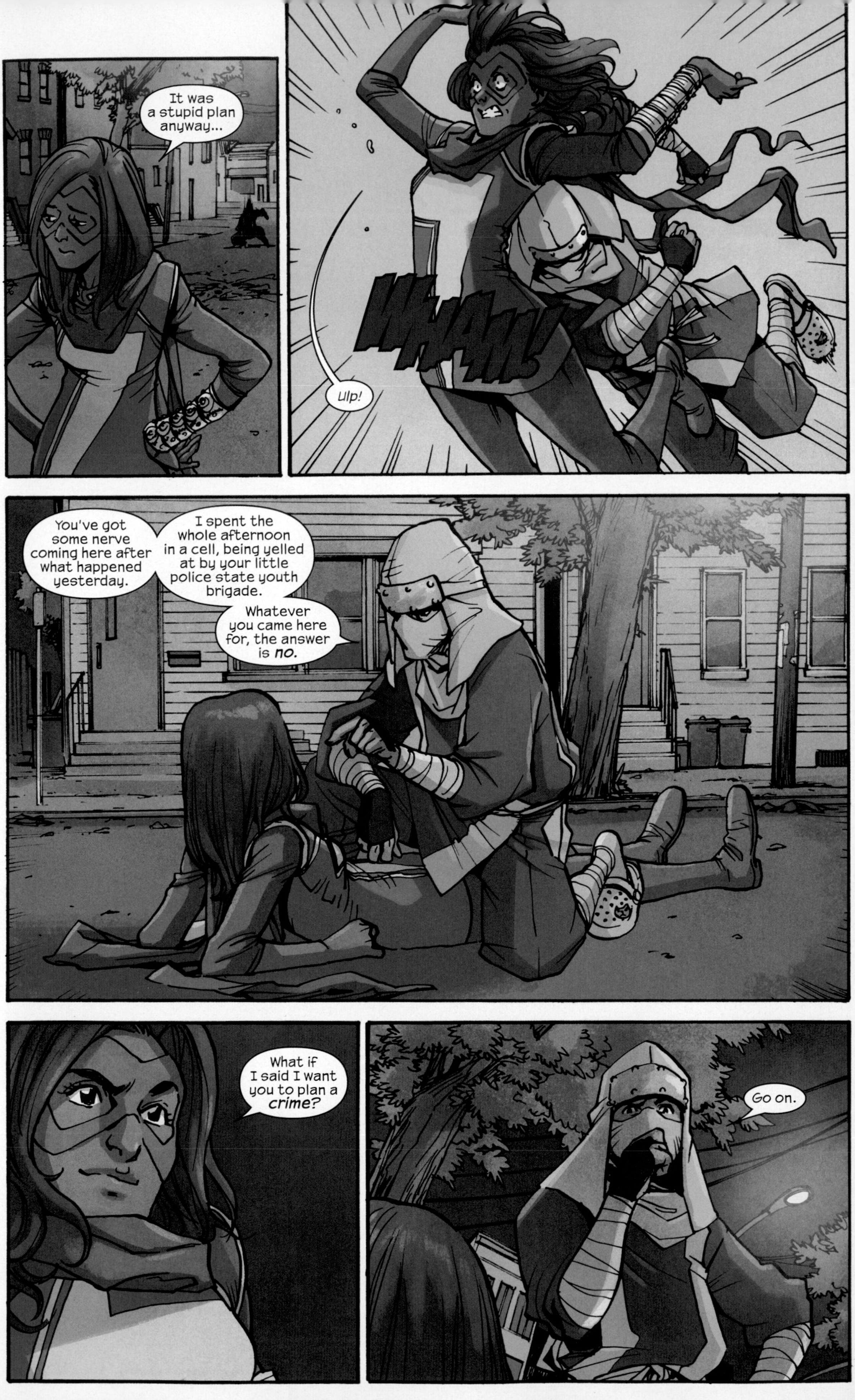
It was a stupid plan anyway...
WHAM!
Ulp!
You've got some nerve coming here after what happened yesterday.
I spent the whole afternoon in a cell, being yelled at by your little police state youth brigade.
Whatever you came here for, the answer is *no.*
What if I said I want you to plan a *crime?*
Go on.

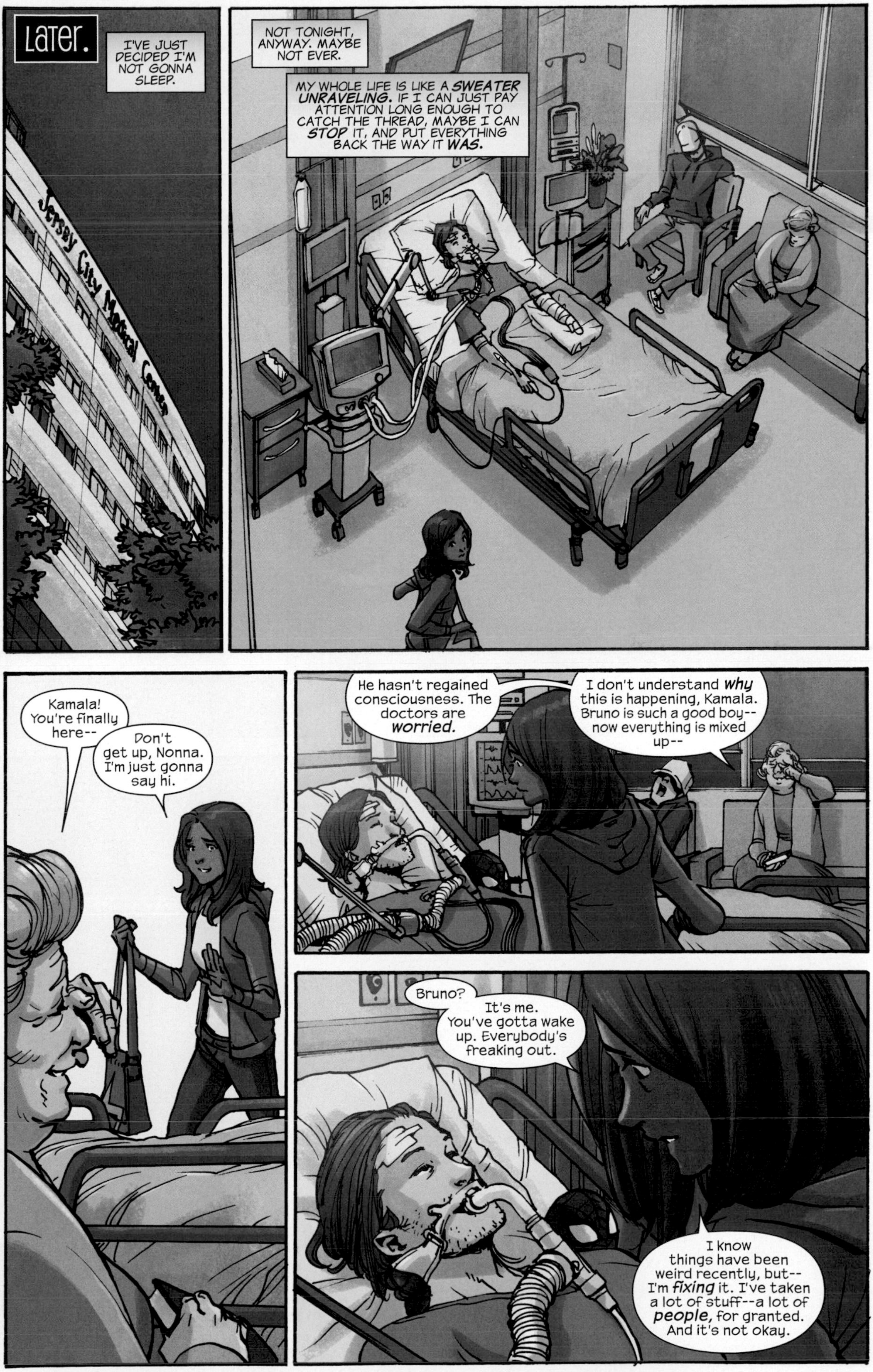
LATER.
I'VE JUST DECIDED I'M NOT GONNA SLEEP.
Jersey City Medical Center
NOT TONIGHT, ANYWAY. MAYBE NOT EVER.
MY WHOLE LIFE IS LIKE A SWEATER UNRAVELING. IF I CAN JUST PAY ATTENTION LONG ENOUGH TO CATCH THE THREAD, MAYBE I CAN STOP IT, AND PUT EVERYTHING BACK THE WAY IT WAS.
Kamala! You're finally here--
Don't get up, Nonna. I'm just gonna say hi.
He hasn't regained consciousness. The doctors are worried.
I don't understand why this is happening, Kamala. Bruno is such a good boy-- now everything is mixed up--
Bruno?
It's me. You've gotta wake up. Everybody's freaking out.
I know things have been weird recently, but-- I'm fixing it. I've taken a lot of stuff--a lot of people, for granted. And it's not okay.

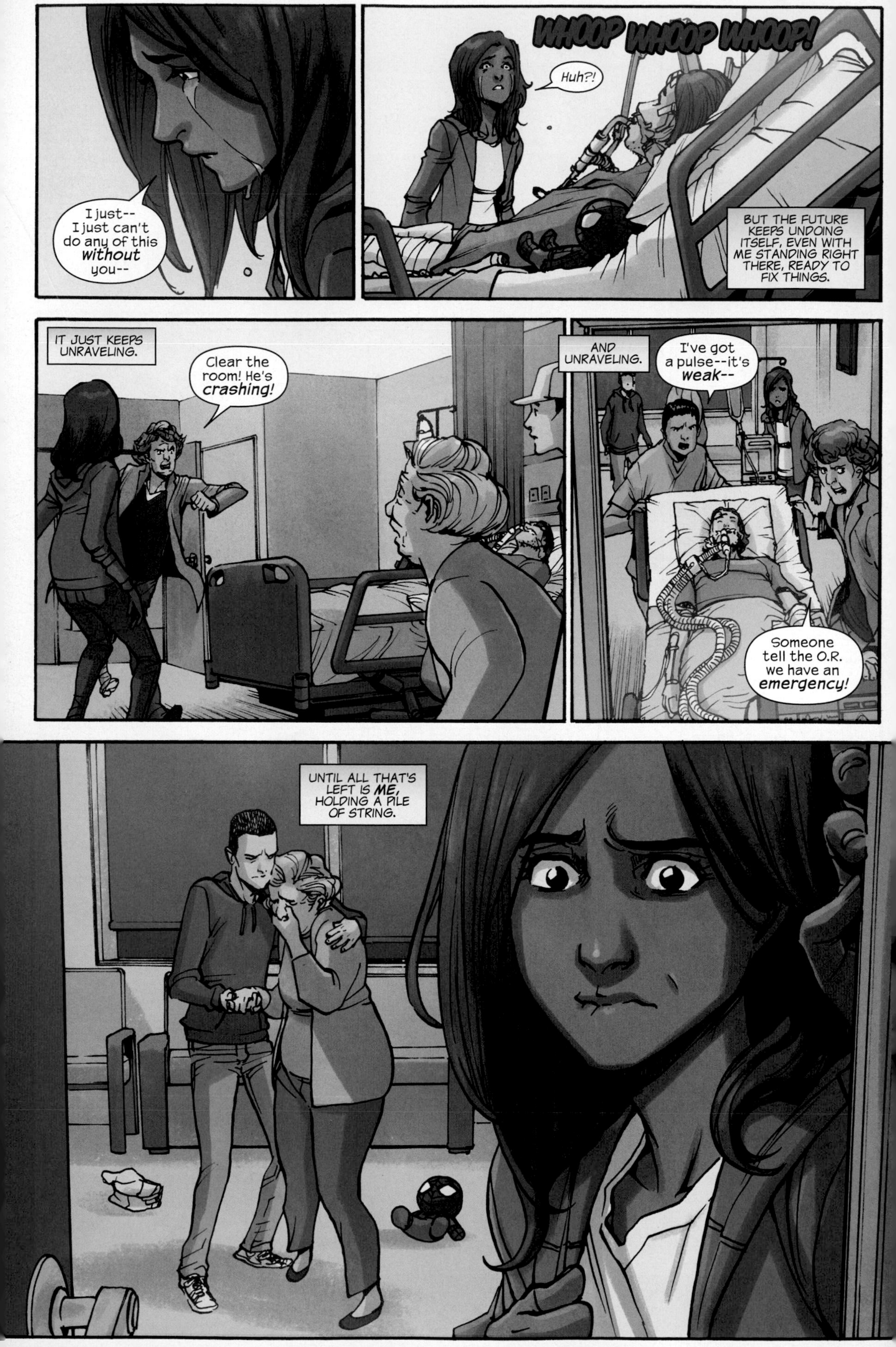

I just-- I just can't do any of this *without* you--
WHOOP WHOOP WHOOP!
Huh?!
BUT THE FUTURE KEEPS UNDOING ITSELF, EVEN WITH ME STANDING RIGHT THERE, READY TO FIX THINGS.
IT JUST KEEPS UNRAVELING.
Clear the room! He's *crashing!*
AND UNRAVELING.
I've got a pulse--it's *weak--*
Someone tell the O.R. we have an *emergency!*
UNTIL ALL THAT'S LEFT IS *ME,* HOLDING A PILE OF STRING.

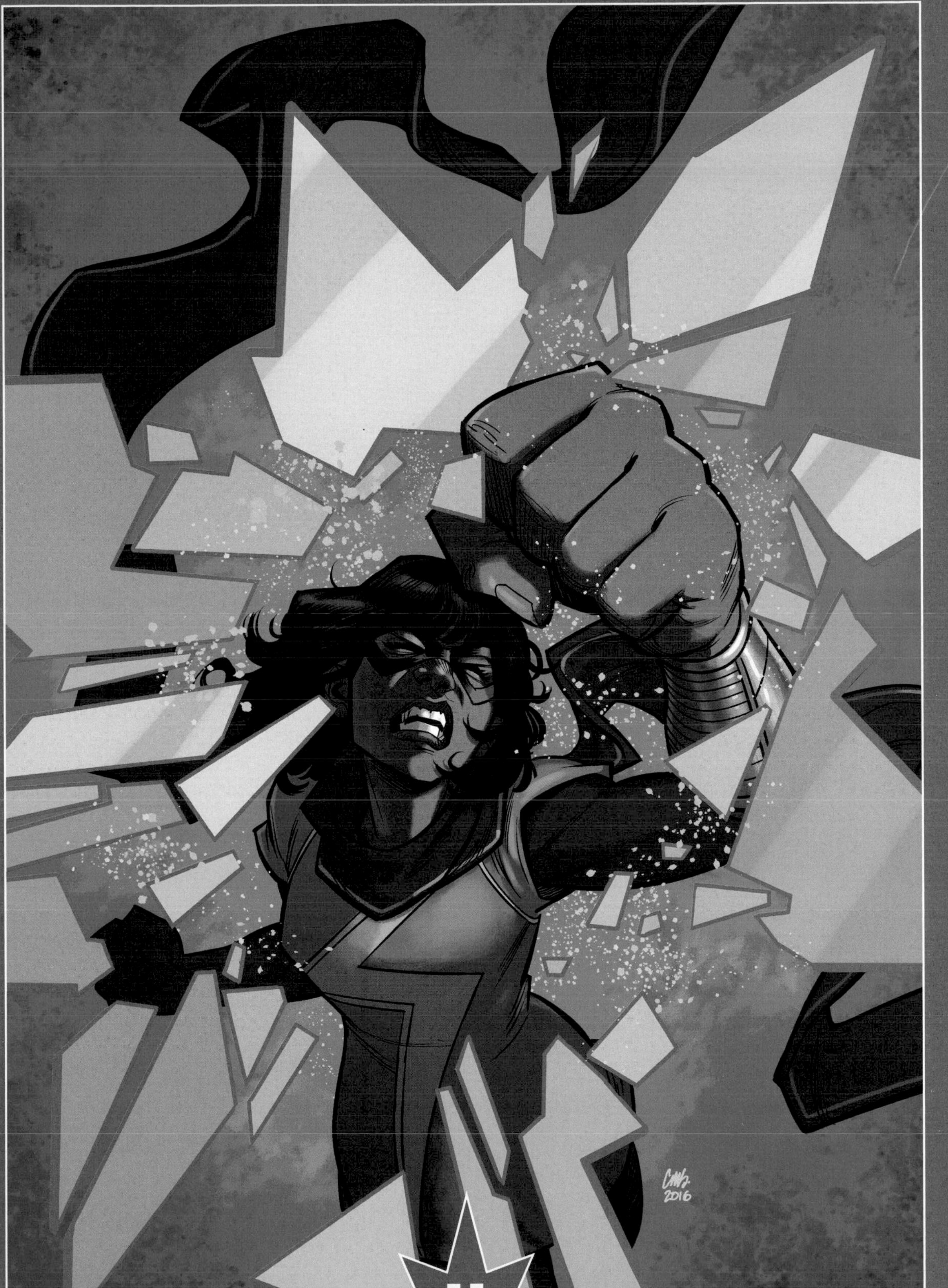
11

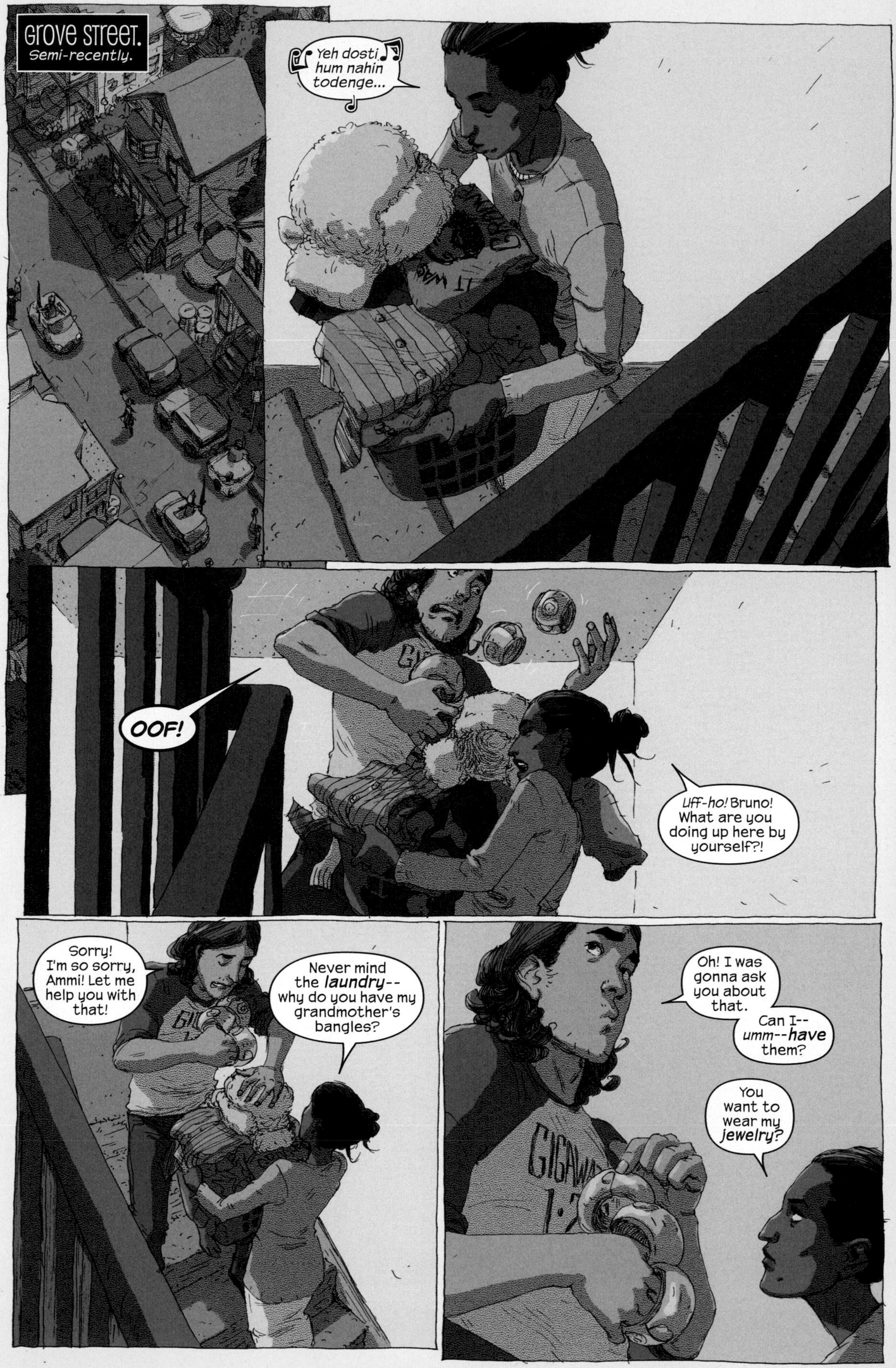
Grove Street.
Semi-recently.
Yeh dosti hum nahin todenge...
OOF!
Uff-ho! Bruno! What are you doing up here by yourself?!
Sorry! I'm so sorry, Ammi! Let me help you with that!
Never mind the laundry-- why do you have my grandmother's bangles?
Oh! I was gonna ask you about that.
Can I-- umm--have them?
You want to wear my jewelry?

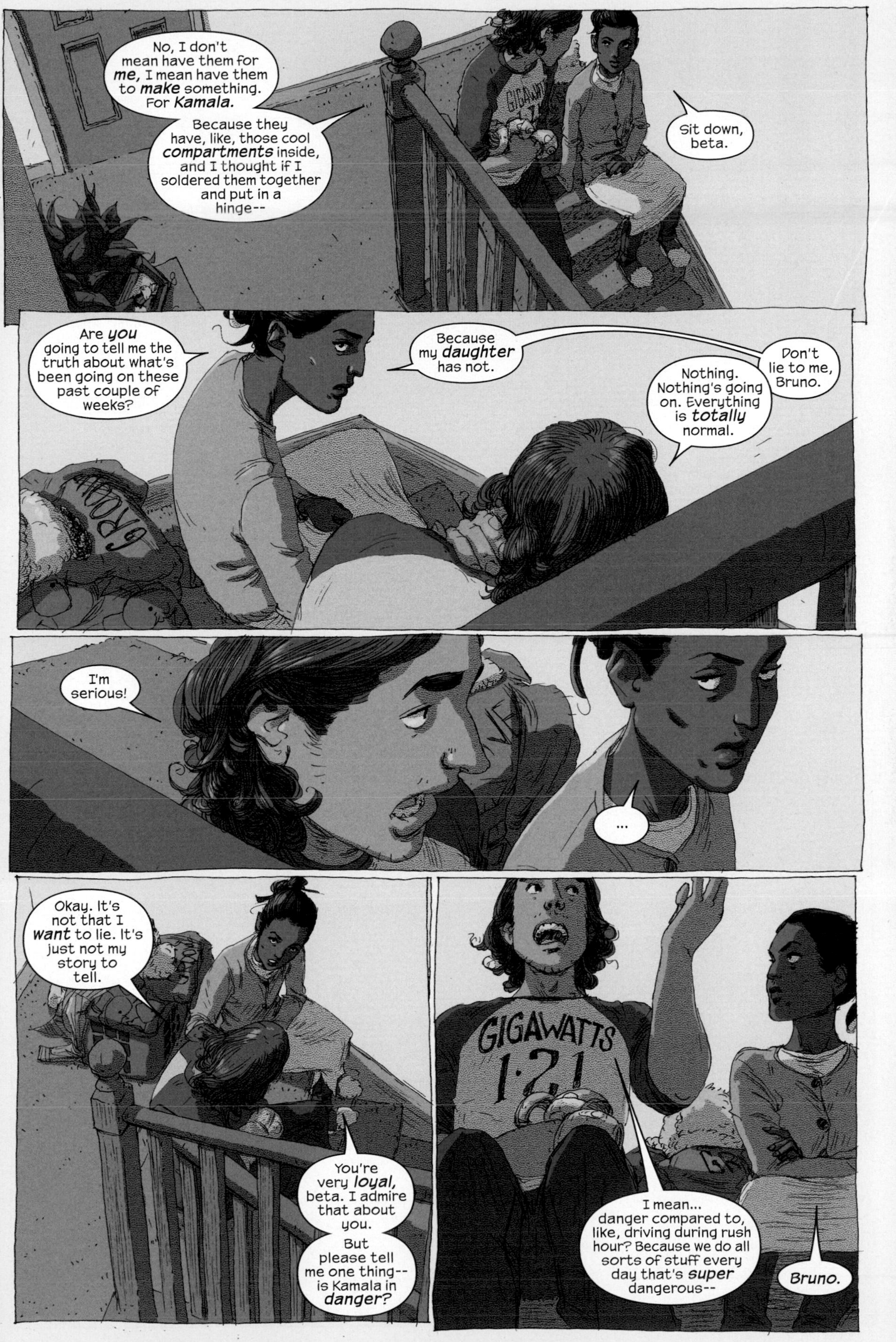

No, I don't mean have them for *me,* I mean have them to *make* something. For *Kamala.*
Because they have, like, those cool *compartments* inside, and I thought if I soldered them together and put in a hinge--
Sit down, beta.
Are *you* going to tell me the truth about what's been going on these past couple of weeks?
Because my *daughter* has not.
Nothing. Nothing's going on. Everything is *totally* normal.
Don't lie to me, Bruno.
I'm serious!
...
Okay. It's not that I *want* to lie. It's just not my story to tell.
You're very *loyal,* beta. I admire that about you.
But please tell me one thing-- is Kamala in *danger?*
GIGAWATTS 1.21
I mean... danger compared to, like, driving during rush hour? Because we do all sorts of stuff every day that's *super* dangerous--
Bruno.

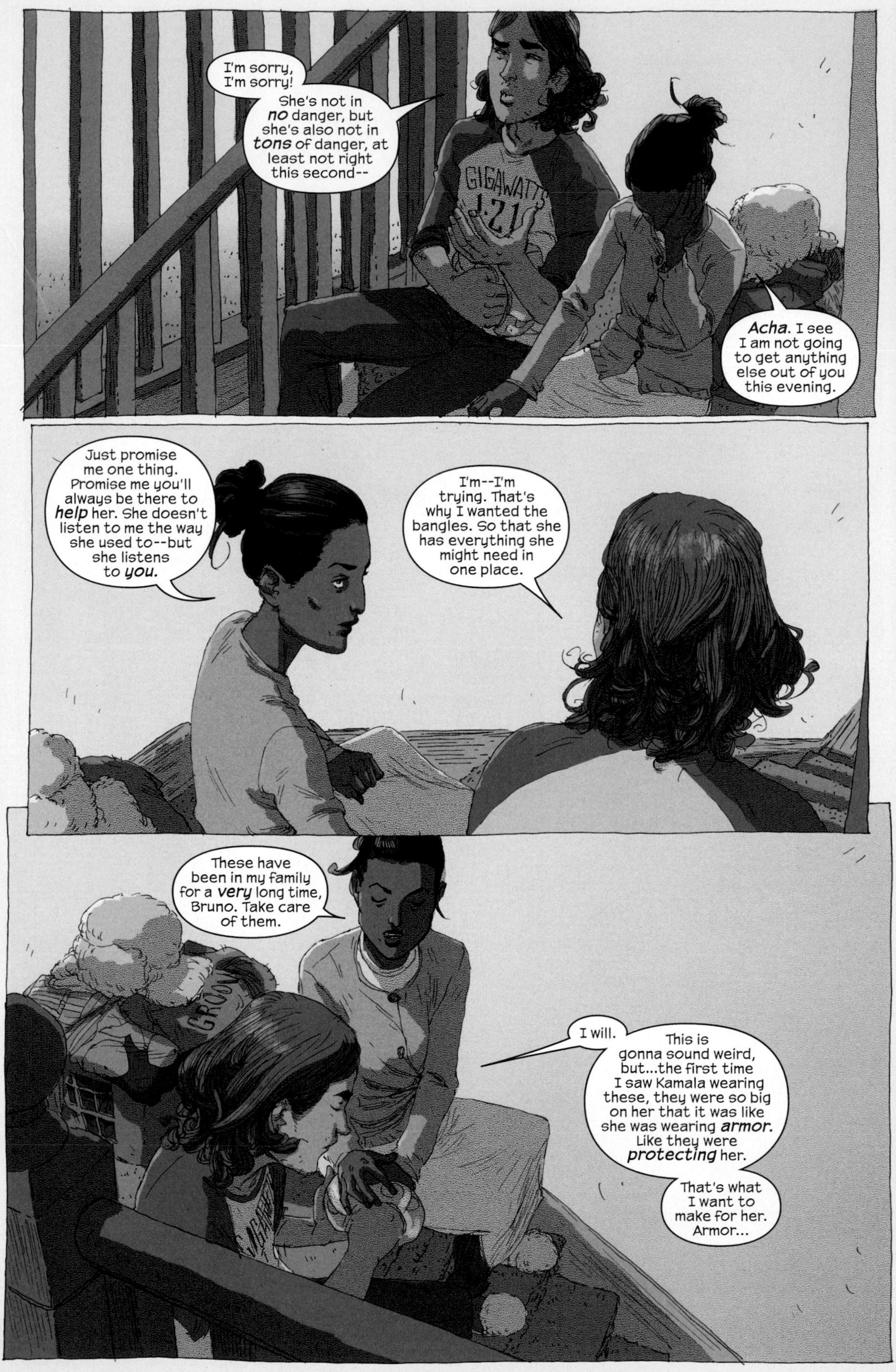
I'm sorry, I'm sorry!
She's not in *no* danger, but she's also not in *tons* of danger, at least not right this second--
Acha. I see I am not going to get anything else out of you this evening.
Just promise me one thing. Promise me you'll always be there to *help* her. She doesn't listen to me the way she used to--but she listens to *you.*
I'm--I'm trying. That's why I wanted the bangles. So that she has everything she might need in one place.
These have been in my family for a *very* long time, Bruno. Take care of them.
I will.
This is gonna sound weird, but...the first time I saw Kamala wearing these, they were so big on her that it was like she was wearing *armor.* Like they were *protecting* her.
That's what I want to make for her. Armor...

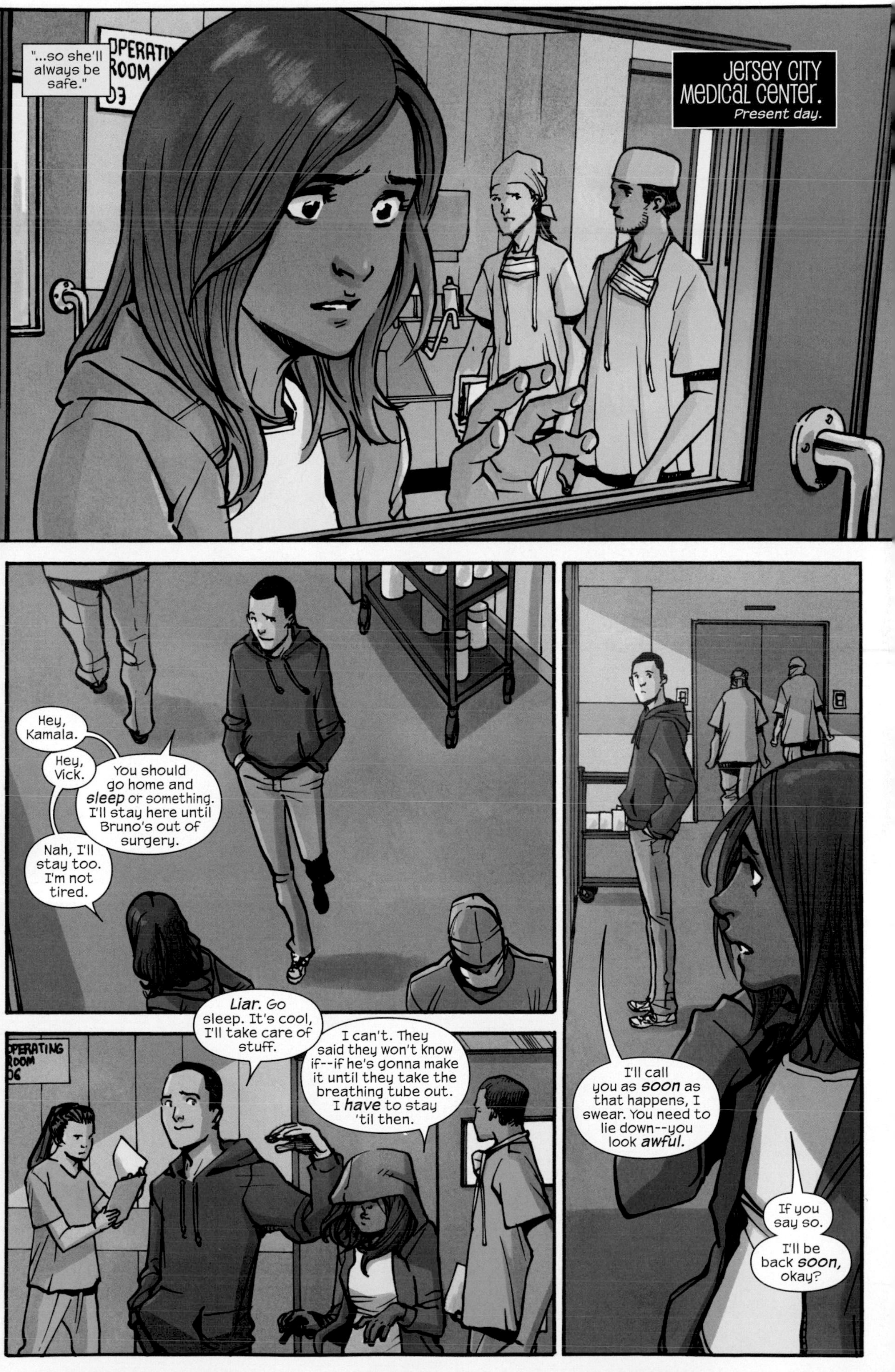
"...so she'll always be safe."
OPERATING ROOM 03
Jersey City Medical Center.
Present day.
Hey, Kamala.
Hey, Vick.
You should go home and *sleep* or something. I'll stay here until Bruno's out of surgery.
Nah, I'll stay too. I'm not tired.
OPERATING ROOM 06
Liar. Go sleep. It's cool, I'll take care of stuff.
I can't. They said they won't know if--if he's gonna make it until they take the breathing tube out. I *have* to stay 'til then.
I'll call you as *soon* as that happens, I swear. You need to lie down--you look *awful.*
If you say so.
I'll be back *soon,* okay?

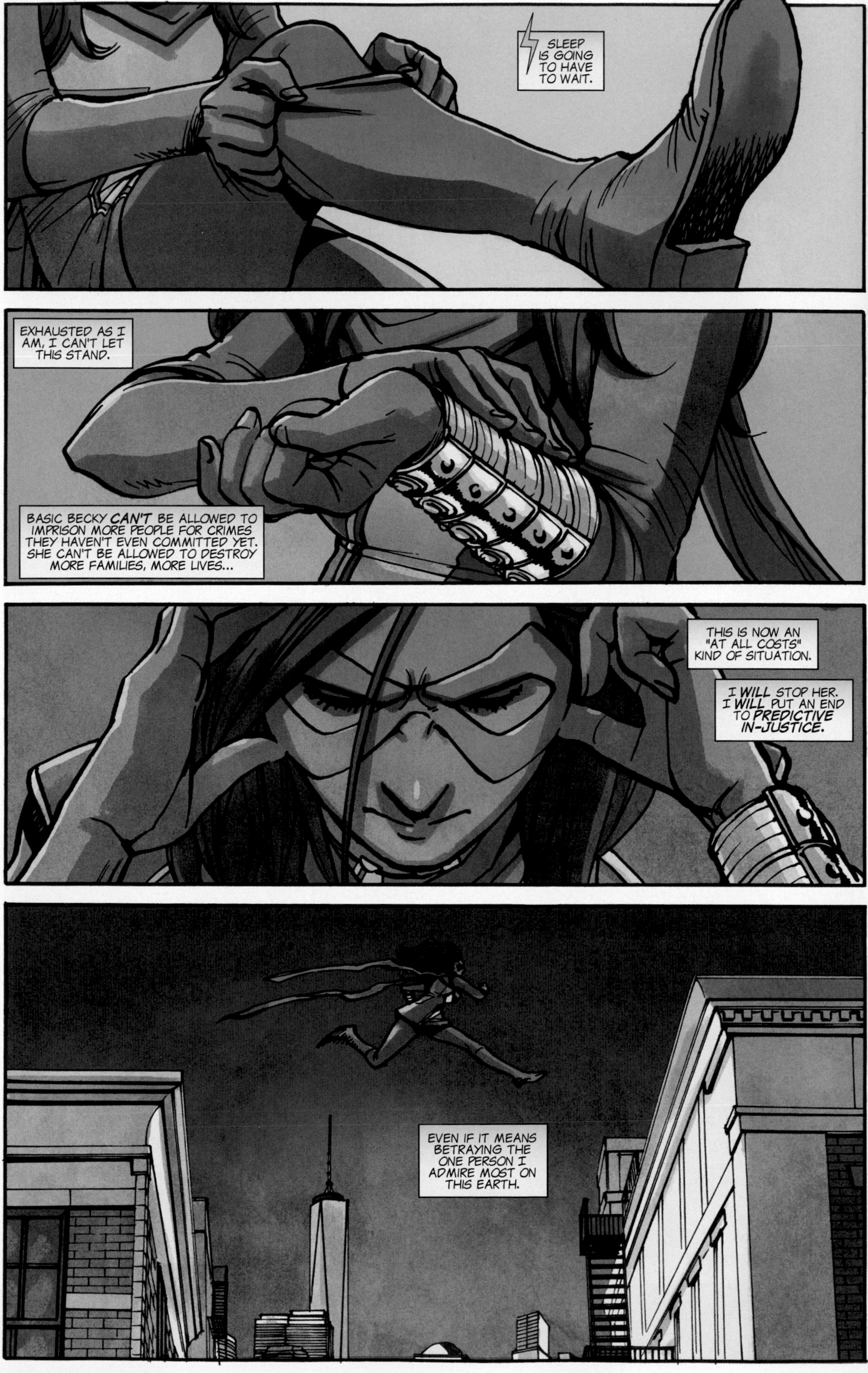
SLEEP IS GOING TO HAVE TO WAIT.
EXHAUSTED AS I AM, I CAN'T LET THIS STAND.
BASIC BECKY **CAN'T** BE ALLOWED TO IMPRISON MORE PEOPLE FOR CRIMES THEY HAVEN'T EVEN COMMITTED YET. SHE CAN'T BE ALLOWED TO DESTROY MORE FAMILIES, MORE LIVES...
THIS IS NOW AN "AT ALL COSTS" KIND OF SITUATION.
I **WILL** STOP HER. I **WILL** PUT AN END TO **PREDICTIVE IN-JUSTICE.**
EVEN IF IT MEANS BETRAYING THE ONE PERSON I ADMIRE MOST ON THIS EARTH.

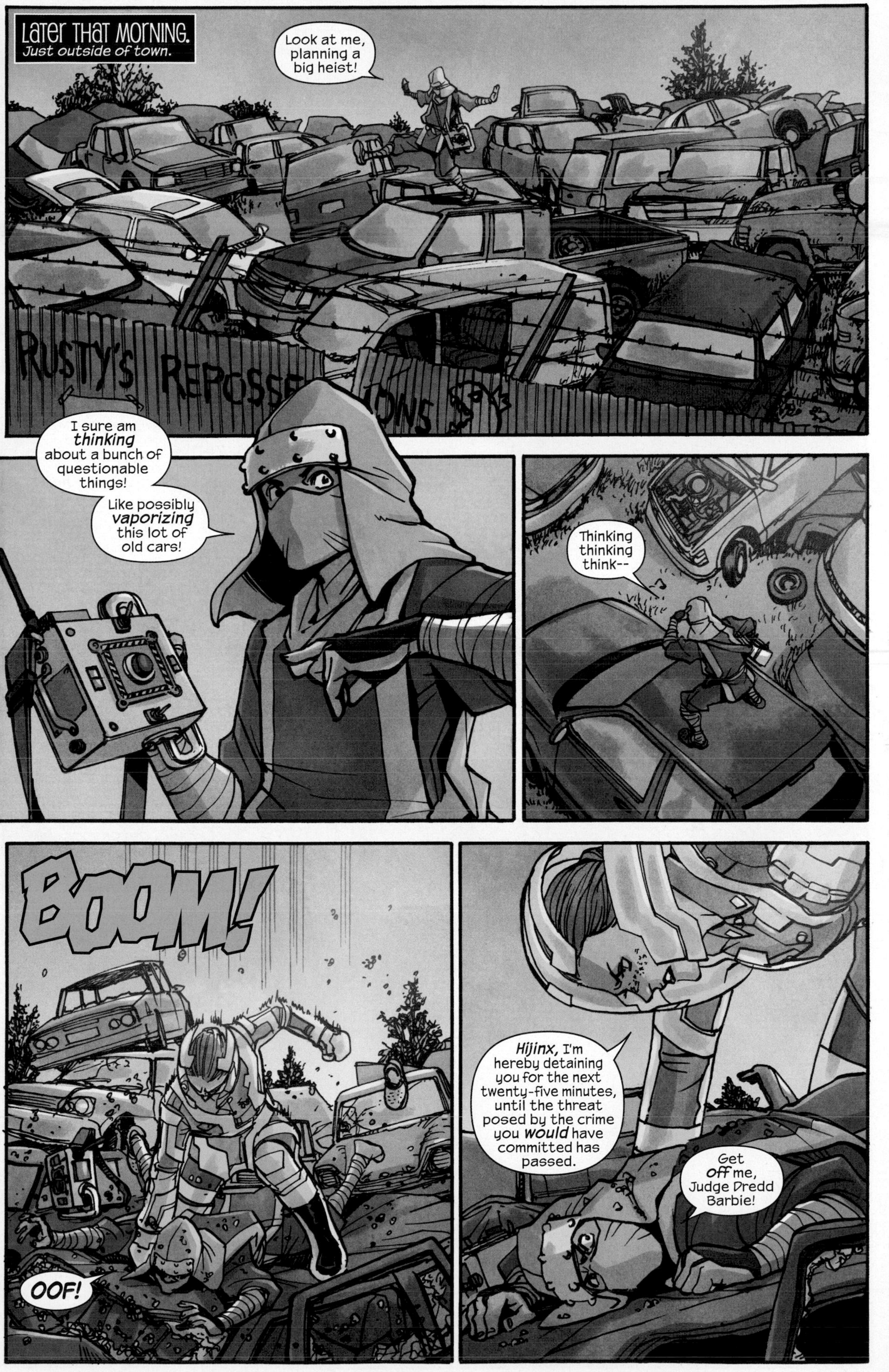
LATER THAT MORNING.
Just outside of town.
Look at me, planning a big heist!
RUSTY'S REPOSSE IONS
I sure am thinking about a bunch of questionable things!
Like possibly vaporizing this lot of old cars!
Thinking thinking think--
BOOM!
OOF!
Hijinx, I'm hereby detaining you for the next twenty-five minutes, until the threat posed by the crime you would have committed has passed.
Get off me, Judge Dredd Barbie!

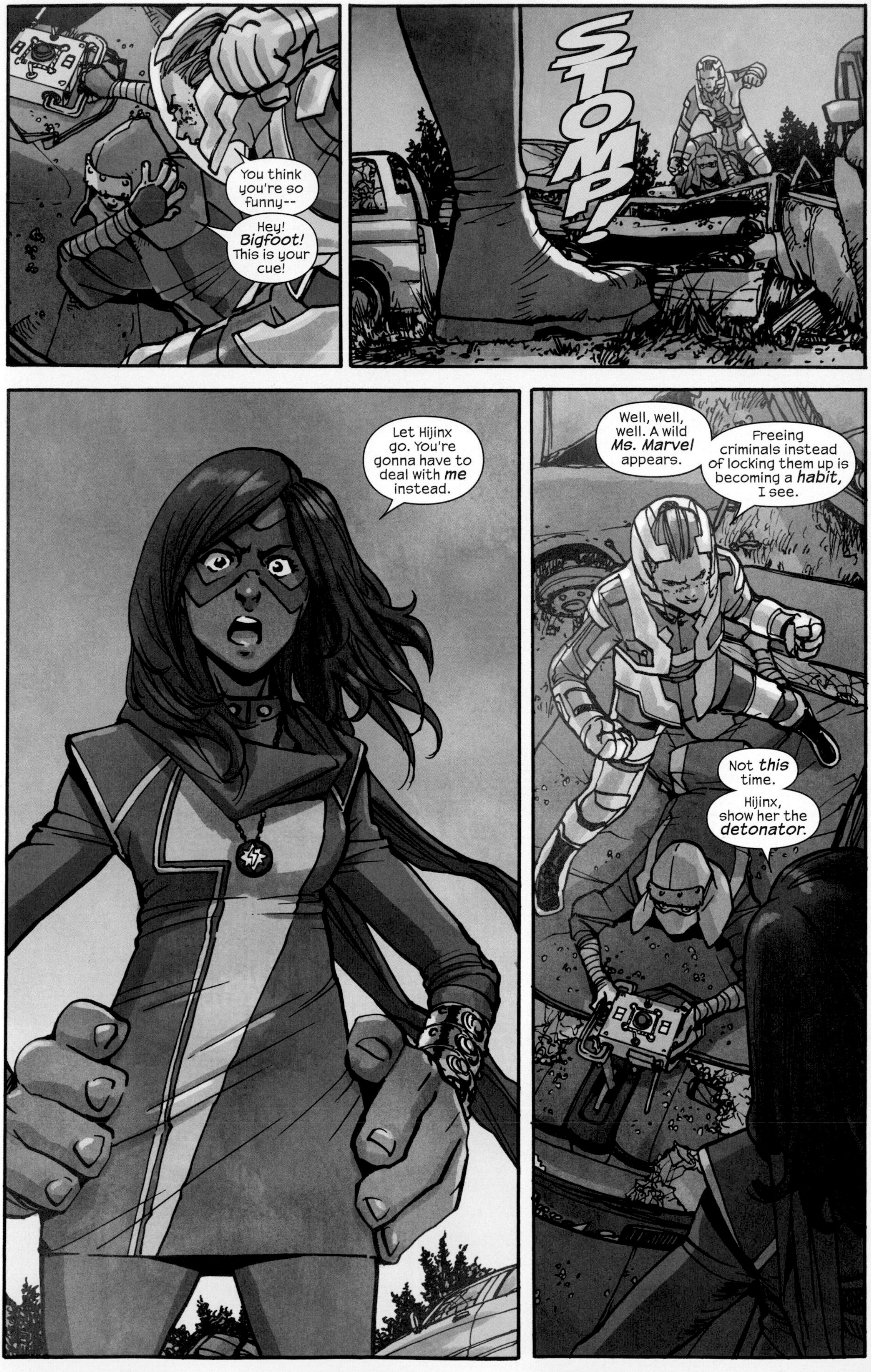
You think you're so funny--
Hey! *Bigfoot!* This is your cue!
STOMP!
Let Hijinx go. You're gonna have to deal with *me* instead.
Well, well, well. A wild *Ms. Marvel* appears.
Freeing criminals instead of locking them up is becoming a *habit,* I see.
Not *this* time.
Hijinx, show her the *detonator*.

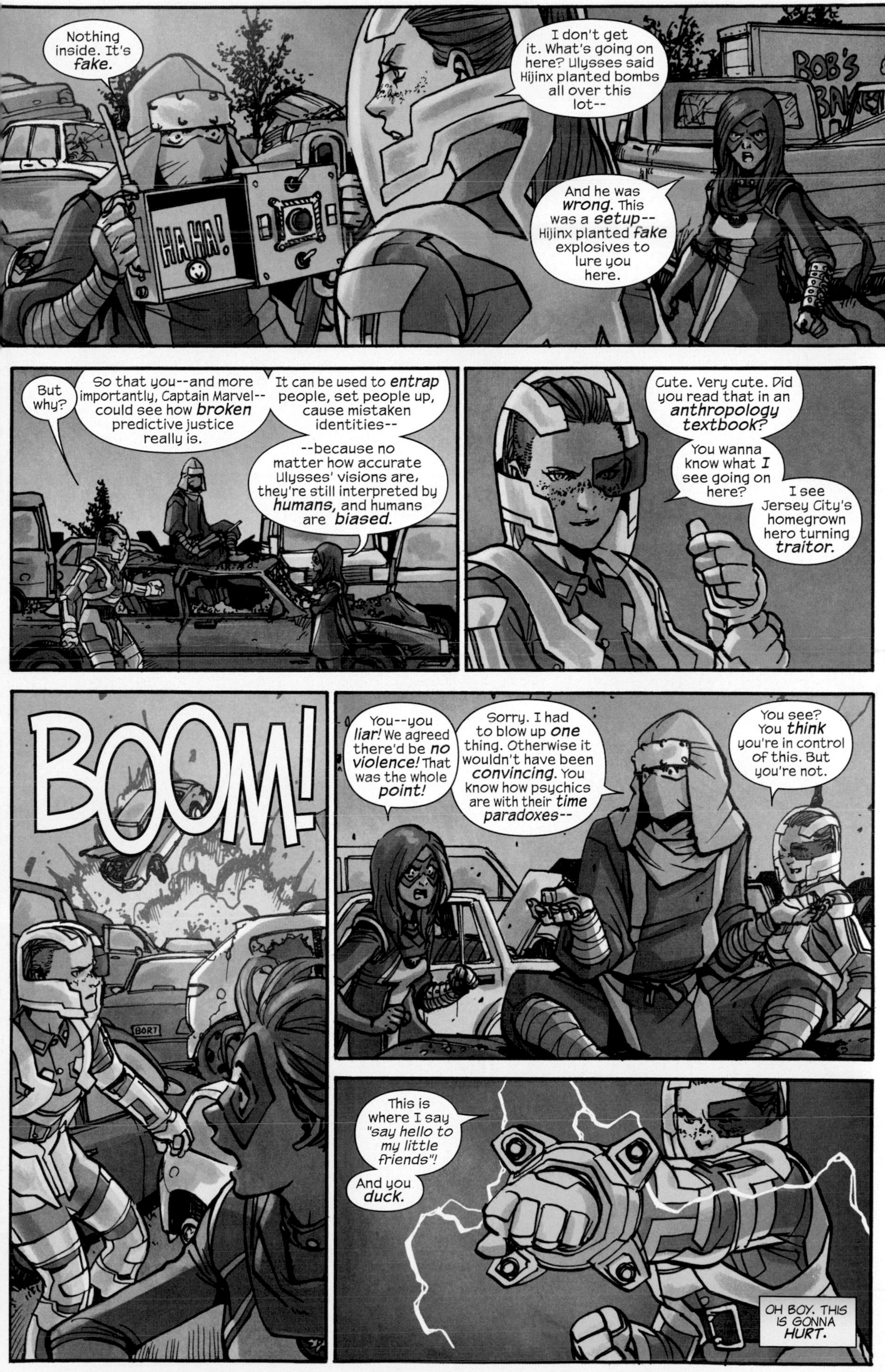
Nothing inside. It's fake.
I don't get it. What's going on here? Ulysses said Hijinx planted bombs all over this lot--
And he was wrong. This was a setup-- Hijinx planted fake explosives to lure you here.
HAHA!
BOB'S BAKERY
But why?
So that you--and more importantly, Captain Marvel-- could see how broken predictive justice really is.
It can be used to entrap people, set people up, cause mistaken identities--
--because no matter how accurate Ulysses' visions are, they're still interpreted by humans, and humans are biased.
Cute. Very cute. Did you read that in an anthropology textbook?
You wanna know what I see going on here?
I see Jersey City's homegrown hero turning traitor.
BOOM!
BORT
You--you liar! We agreed there'd be no violence! That was the whole point!
Sorry. I had to blow up one thing. Otherwise it wouldn't have been convincing. You know how psychics are with their time paradoxes--
You see? You think you're in control of this. But you're not.
This is where I say "say hello to my little friends"!
And you duck.
OH BOY. THIS IS GONNA HURT.

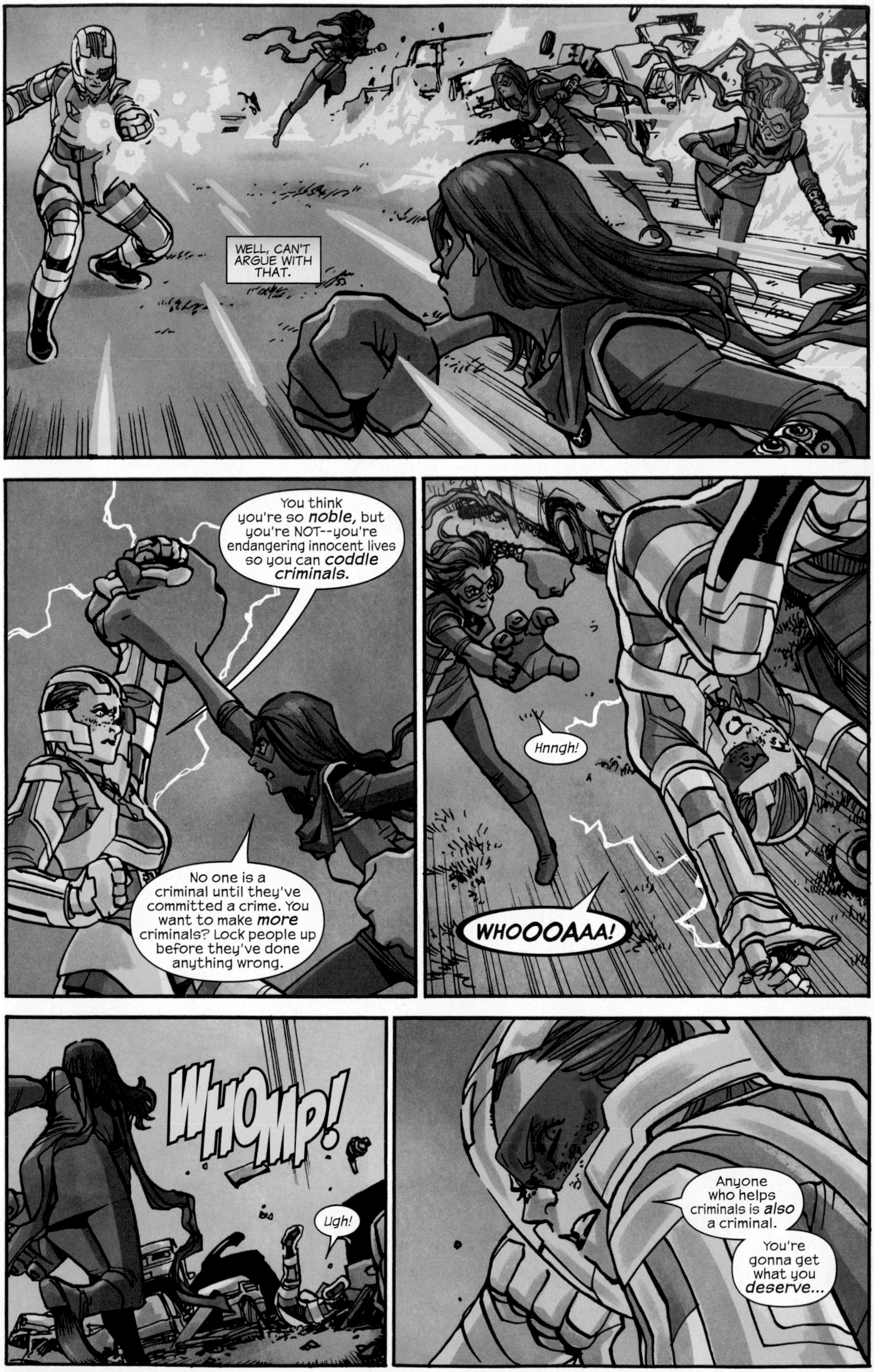
WELL, CAN'T ARGUE WITH THAT.
You think you're so *noble,* but you're NOT--you're endangering innocent lives so you can *coddle criminals.*
No one is a criminal until they've committed a crime. You want to make *more* criminals? Lock people up before they've done anything wrong.
Hnngh!
WHOOOAAA!
WHOMP!
Ugh!
Anyone who helps criminals is *also* a criminal.
You're gonna get what you *deserve...*

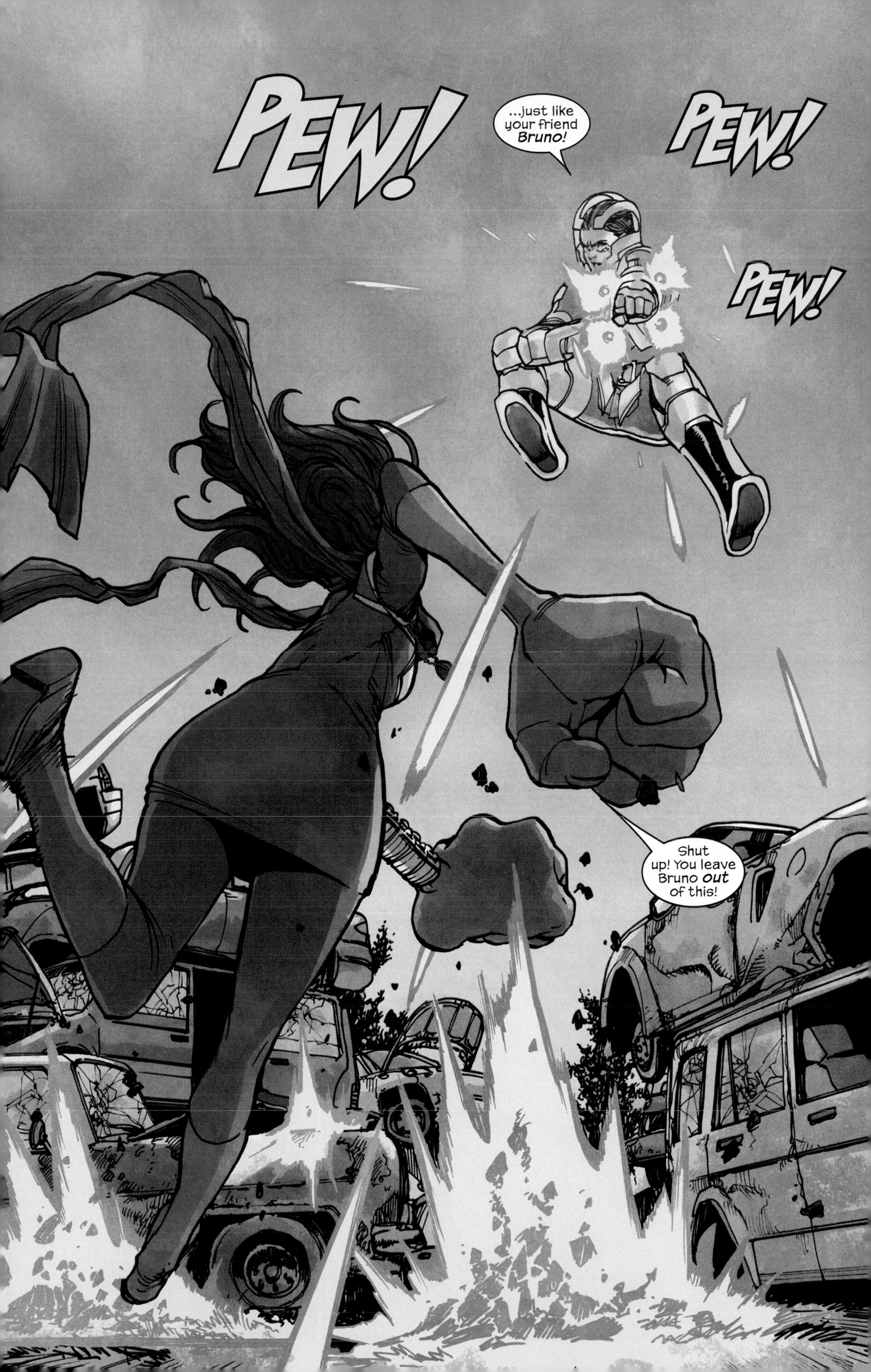
PEW!
...just like your friend Bruno!
PEW!
PEW!
Shut up! You leave Bruno out of this!

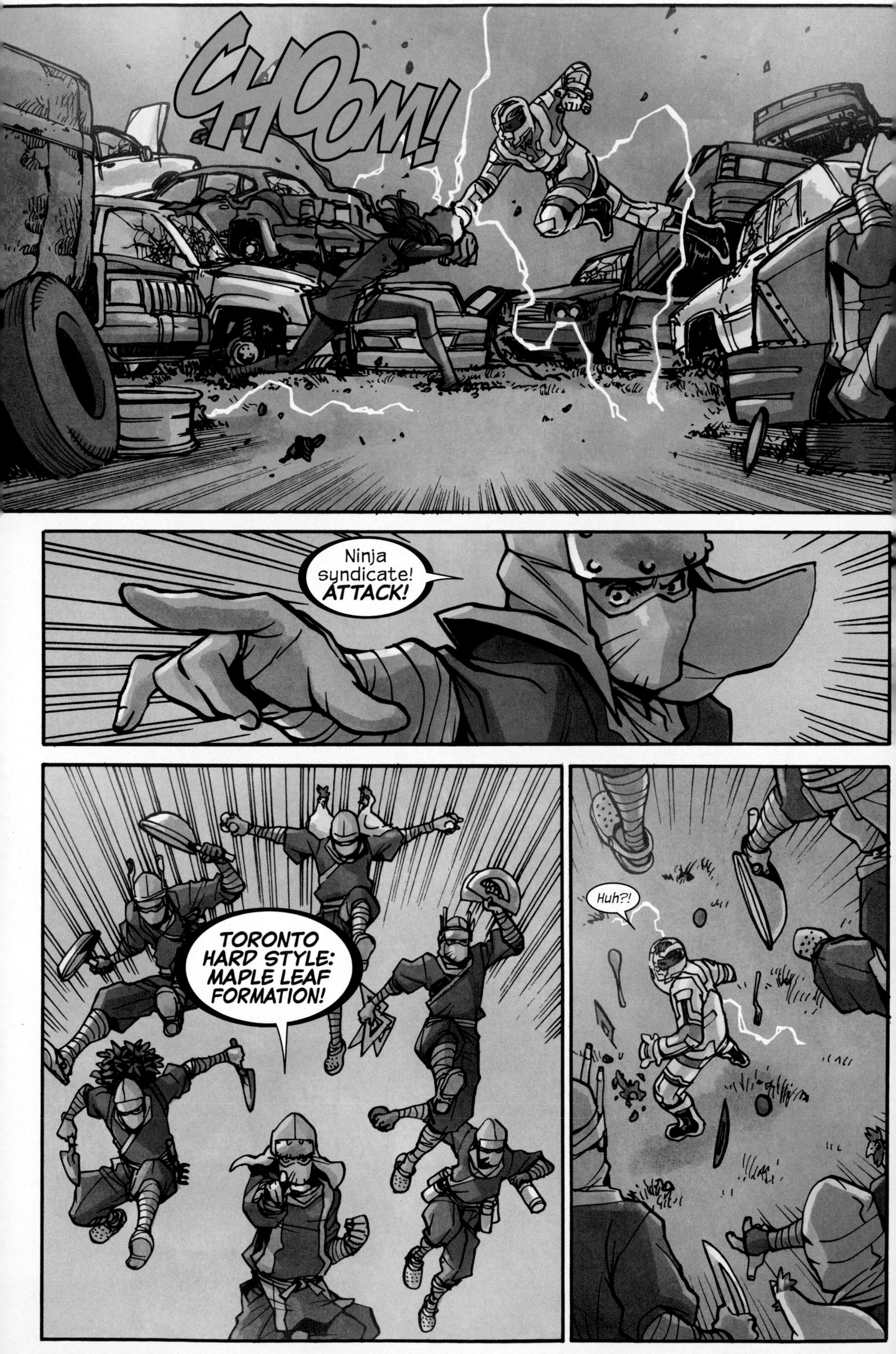
CHOOM!
Ninja syndicate! ATTACK!
TORONTO HARD STYLE: MAPLE LEAF FORMATION!
Huh?!

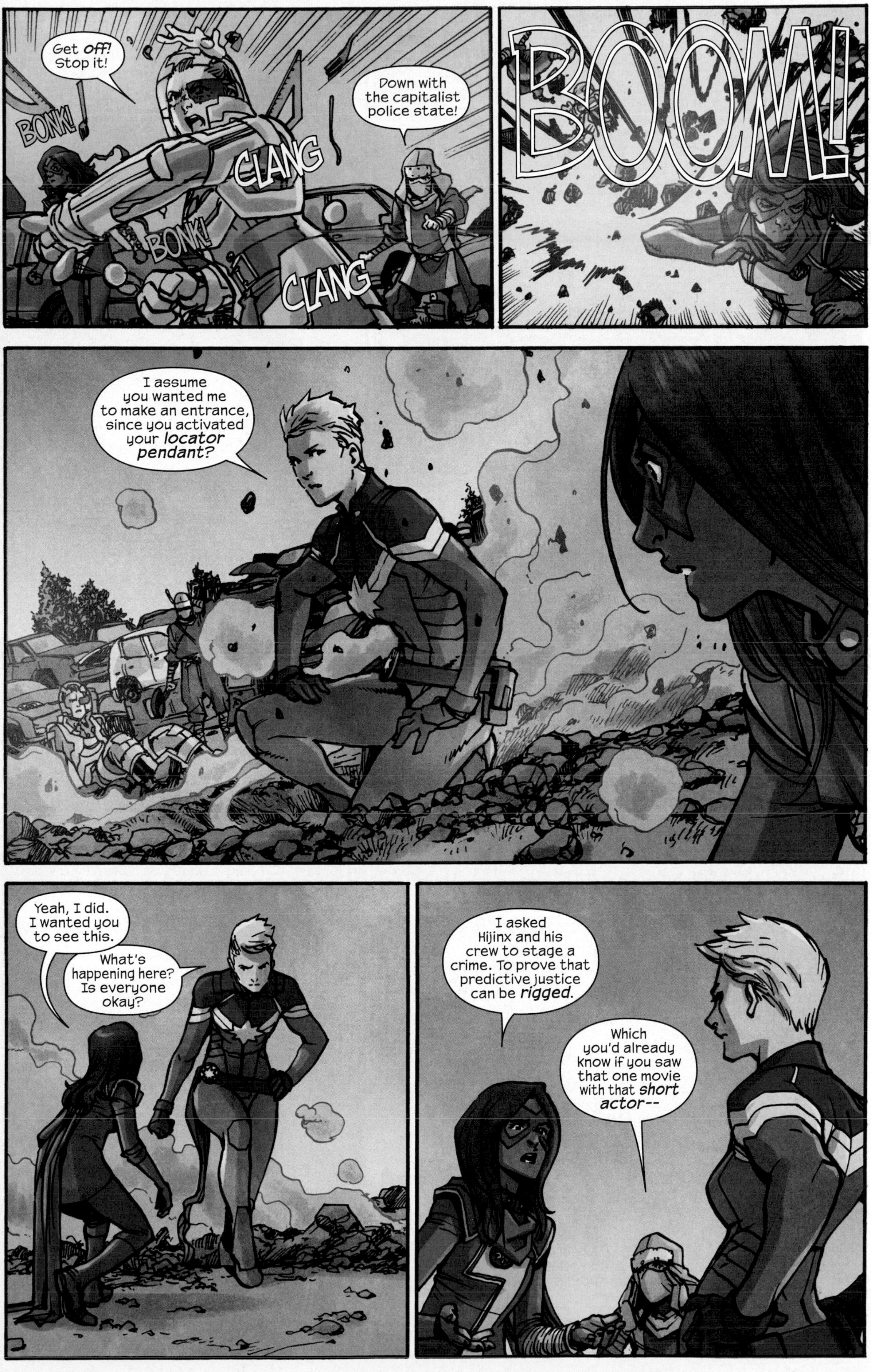
Get off! Stop it!
BONK!
CLANG
BONK!
CLANG
Down with the capitalist police state!
BOOM!
I assume you wanted me to make an entrance, since you activated your locator pendant?
Yeah, I did. I wanted you to see this.
What's happening here? Is everyone okay?
I asked Hijinx and his crew to stage a crime. To prove that predictive justice can be rigged.
Which you'd already know if you saw that one movie with that short actor--

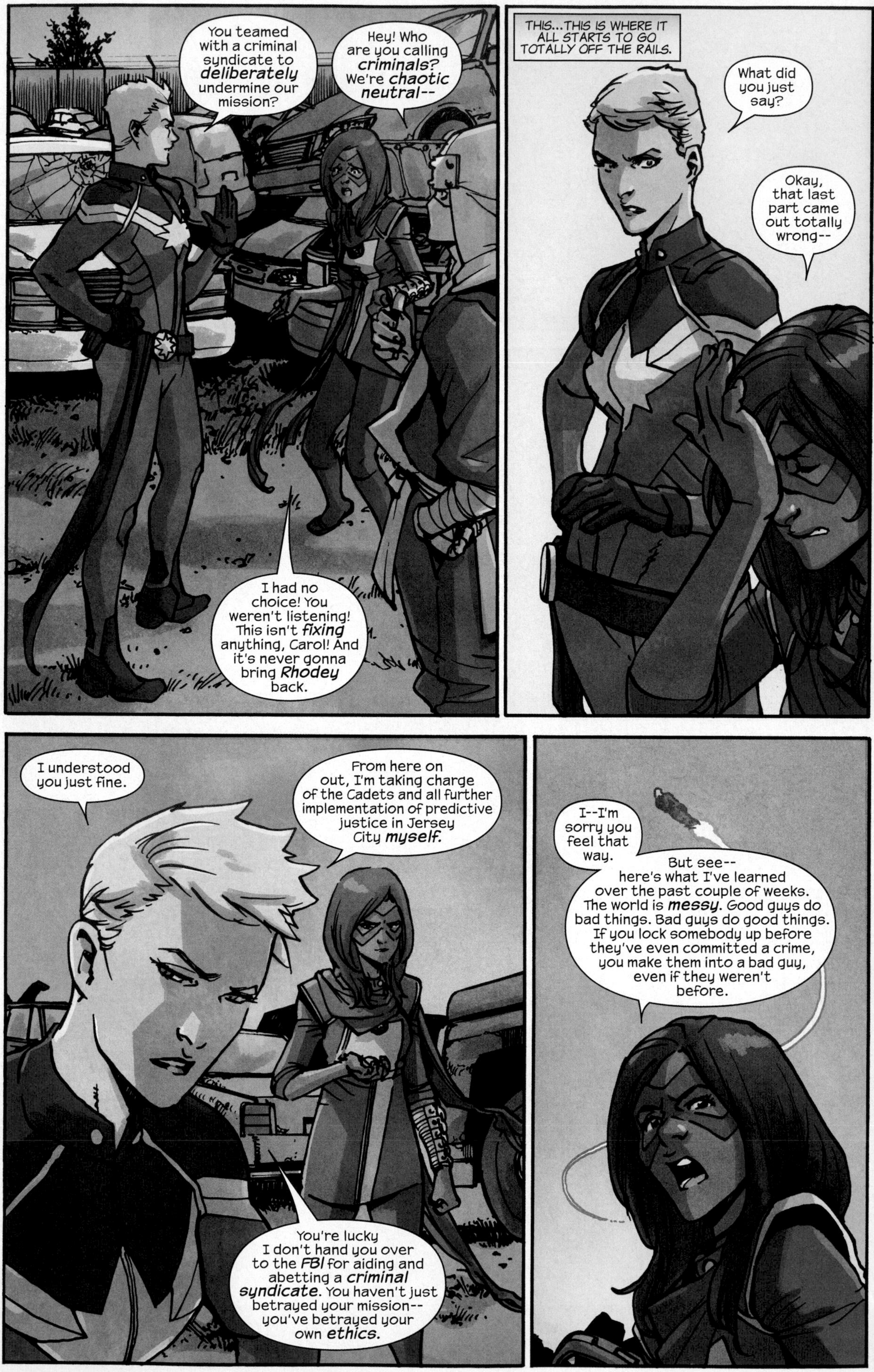
You teamed with a criminal syndicate to *deliberately* undermine our mission?
Hey! Who are you calling *criminals?* We're *chaotic neutral--*
I had no choice! You weren't listening! This isn't *fixing* anything, Carol! And it's never gonna bring *Rhodey* back.
THIS...THIS IS WHERE IT ALL STARTS TO GO TOTALLY OFF THE RAILS.
What did you just say?
Okay, that last part came out totally wrong--
I understood you just fine.
From here on out, I'm taking charge of the Cadets and all further implementation of predictive justice in Jersey City *myself.*
You're lucky I don't hand you over to the *FBI* for aiding and abetting a *criminal syndicate*. You haven't just betrayed your mission-- you've betrayed your own *ethics.*
I--I'm sorry you feel that way.
But see-- here's what I've learned over the past couple of weeks. The world is *messy*. Good guys do bad things. Bad guys do good things. If you lock somebody up before they've even committed a crime, you make them into a bad guy, even if they weren't before.

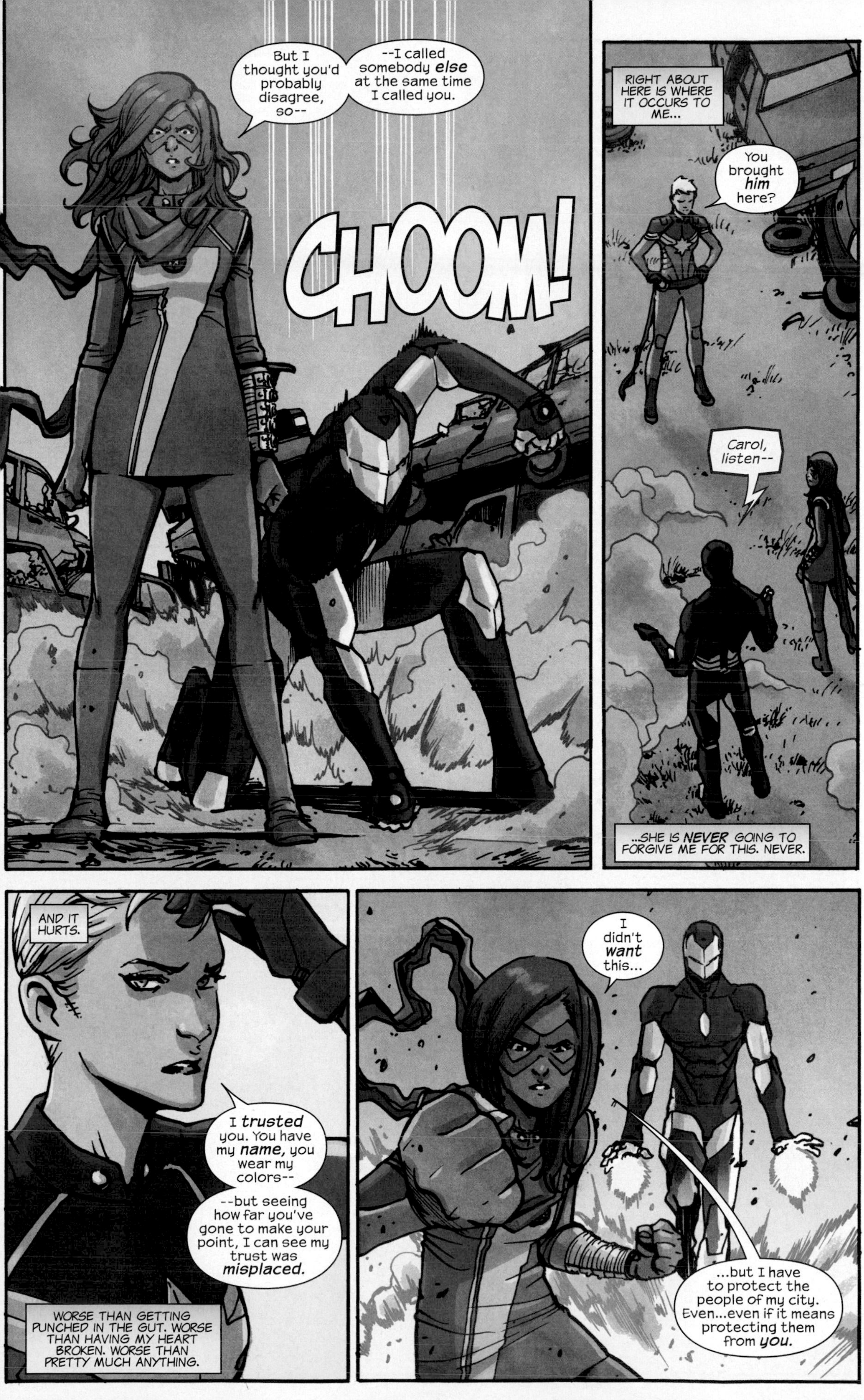

But I thought you'd probably disagree, so--
--I called somebody else at the same time I called you.
CHOOM!
RIGHT ABOUT HERE IS WHERE IT OCCURS TO ME...
You brought him here?
Carol, listen--
...SHE IS NEVER GOING TO FORGIVE ME FOR THIS. NEVER.
AND IT HURTS.
I trusted you. You have my name, you wear my colors--
--but seeing how far you've gone to make your point, I can see my trust was misplaced.
WORSE THAN GETTING PUNCHED IN THE GUT. WORSE THAN HAVING MY HEART BROKEN. WORSE THAN PRETTY MUCH ANYTHING.
I didn't want this...
...but I have to protect the people of my city. Even...even if it means protecting them from you.

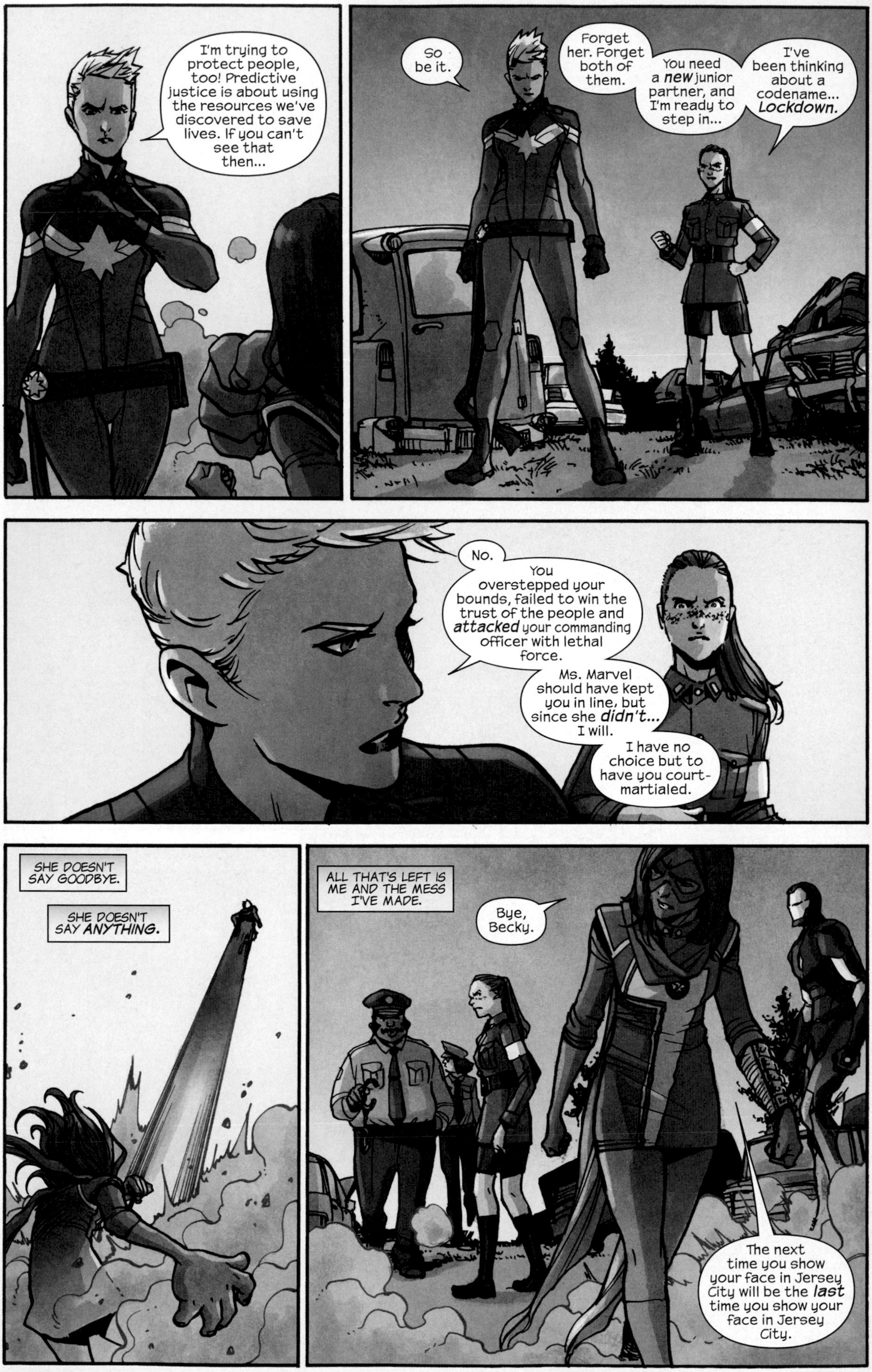

I'm trying to protect people, too! Predictive justice is about using the resources we've discovered to save lives. If you can't see that then...
So be it.
Forget her. Forget both of them.
You need a *new* junior partner, and I'm ready to step in...
I've been thinking about a codename... *Lockdown.*
No.
You overstepped your bounds, failed to win the trust of the people and *attacked* your commanding officer with lethal force.
Ms. Marvel should have kept you in line, but since she *didn't...* I will.
I have no choice but to have you court-martialed.
SHE DOESN'T SAY GOODBYE.
SHE DOESN'T SAY *ANYTHING.*
ALL THAT'S LEFT IS ME AND THE MESS I'VE MADE.
Bye, Becky.
The next time you show your face in Jersey City will be the *last* time you show your face in Jersey City.

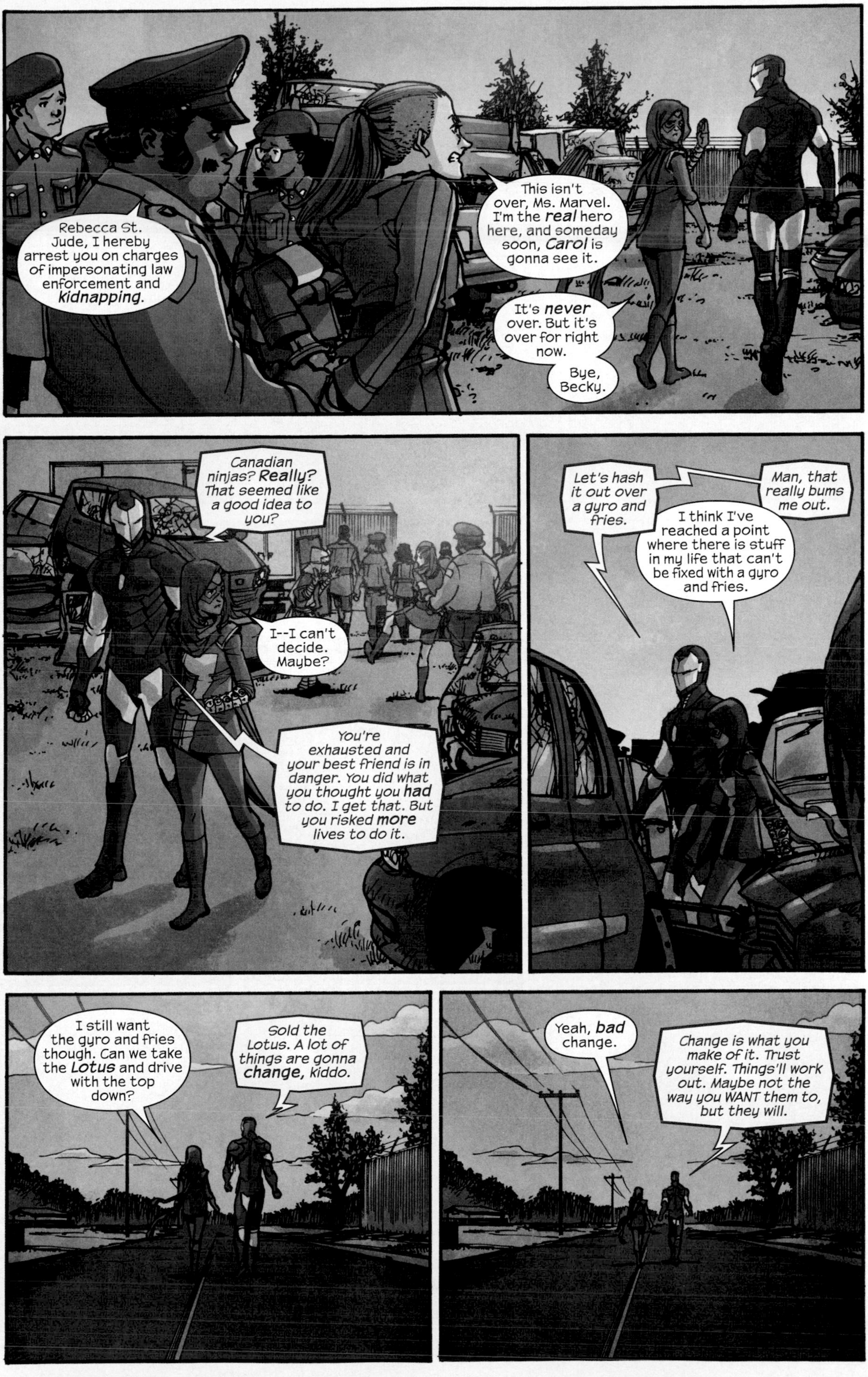
Rebecca St. Jude, I hereby arrest you on charges of impersonating law enforcement and *kidnapping*.
This isn't over, Ms. Marvel. I'm the *real* hero here, and someday soon, *Carol* is gonna see it.
It's *never* over. But it's over for right now.
Bye, Becky.
Canadian ninjas? *Really?* That seemed like a good idea to you?
I--I can't decide. Maybe?
You're exhausted and your best friend is in danger. You did what you thought you *had* to do. I get that. But you risked *more* lives to do it.
Let's hash it out over a gyro and fries.
Man, that really bums me out.
I think I've reached a point where there is stuff in my life that can't be fixed with a gyro and fries.
I still want the gyro and fries though. Can we take the *Lotus* and drive with the top down?
Sold the Lotus. A lot of things are gonna *change,* kiddo.
Yeah, *bad* change.
Change is what you make of it. Trust yourself. Things'll work out. Maybe not the way you WANT them to, but they will.

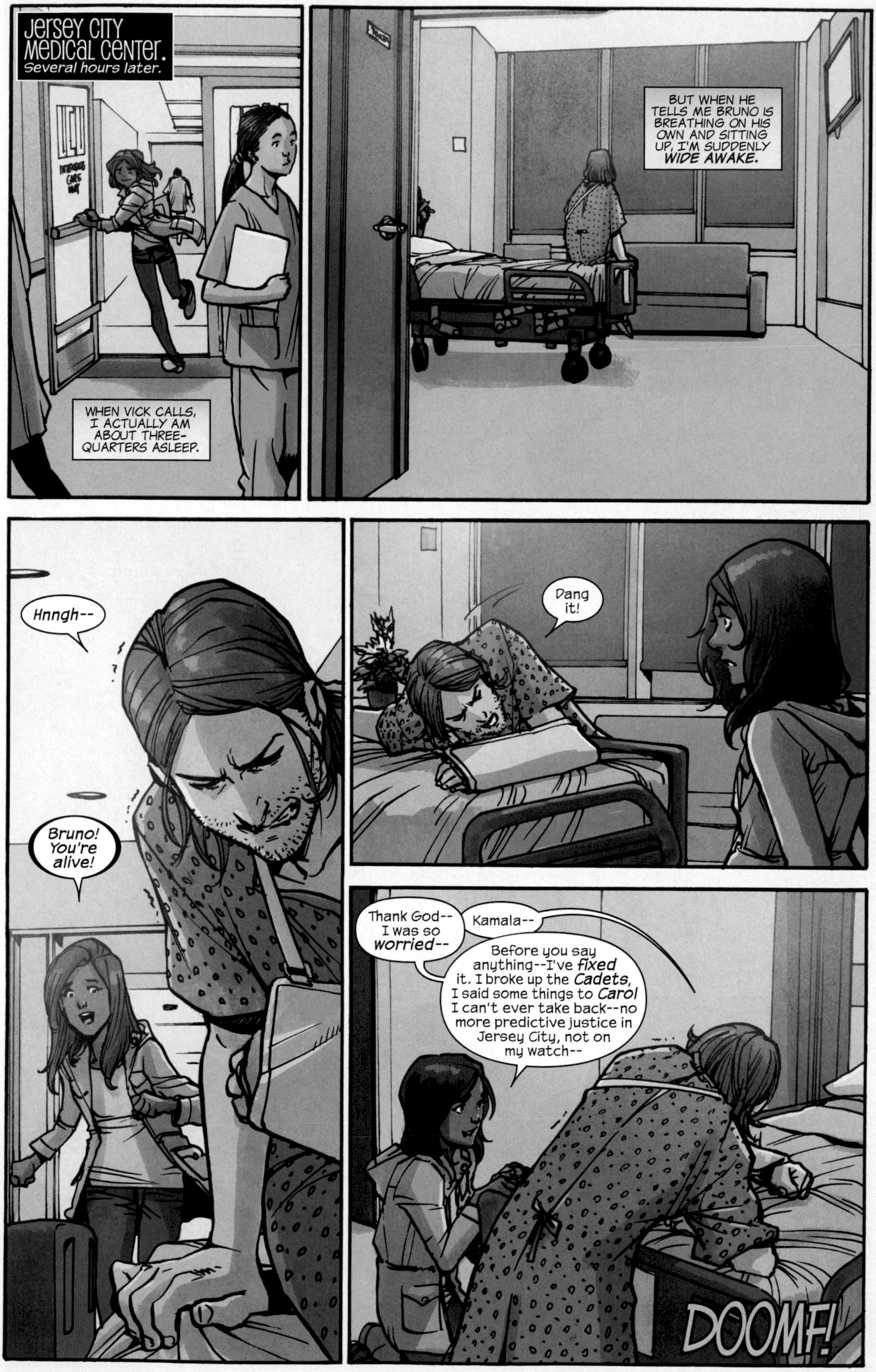
Jersey City Medical Center.
Several hours later.
WHEN VICK CALLS, I ACTUALLY AM ABOUT THREE-QUARTERS ASLEEP.
BUT WHEN HE TELLS ME BRUNO IS BREATHING ON HIS OWN AND SITTING UP, I'M SUDDENLY WIDE AWAKE.
Hnngh--
Bruno! You're alive!
Dang it!
Thank God-- I was so worried--
Kamala--
Before you say anything--I've fixed it. I broke up the Cadets, I said some things to Carol I can't ever take back--no more predictive justice in Jersey City, not on my watch--
DOOMF!

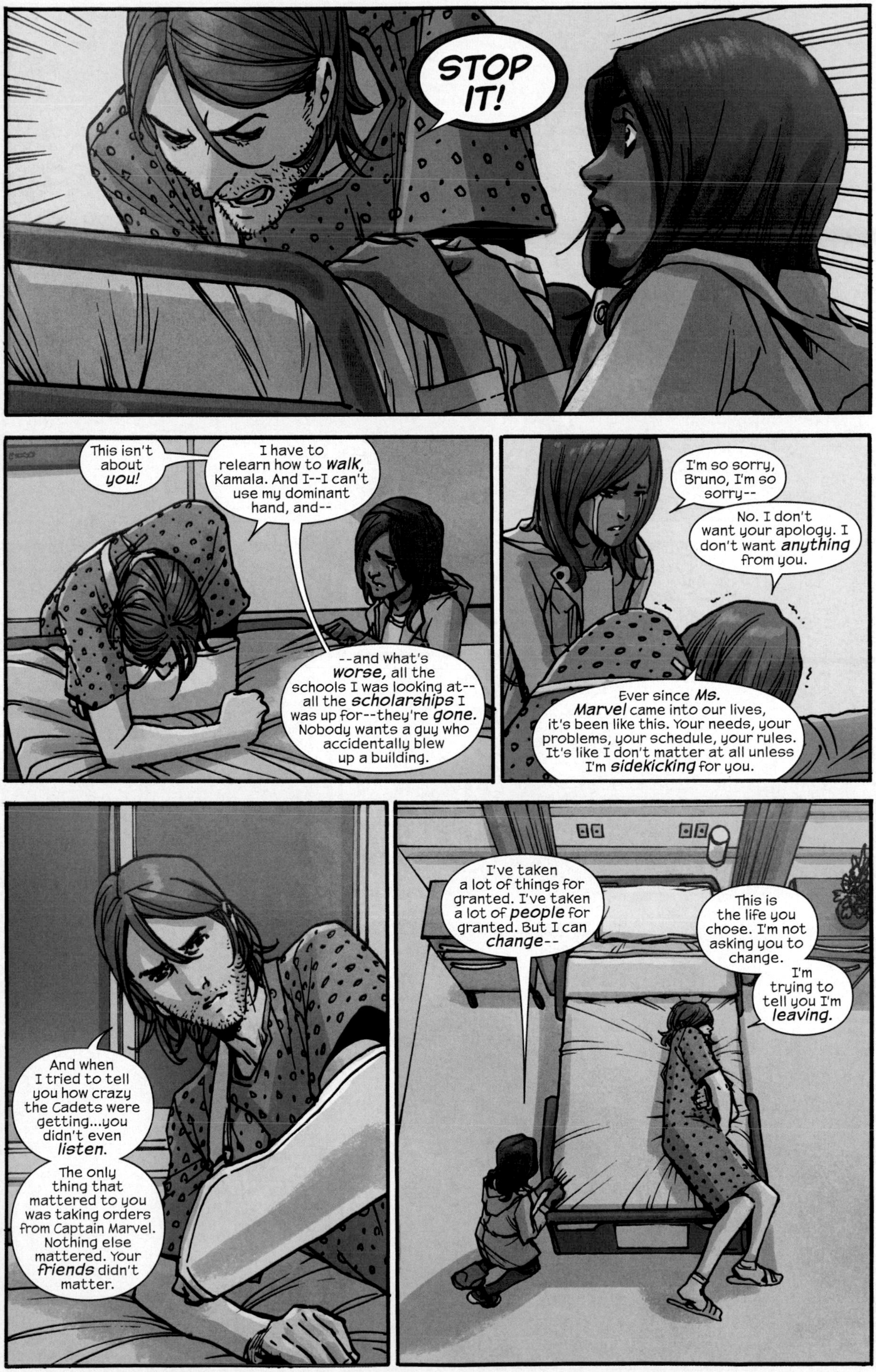
STOP IT!
This isn't about *you!*
I have to relearn how to *walk,* Kamala. And I--I can't use my dominant hand, and--
--and what's *worse,* all the schools I was looking at--all the *scholarships* I was up for--they're *gone.* Nobody wants a guy who accidentally blew up a building.
I'm so sorry, Bruno, I'm so sorry--
No. I don't want your apology. I don't want *anything* from you.
Ever since *Ms. Marvel* came into our lives, it's been like this. Your needs, your problems, your schedule, your rules. It's like I don't matter at all unless I'm *sidekicking* for you.
And when I tried to tell you how crazy the Cadets were getting...you didn't even *listen.*
The only thing that mattered to you was taking orders from Captain Marvel. Nothing else mattered. Your *friends* didn't matter.
I've taken a lot of things for granted. I've taken a lot of *people* for granted. But I can *change*--
This is the life you chose. I'm not asking you to change.
I'm trying to tell you I'm *leaving.*

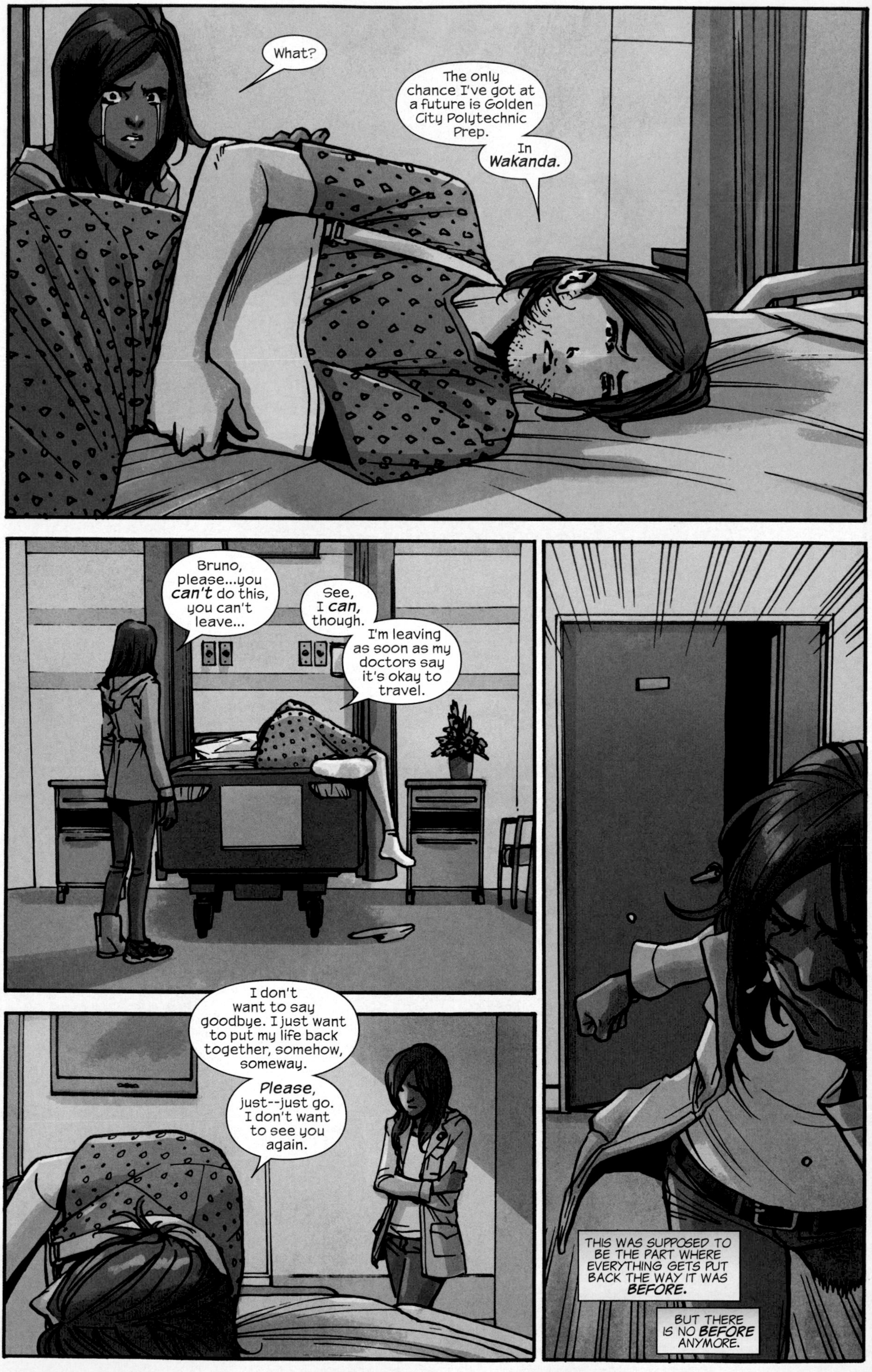
What?
The only chance I've got at a future is Golden City Polytechnic Prep.
In *Wakanda.*
Bruno, please...you ***can't*** do this, you can't leave...
See, I ***can,*** though.
I'm leaving as soon as my doctors say it's okay to travel.
I don't want to say goodbye. I just want to put my life back together, somehow, someway.
Please, just--just go. I don't want to see you again.
THIS WAS SUPPOSED TO BE THE PART WHERE EVERYTHING GETS PUT BACK THE WAY IT WAS ***BEFORE.***
BUT THERE IS NO ***BEFORE*** ANYMORE.

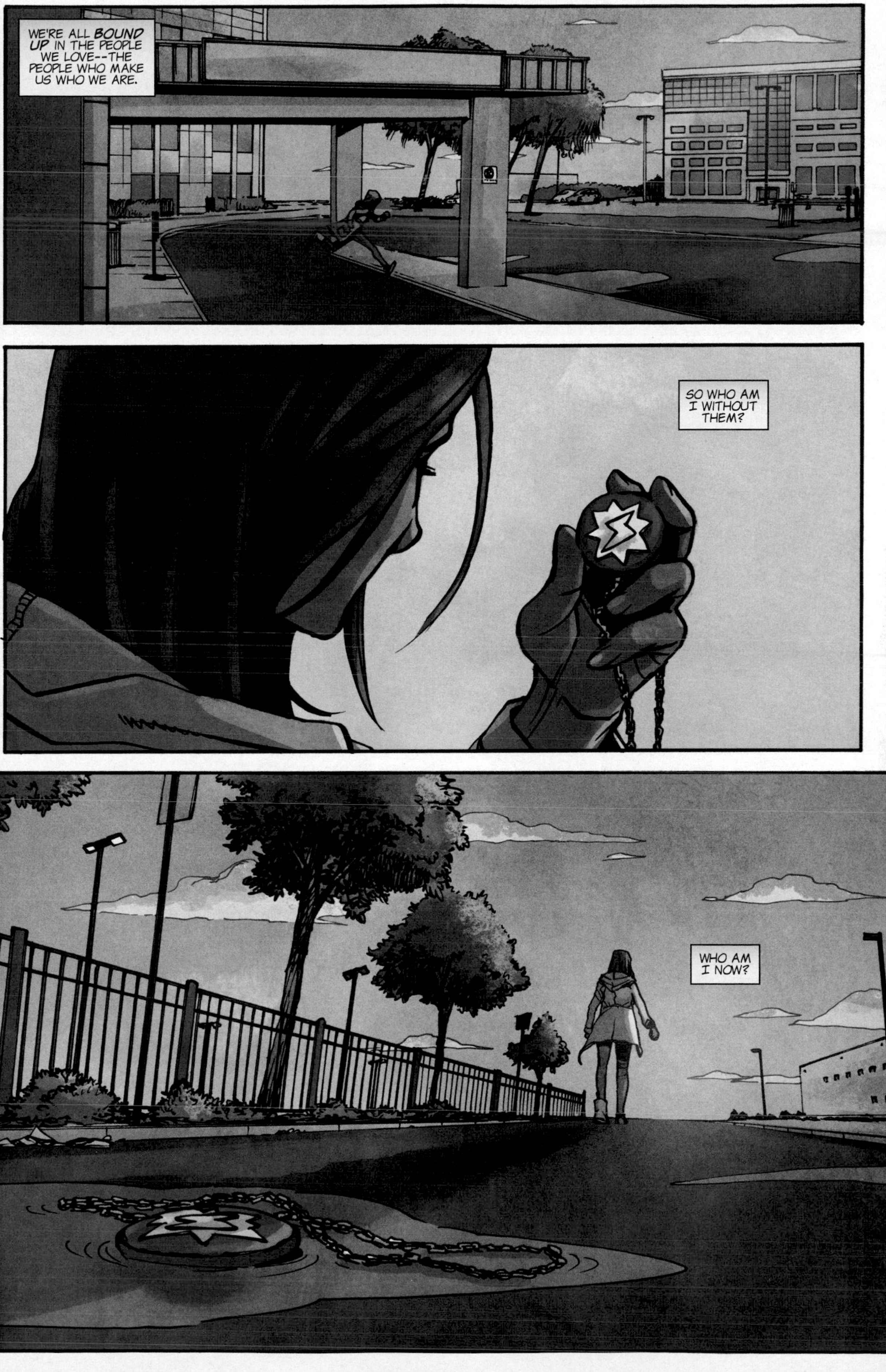
WE'RE ALL BOUND UP IN THE PEOPLE WE LOVE--THE PEOPLE WHO MAKE US WHO WE ARE.
SO WHO AM I WITHOUT THEM?
WHO AM I NOW?

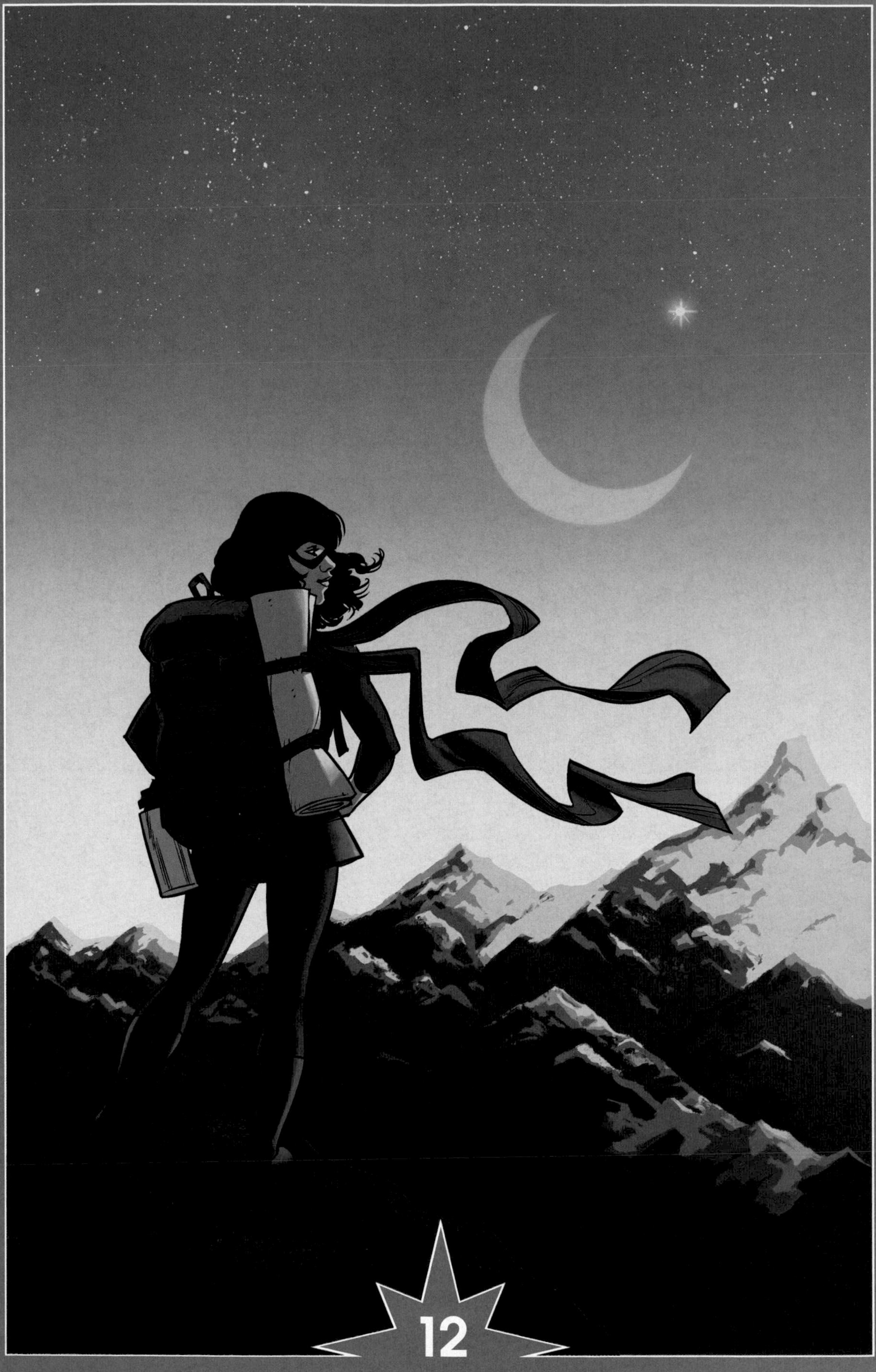
12

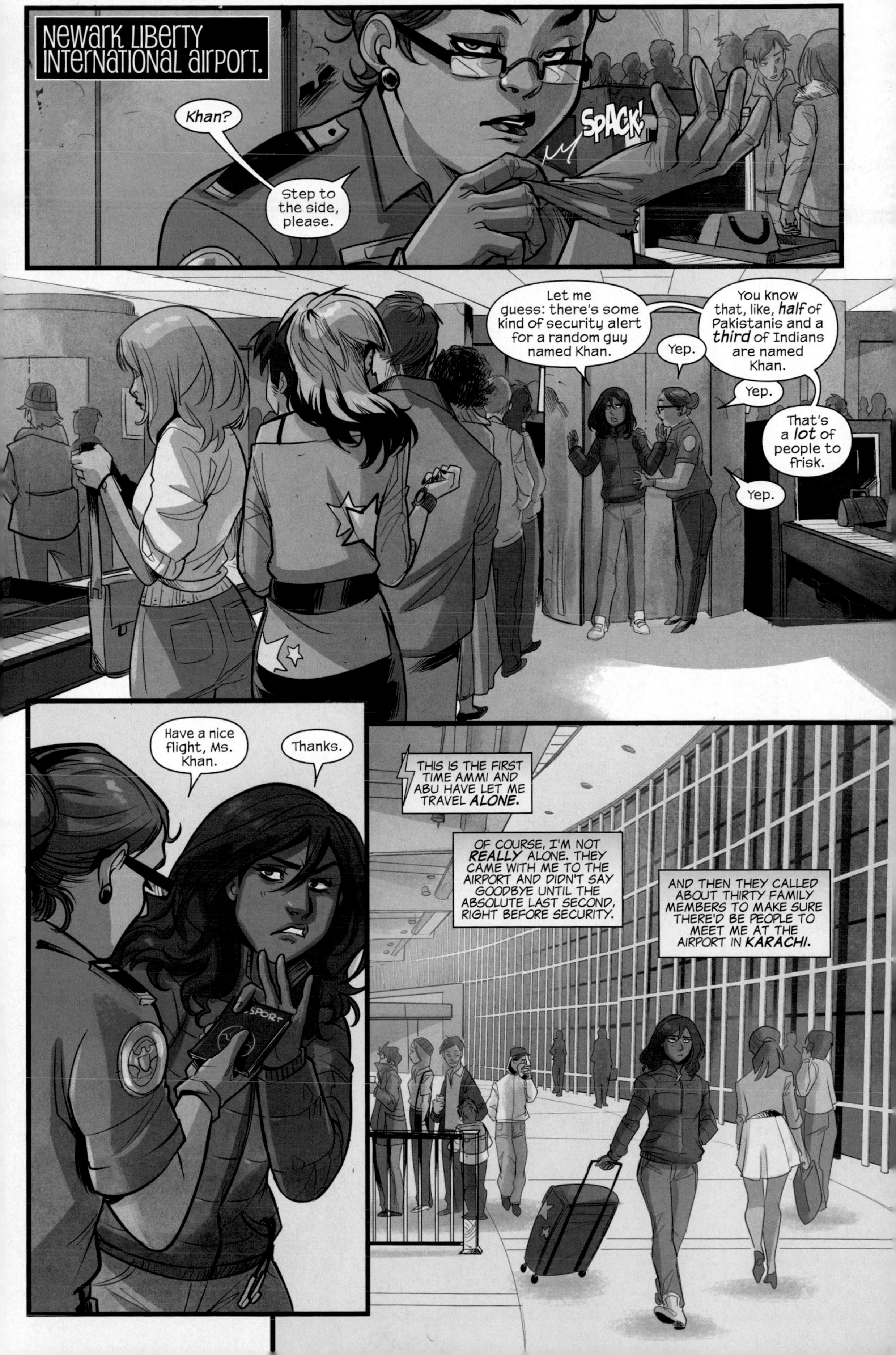

Newark Liberty International airport.
Khan?
Step to the side, please.
SPACK!
Let me guess: there's some kind of security alert for a random guy named Khan.
Yep.
You know that, like, half of Pakistanis and a third of Indians are named Khan.
Yep.
That's a lot of people to frisk.
Yep.
Have a nice flight, Ms. Khan.
Thanks.
THIS IS THE FIRST TIME AMMI AND ABU HAVE LET ME TRAVEL ALONE.
OF COURSE, I'M NOT REALLY ALONE. THEY CAME WITH ME TO THE AIRPORT AND DIDN'T SAY GOODBYE UNTIL THE ABSOLUTE LAST SECOND, RIGHT BEFORE SECURITY.
AND THEN THEY CALLED ABOUT THIRTY FAMILY MEMBERS TO MAKE SURE THERE'D BE PEOPLE TO MEET ME AT THE AIRPORT IN KARACHI.

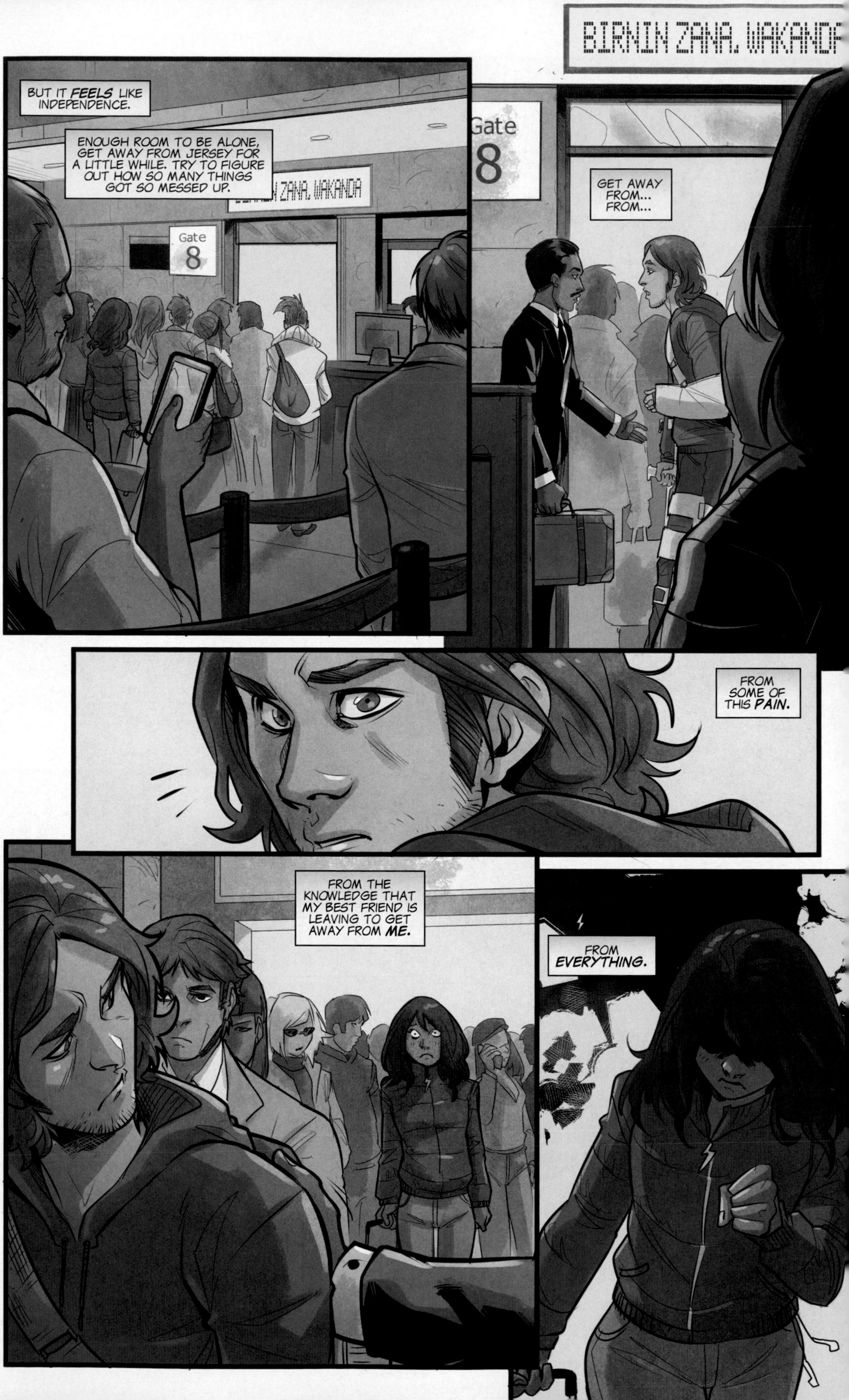

BIRNIN ZANA, WAKANDA
BUT IT FEELS LIKE INDEPENDENCE.
ENOUGH ROOM TO BE ALONE, GET AWAY FROM JERSEY FOR A LITTLE WHILE. TRY TO FIGURE OUT HOW SO MANY THINGS GOT SO MESSED UP.
Gate 8
GET AWAY FROM... FROM...
FROM SOME OF THIS PAIN.
FROM THE KNOWLEDGE THAT MY BEST FRIEND IS LEAVING TO GET AWAY FROM ME.
FROM EVERYTHING.

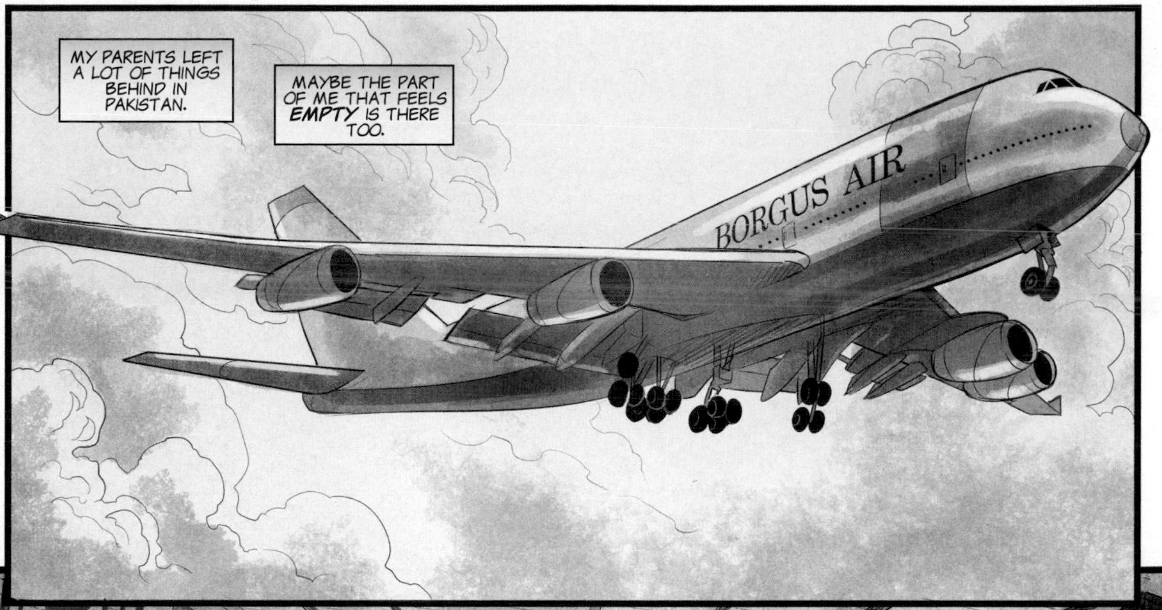
MY PARENTS LEFT A LOT OF THINGS BEHIND IN PAKISTAN.
MAYBE THE PART OF ME THAT FEELS EMPTY IS THERE TOO.
BORGUS AIR

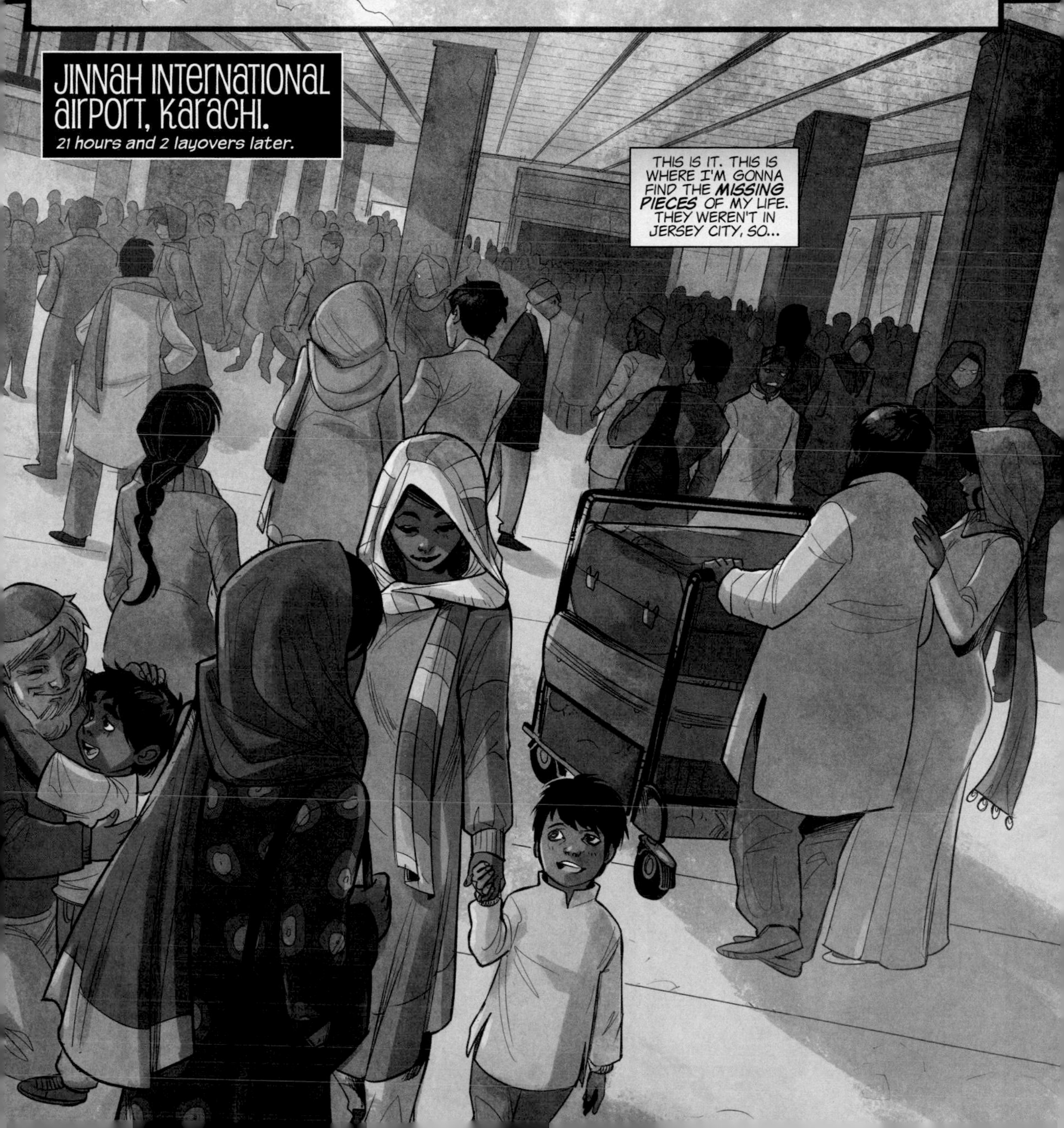
JINNAH INTERNATIONAL AIRPORT, KARACHI.
21 hours and 2 layovers later.
THIS IS IT. THIS IS WHERE I'M GONNA FIND THE MISSING PIECES OF MY LIFE. THEY WEREN'T IN JERSEY CITY, SO...

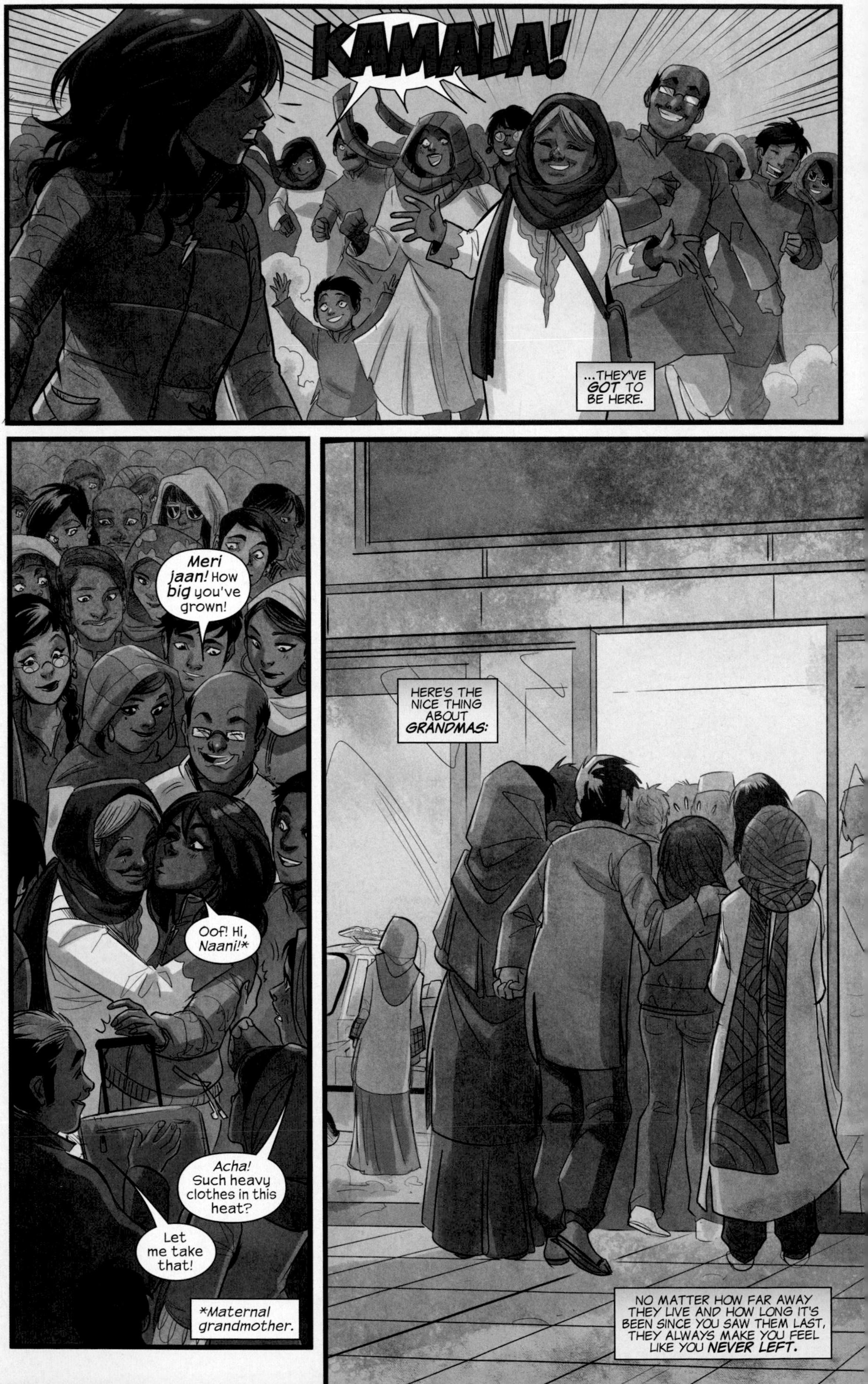
KAMALA!
...THEY'VE GOT TO BE HERE.
Meri jaan! How big you've grown!
Oof! Hi, Naani!*
Acha! Such heavy clothes in this heat?
Let me take that!
*Maternal grandmother.
HERE'S THE NICE THING ABOUT GRANDMAS:
NO MATTER HOW FAR AWAY THEY LIVE AND HOW LONG IT'S BEEN SINCE YOU SAW THEM LAST, THEY ALWAYS MAKE YOU FEEL LIKE YOU NEVER LEFT.

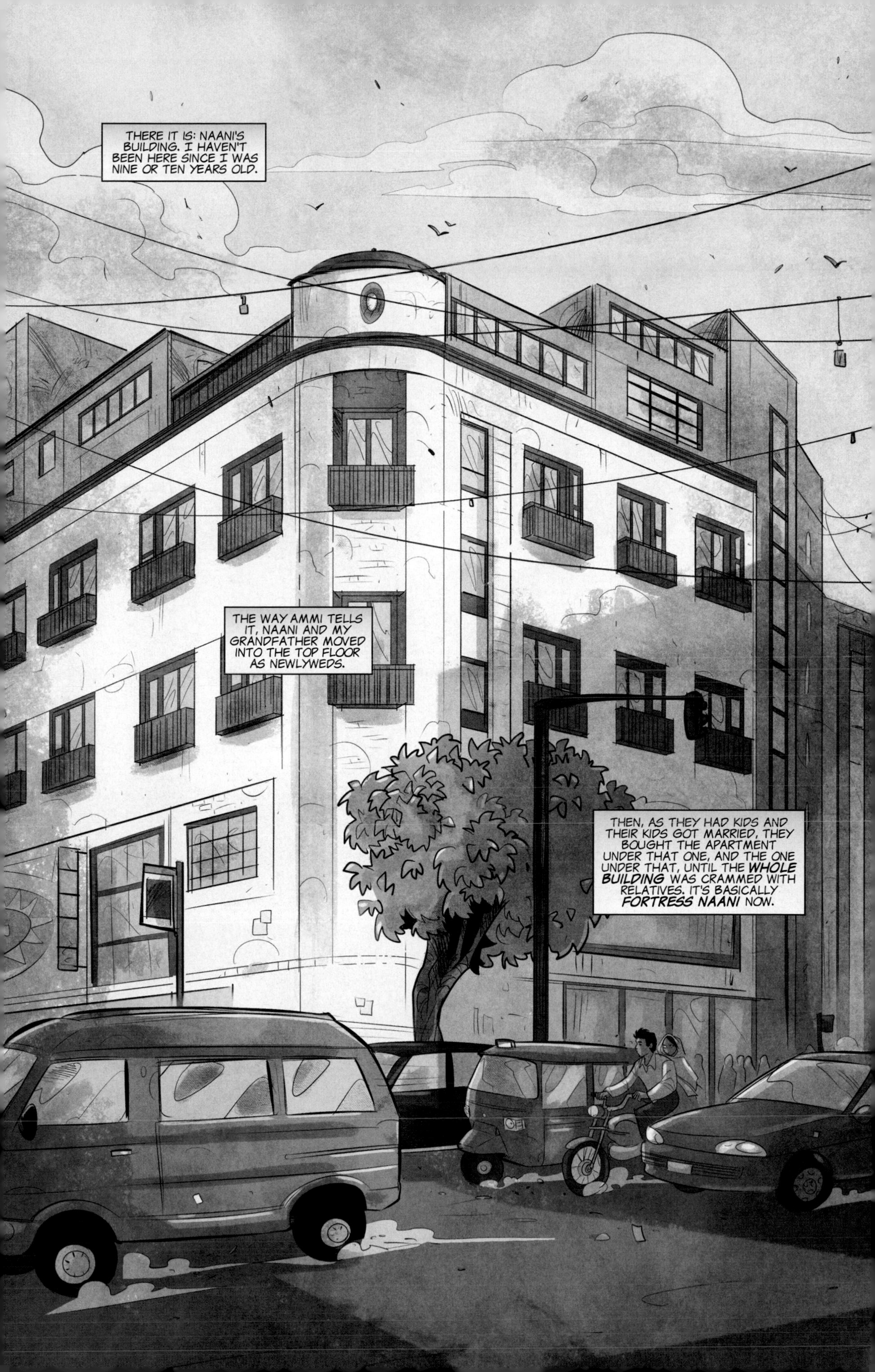
THERE IT IS: NAANI'S BUILDING. I HAVEN'T BEEN HERE SINCE I WAS NINE OR TEN YEARS OLD.
THE WAY AMMI TELLS IT, NAANI AND MY GRANDFATHER MOVED INTO THE TOP FLOOR AS NEWLYWEDS.
THEN, AS THEY HAD KIDS AND THEIR KIDS GOT MARRIED, THEY BOUGHT THE APARTMENT UNDER THAT ONE, AND THE ONE UNDER THAT, UNTIL THE WHOLE BUILDING WAS CRAMMED WITH RELATIVES. IT'S BASICALLY FORTRESS NAANI NOW.

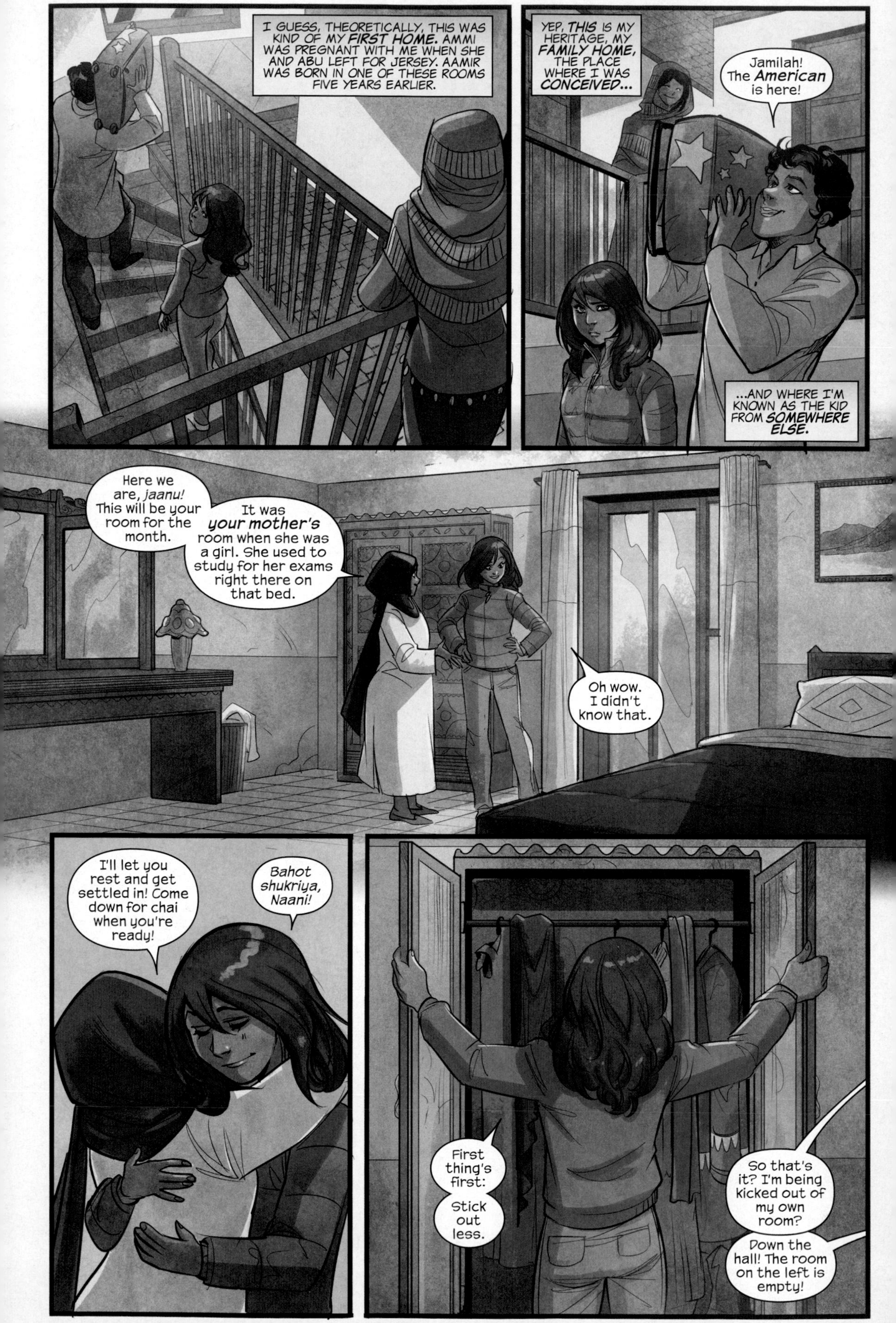
I GUESS, THEORETICALLY, THIS WAS KIND OF MY FIRST HOME. AMMI WAS PREGNANT WITH ME WHEN SHE AND ABU LEFT FOR JERSEY. AAMIR WAS BORN IN ONE OF THESE ROOMS FIVE YEARS EARLIER.
YEP, THIS IS MY HERITAGE, MY FAMILY HOME, THE PLACE WHERE I WAS CONCEIVED...
Jamilah! The American is here!
...AND WHERE I'M KNOWN AS THE KID FROM SOMEWHERE ELSE.
Here we are, jaanu! This will be your room for the month.
It was your mother's room when she was a girl. She used to study for her exams right there on that bed.
Oh wow. I didn't know that.
I'll let you rest and get settled in! Come down for chai when you're ready!
Bahot shukriya, Naani!
First thing's first:
Stick out less.
So that's it? I'm being kicked out of my own room?
Down the hall! The room on the left is empty!

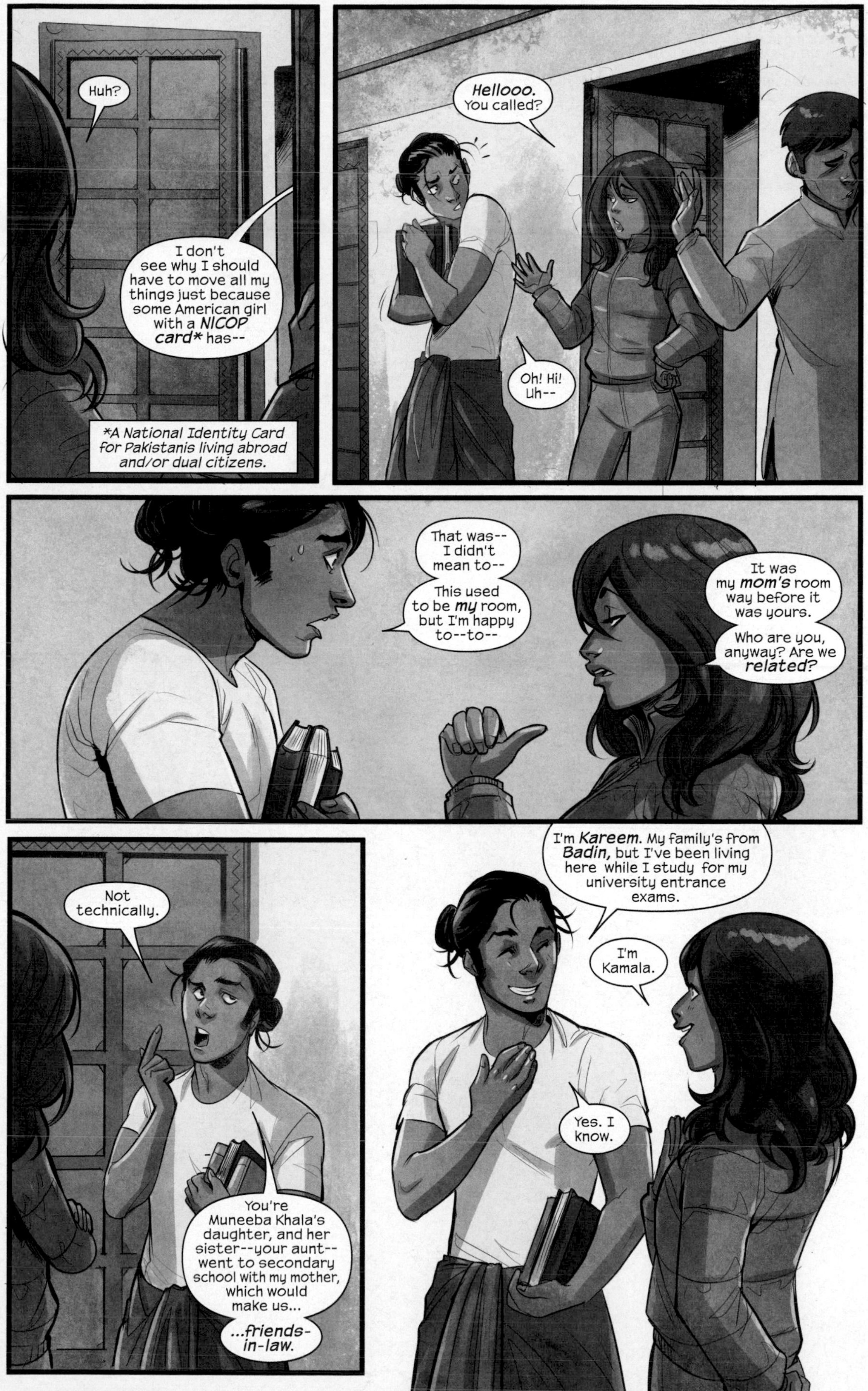

Huh?
I don't see why I should have to move all my things just because some American girl with a NICOP card* has--
*A National Identity Card for Pakistanis living abroad and/or dual citizens.
Hellooo. You called?
Oh! Hi! Uh--
That was-- I didn't mean to--
This used to be my room, but I'm happy to--to--
It was my mom's room way before it was yours.
Who are you, anyway? Are we related?
Not technically.
You're Muneeba Khala's daughter, and her sister--your aunt--went to secondary school with my mother, which would make us...
...friends-in-law.
I'm Kareem. My family's from Badin, but I've been living here while I study for my university entrance exams.
I'm Kamala.
Yes. I know.

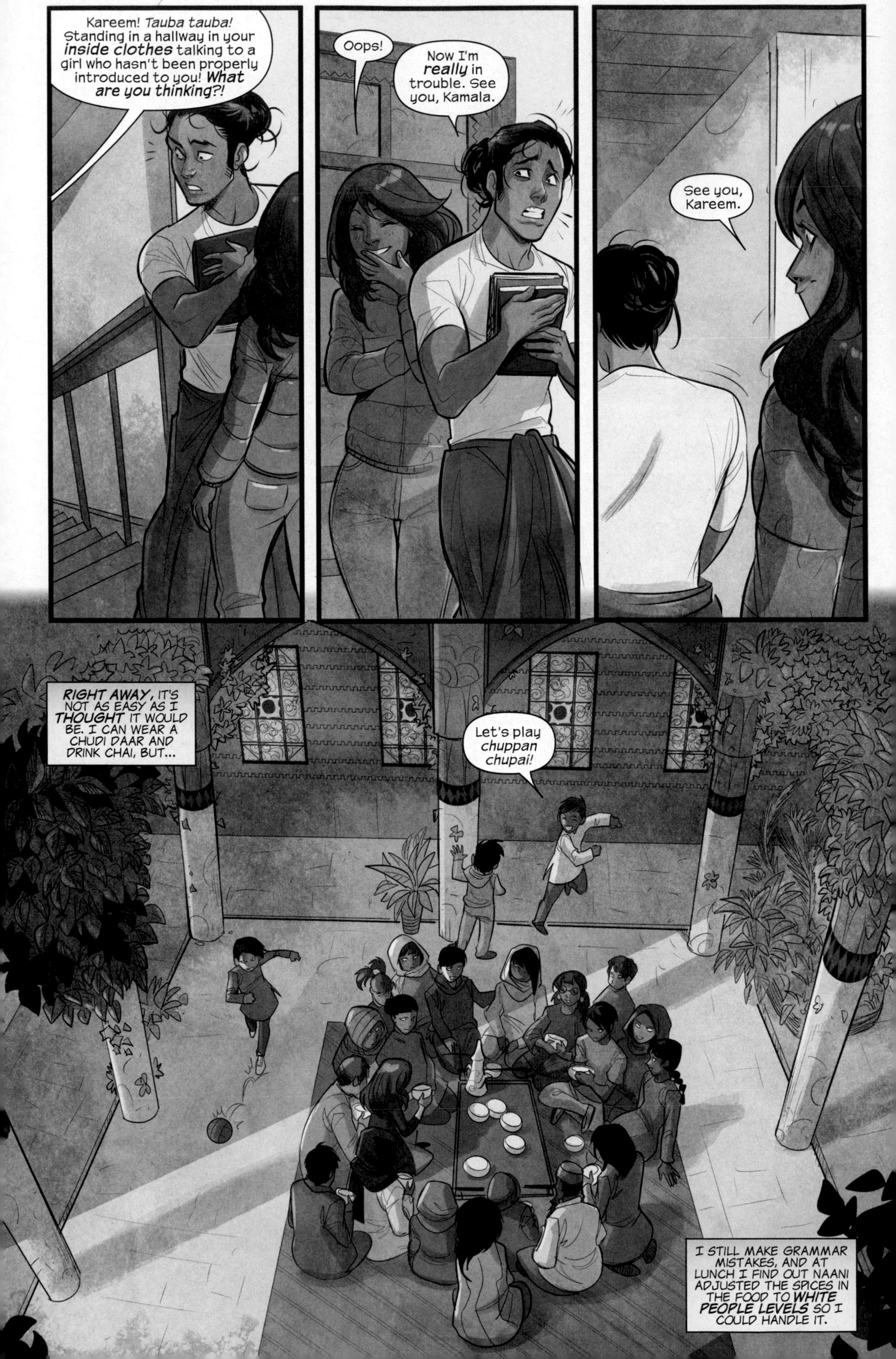

Kareem! *Tauba tauba!* Standing in a hallway in your **inside clothes** talking to a girl who hasn't been properly introduced to you! **What are you thinking?!**
Oops!
Now I'm **really** in trouble. See you, Kamala.
See you, Kareem.
RIGHT AWAY, IT'S NOT AS EASY AS I **THOUGHT** IT WOULD BE. I CAN WEAR A CHUDI DAAR AND DRINK CHAI, BUT...
Let's play *chuppan chupai!*
I STILL MAKE GRAMMAR MISTAKES, AND AT LUNCH I FIND OUT NAANI ADJUSTED THE SPICES IN THE FOOD TO **WHITE PEOPLE LEVELS** SO I COULD HANDLE IT.

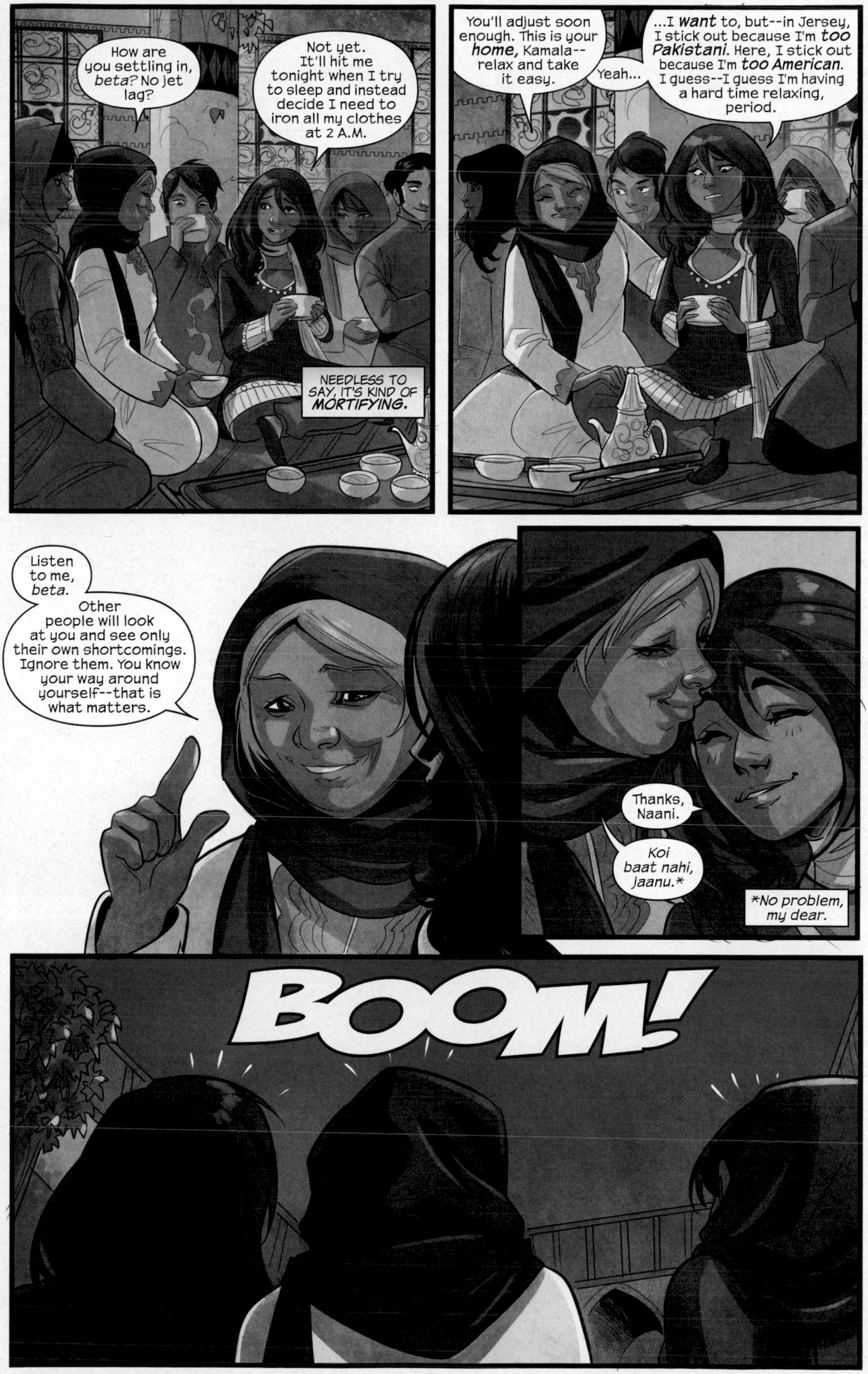
How are you settling in, beta? No jet lag?
Not yet. It'll hit me tonight when I try to sleep and instead decide I need to iron all my clothes at 2 A.M.
NEEDLESS TO SAY, IT'S KIND OF MORTIFYING.
You'll adjust soon enough. This is your home, Kamala-- relax and take it easy.
Yeah...
...I want to, but--in Jersey, I stick out because I'm too Pakistani. Here, I stick out because I'm too American. I guess--I guess I'm having a hard time relaxing, period.
Listen to me, beta. Other people will look at you and see only their own shortcomings. Ignore them. You know your way around yourself--that is what matters.
Thanks, Naani.
Koi baat nahi, jaanu.*
*No problem, my dear.
BOOM!

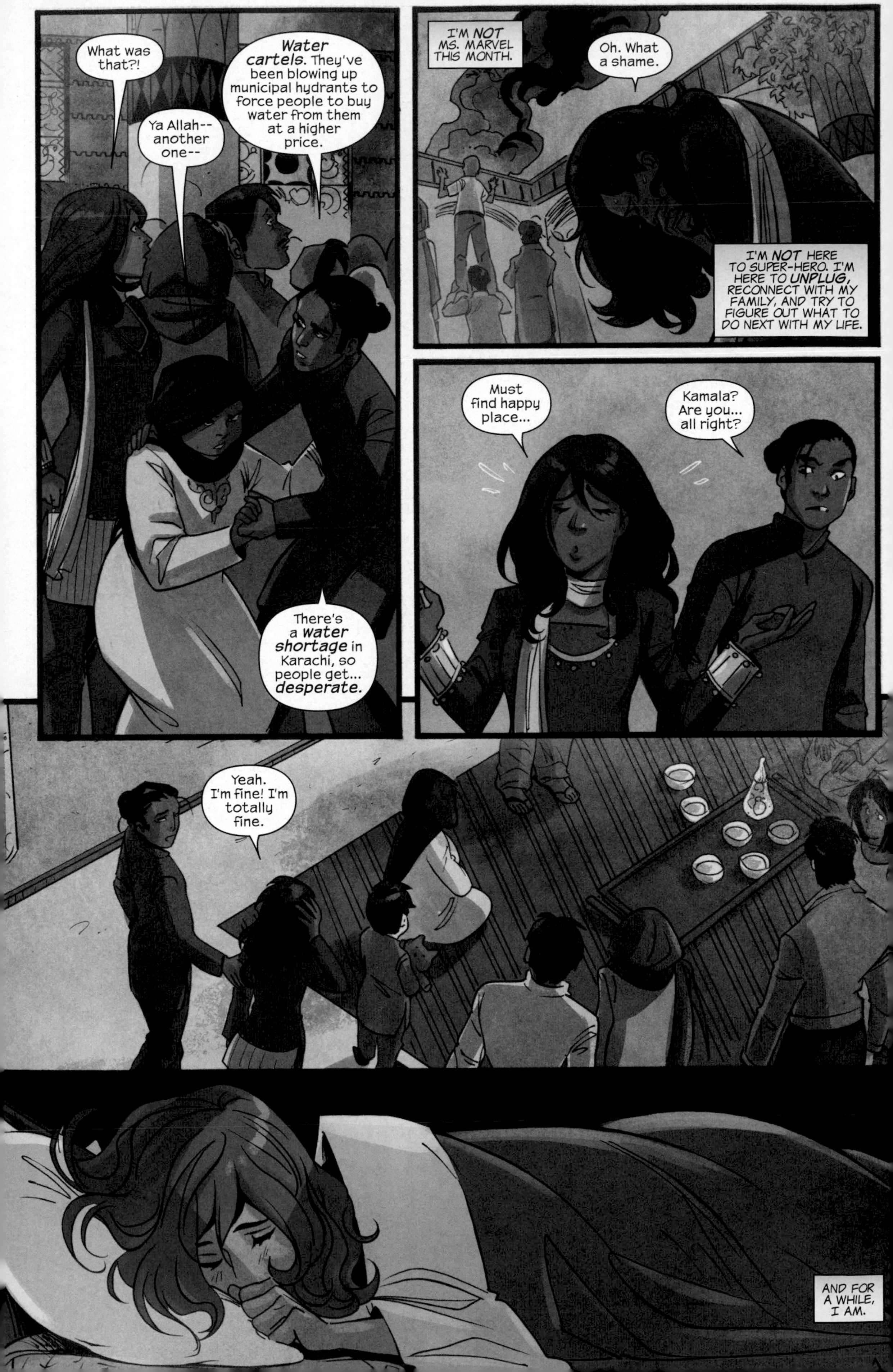
What was that?!
Ya Allah-- another one--
Water cartels. They've been blowing up municipal hydrants to force people to buy water from them at a higher price.
There's a water shortage in Karachi, so people get... desperate.
I'M NOT MS. MARVEL THIS MONTH.
Oh. What a shame.
I'M NOT HERE TO SUPER-HERO. I'M HERE TO UNPLUG, RECONNECT WITH MY FAMILY, AND TRY TO FIGURE OUT WHAT TO DO NEXT WITH MY LIFE.
Must find happy place...
Kamala? Are you... all right?
Yeah. I'm fine! I'm totally fine.
AND FOR A WHILE, I AM.

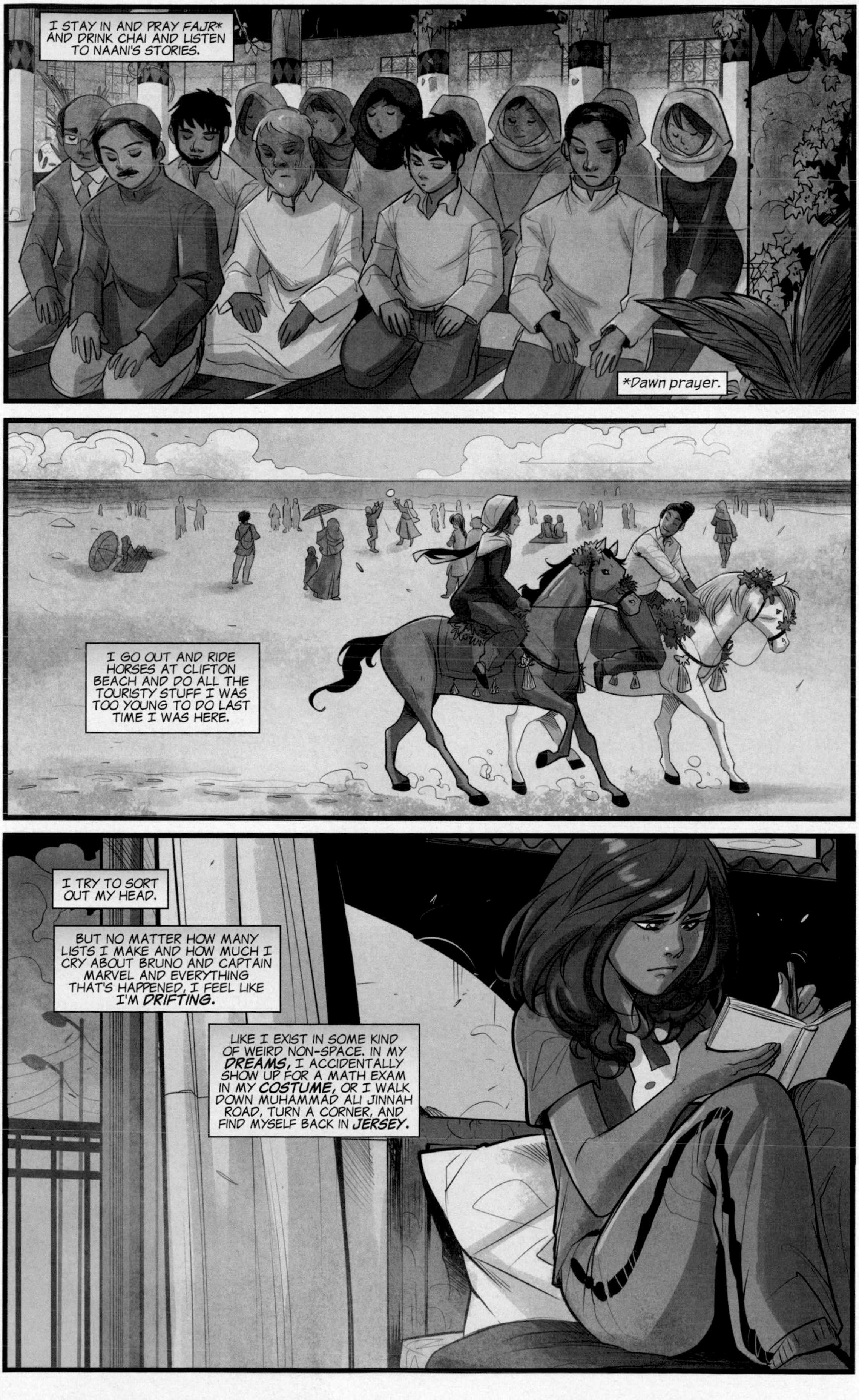
I STAY IN AND PRAY FAJR* AND DRINK CHAI AND LISTEN TO NAANI'S STORIES.
*Dawn prayer.
I GO OUT AND RIDE HORSES AT CLIFTON BEACH AND DO ALL THE TOURISTY STUFF I WAS TOO YOUNG TO DO LAST TIME I WAS HERE.
I TRY TO SORT OUT MY HEAD.
BUT NO MATTER HOW MANY LISTS I MAKE AND HOW MUCH I CRY ABOUT BRUNO AND CAPTAIN MARVEL AND EVERYTHING THAT'S HAPPENED, I FEEL LIKE I'M DRIFTING.
LIKE I EXIST IN SOME KIND OF WEIRD NON-SPACE. IN MY DREAMS, I ACCIDENTALLY SHOW UP FOR A MATH EXAM IN MY COSTUME, OR I WALK DOWN MUHAMMAD ALI JINNAH ROAD, TURN A CORNER, AND FIND MYSELF BACK IN JERSEY.

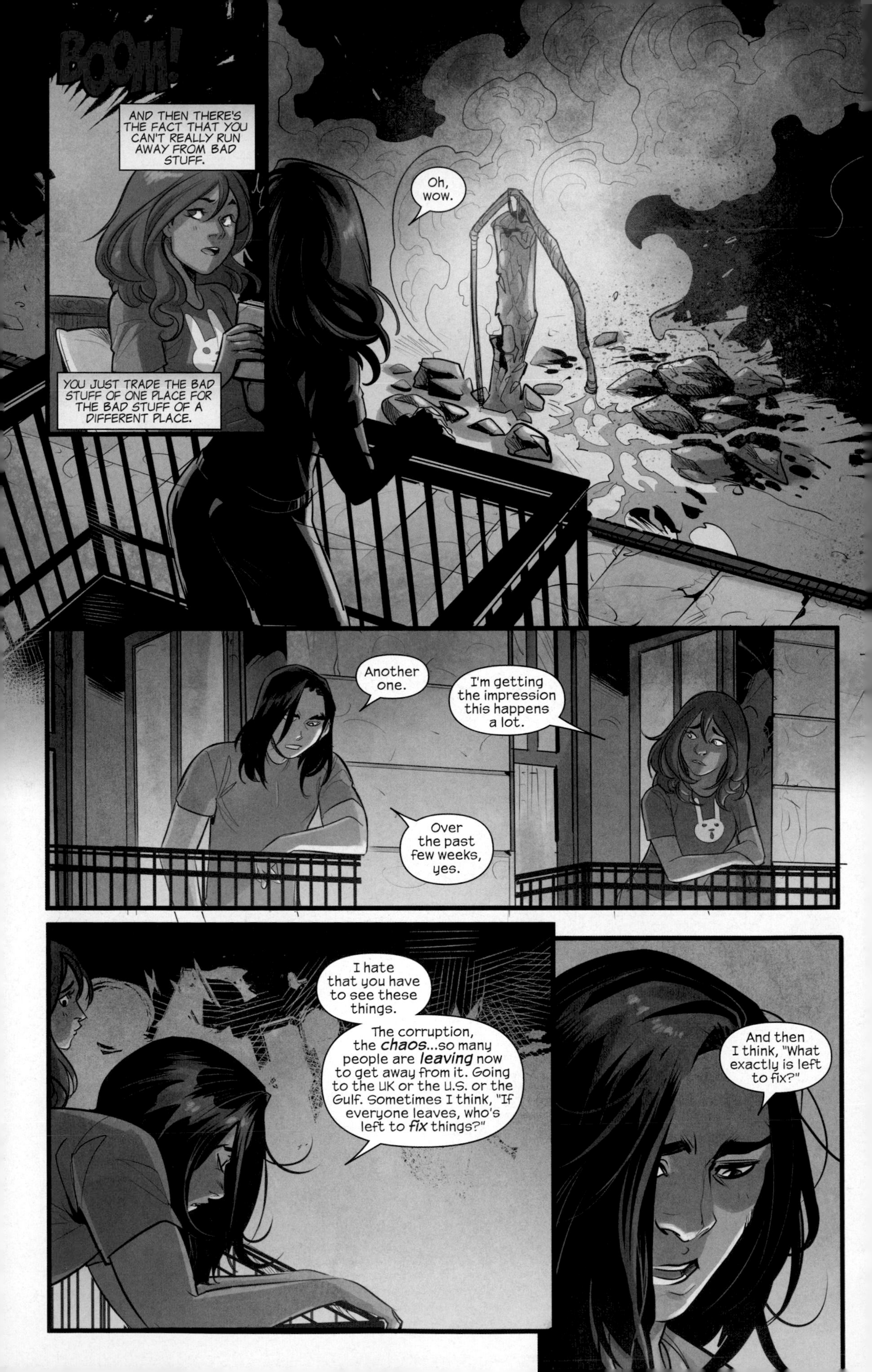
BOOM!
AND THEN THERE'S THE FACT THAT YOU CAN'T REALLY RUN AWAY FROM BAD STUFF.
Oh, wow.
YOU JUST TRADE THE BAD STUFF OF ONE PLACE FOR THE BAD STUFF OF A DIFFERENT PLACE.
Another one.
I'm getting the impression this happens a lot.
Over the past few weeks, yes.
I hate that you have to see these things.
The corruption, the chaos...so many people are leaving now to get away from it. Going to the UK or the U.S. or the Gulf. Sometimes I think, "If everyone leaves, who's left to fix things?"
And then I think, "What exactly is left to fix?"

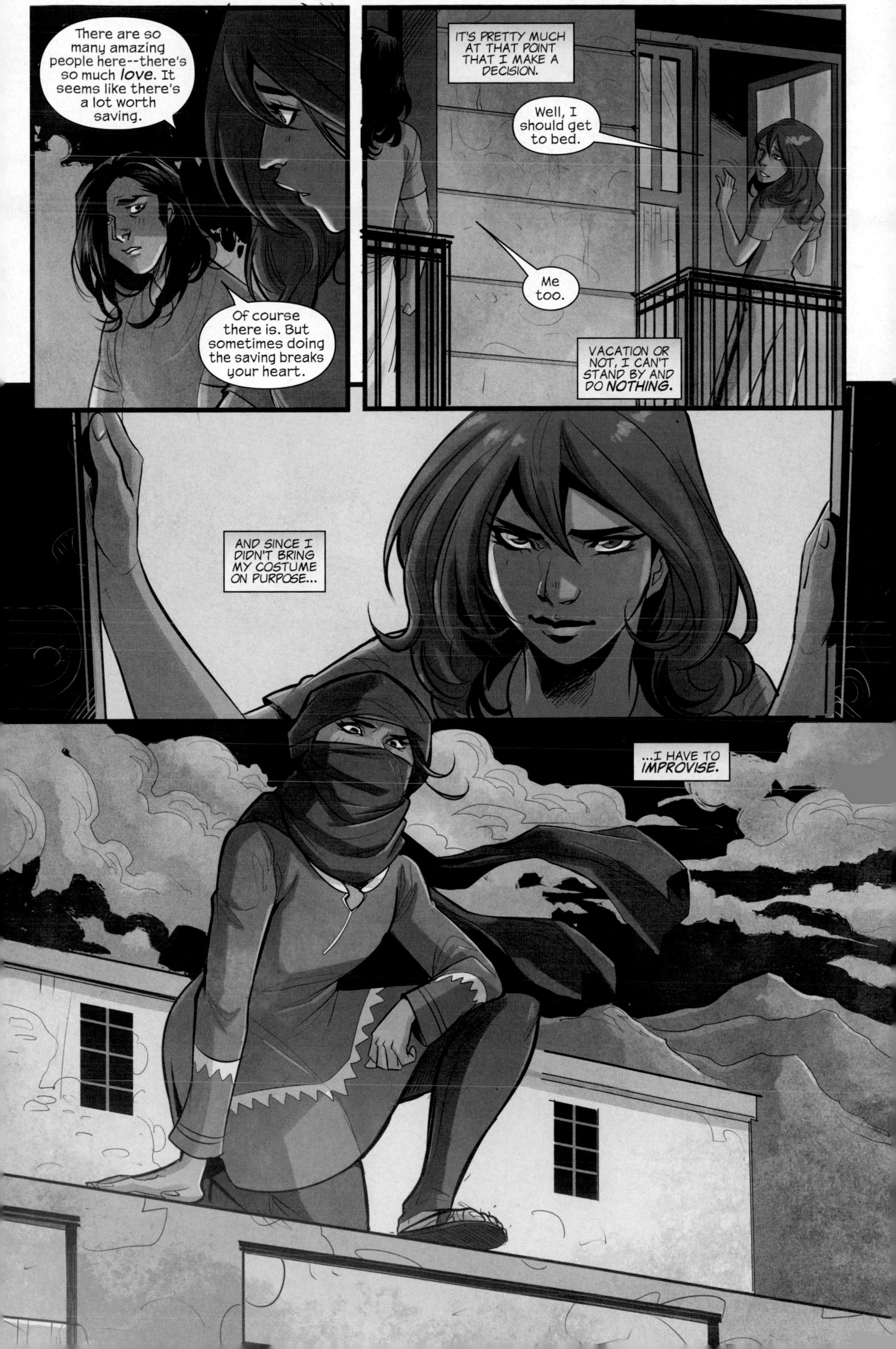
There are so many amazing people here--there's so much *love*. It seems like there's a lot worth saving.
Of course there is. But sometimes doing the saving breaks your heart.
IT'S PRETTY MUCH AT THAT POINT THAT I MAKE A DECISION.
Well, I should get to bed.
Me too.
VACATION OR NOT, I CAN'T STAND BY AND DO ***NOTHING***.
AND SINCE I DIDN'T BRING MY COSTUME ON PURPOSE...
...I HAVE TO ***IMPROVISE***.

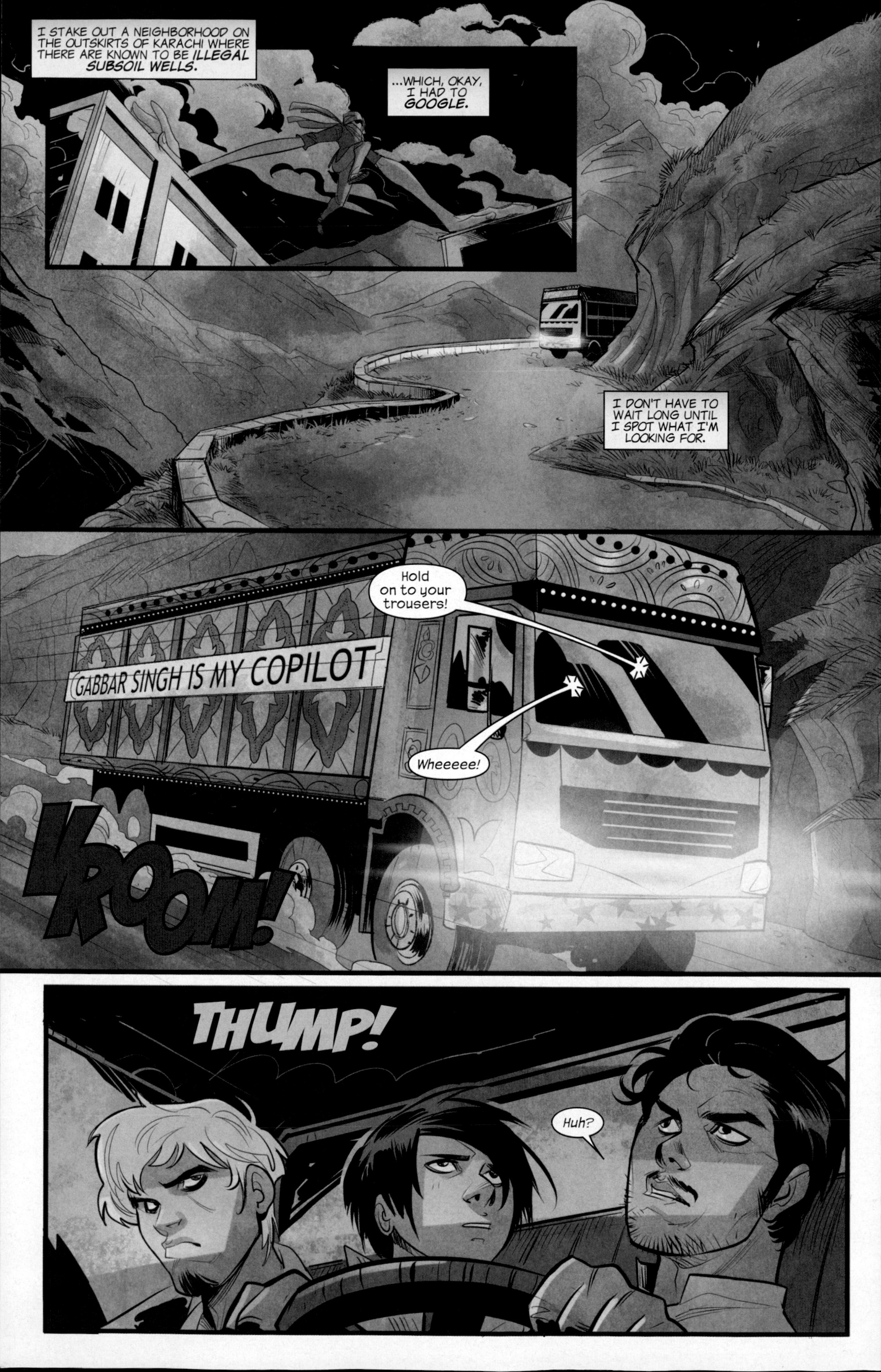
I STAKE OUT A NEIGHBORHOOD ON THE OUTSKIRTS OF KARACHI WHERE THERE ARE KNOWN TO BE ILLEGAL SUBSOIL WELLS.
...WHICH, OKAY, I HAD TO GOOGLE.
I DON'T HAVE TO WAIT LONG UNTIL I SPOT WHAT I'M LOOKING FOR.
GABBAR SINGH IS MY COPILOT
Hold on to your trousers!
Wheeeee!
VROOM!
THUMP!
Huh?

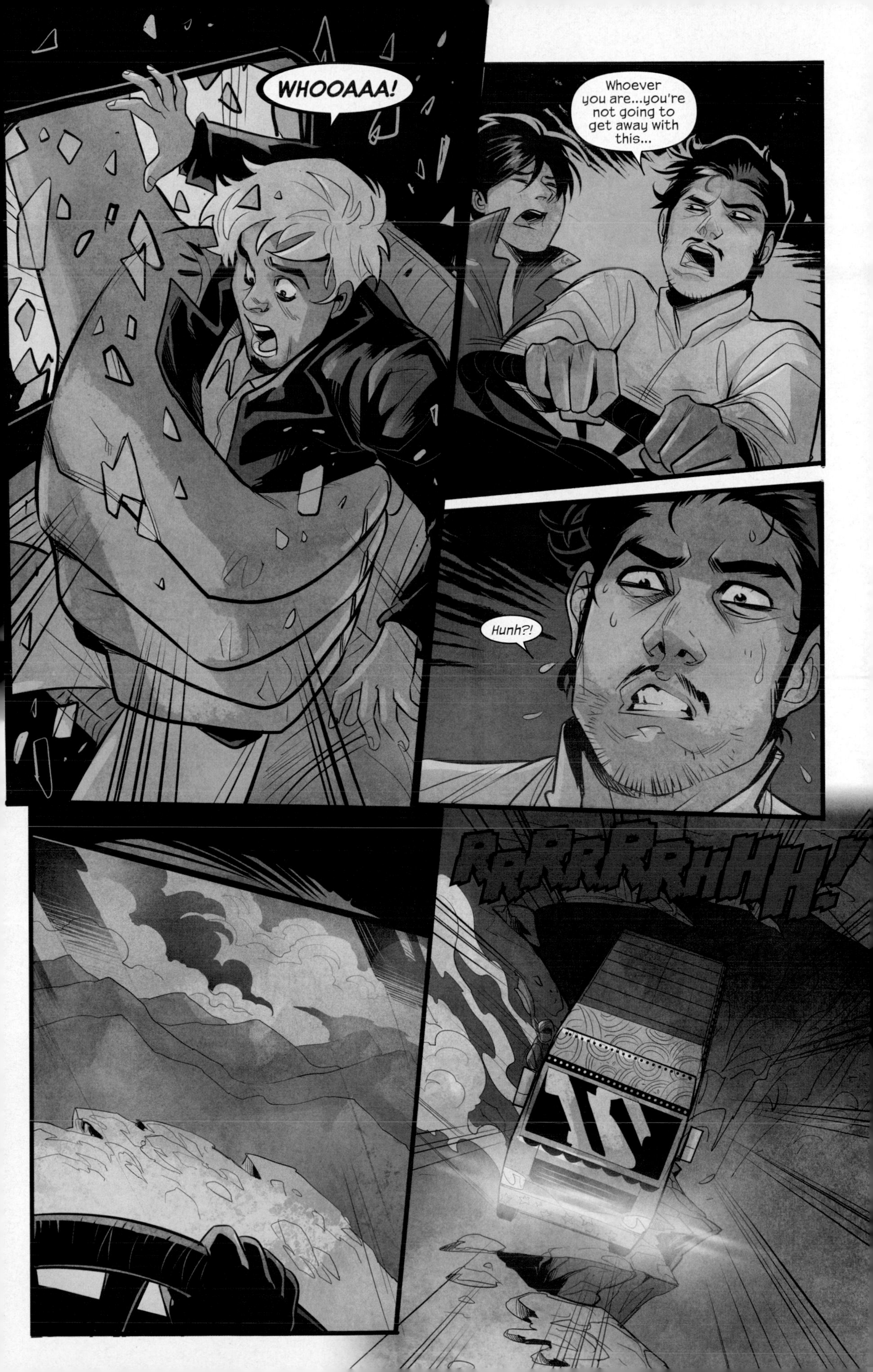
WHOOAAA!
Whoever you are...you're not going to get away with this...
Hunh?!
RRRRRRRHHH!

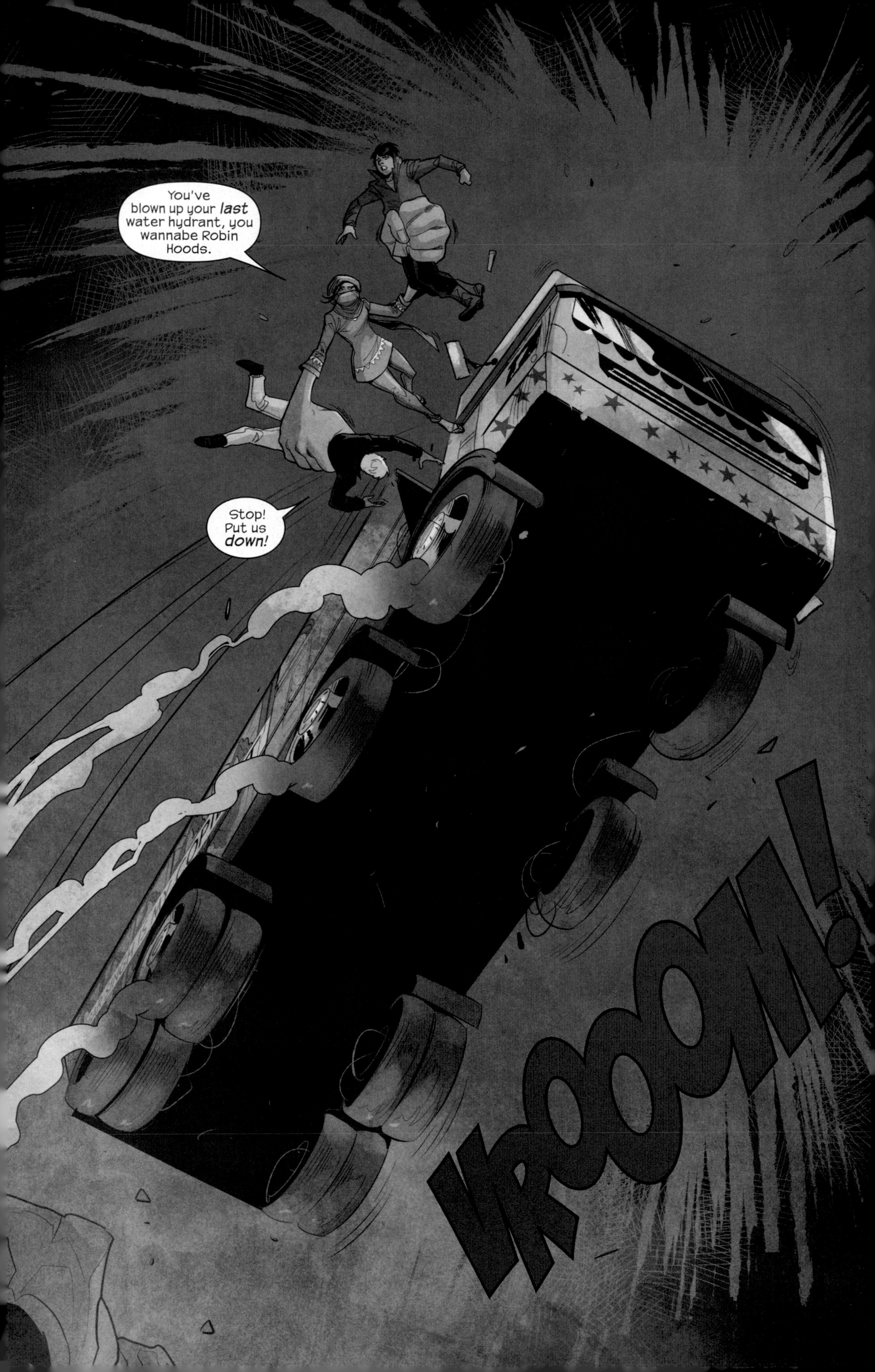
You've blown up your *last* water hydrant, you wannabe Robin Hoods.
Stop! Put us *down*!
VROOOM!!

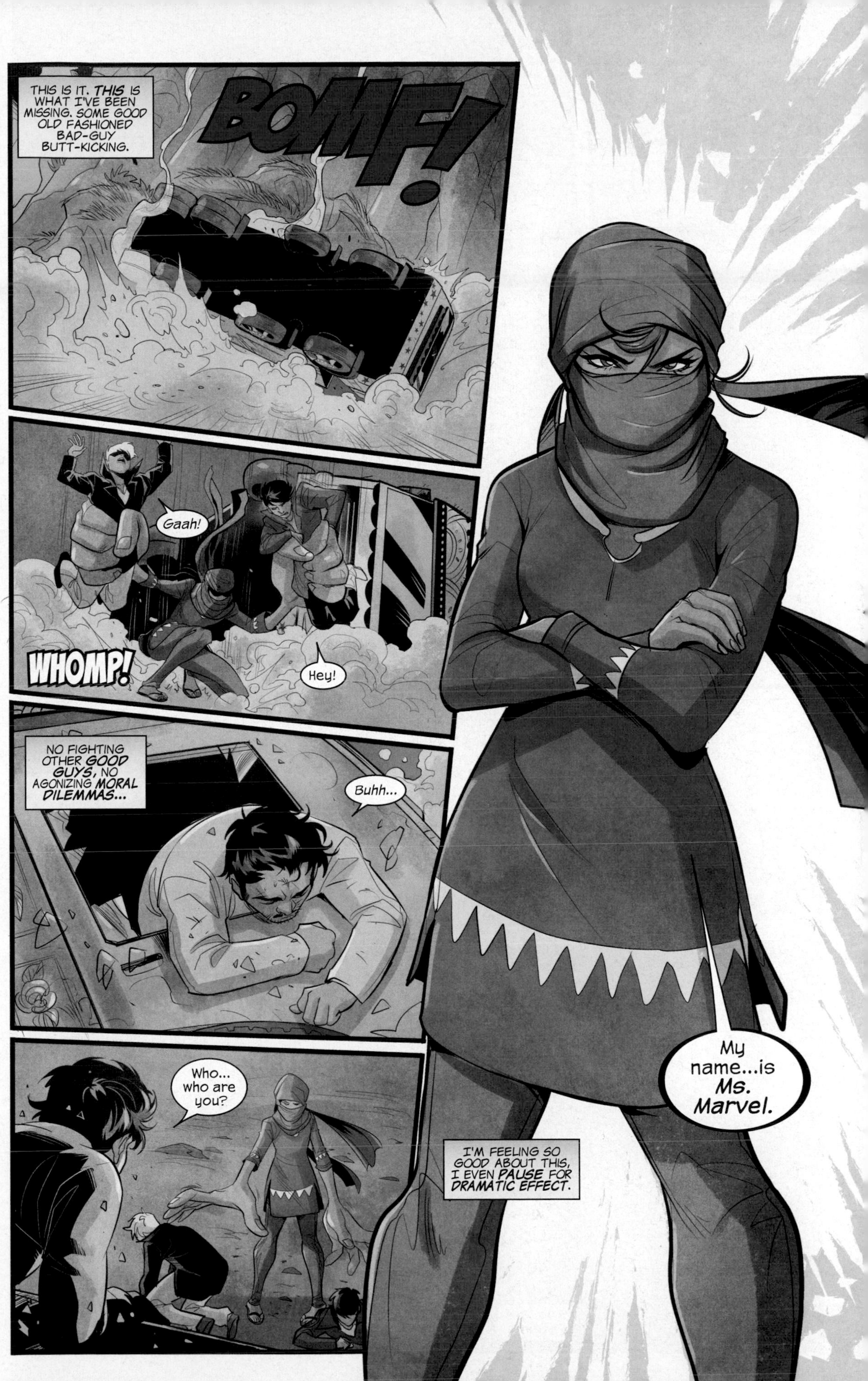
THIS IS IT. THIS IS WHAT I'VE BEEN MISSING. SOME GOOD OLD FASHIONED BAD-GUY BUTT-KICKING.
BOMF!
Gaah!
WHOMP!
Hey!
NO FIGHTING OTHER GOOD GUYS, NO AGONIZING MORAL DILEMMAS...
Buhh...
Who... who are you?
My name...is Ms. Marvel.
I'M FEELING SO GOOD ABOUT THIS, I EVEN PAUSE FOR DRAMATIC EFFECT.

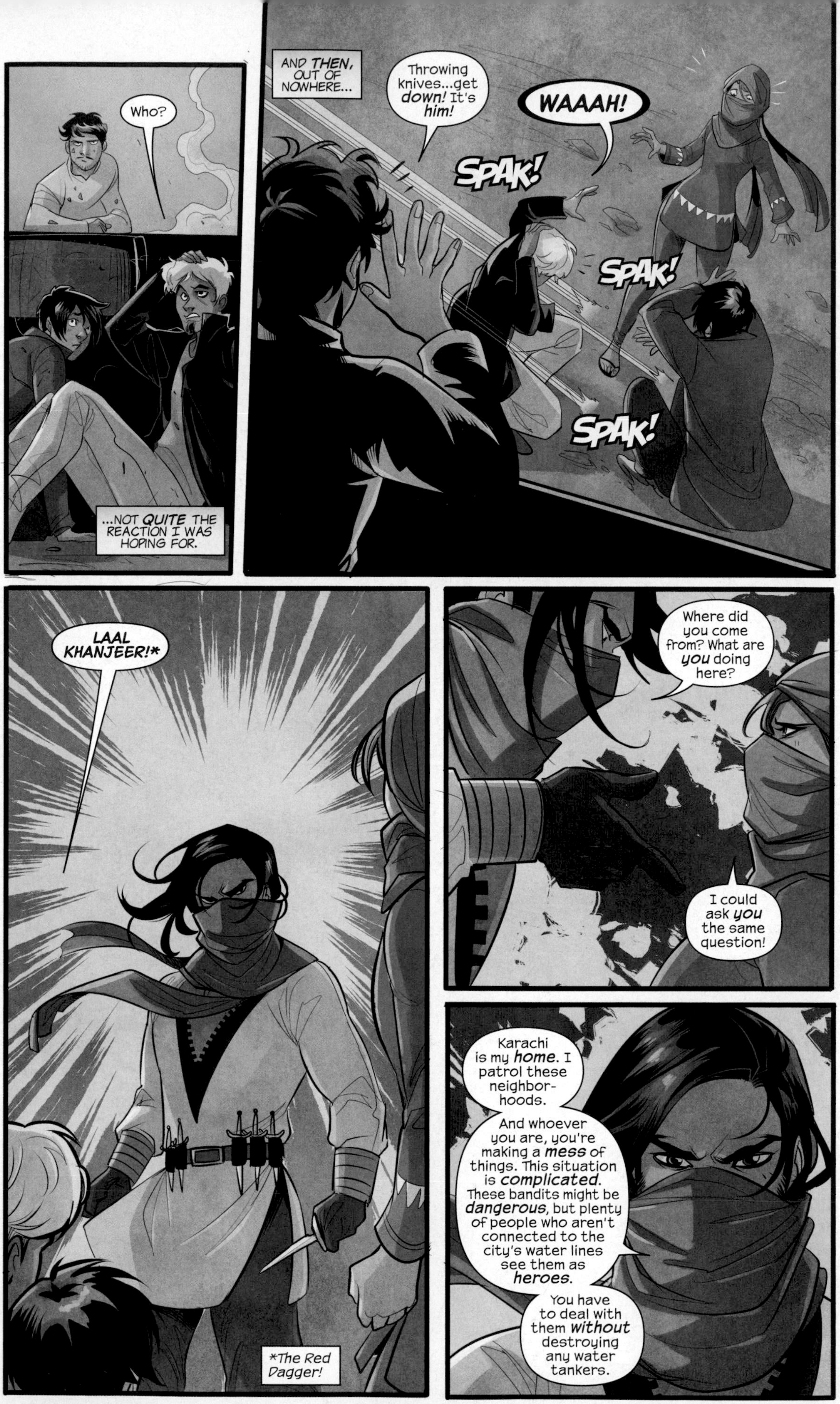
Who?
...NOT QUITE THE REACTION I WAS HOPING FOR.
AND THEN, OUT OF NOWHERE...
Throwing knives...get down! It's him!
WAAAH!
SPAK!
SPAK!
SPAK!
LAAL KHANJEER!*
*The Red Dagger!
Where did you come from? What are you doing here?
I could ask you the same question!
Karachi is my home. I patrol these neighbor-hoods.
And whoever you are, you're making a mess of things. This situation is complicated. These bandits might be dangerous, but plenty of people who aren't connected to the city's water lines see them as heroes.
You have to deal with them without destroying any water tankers.

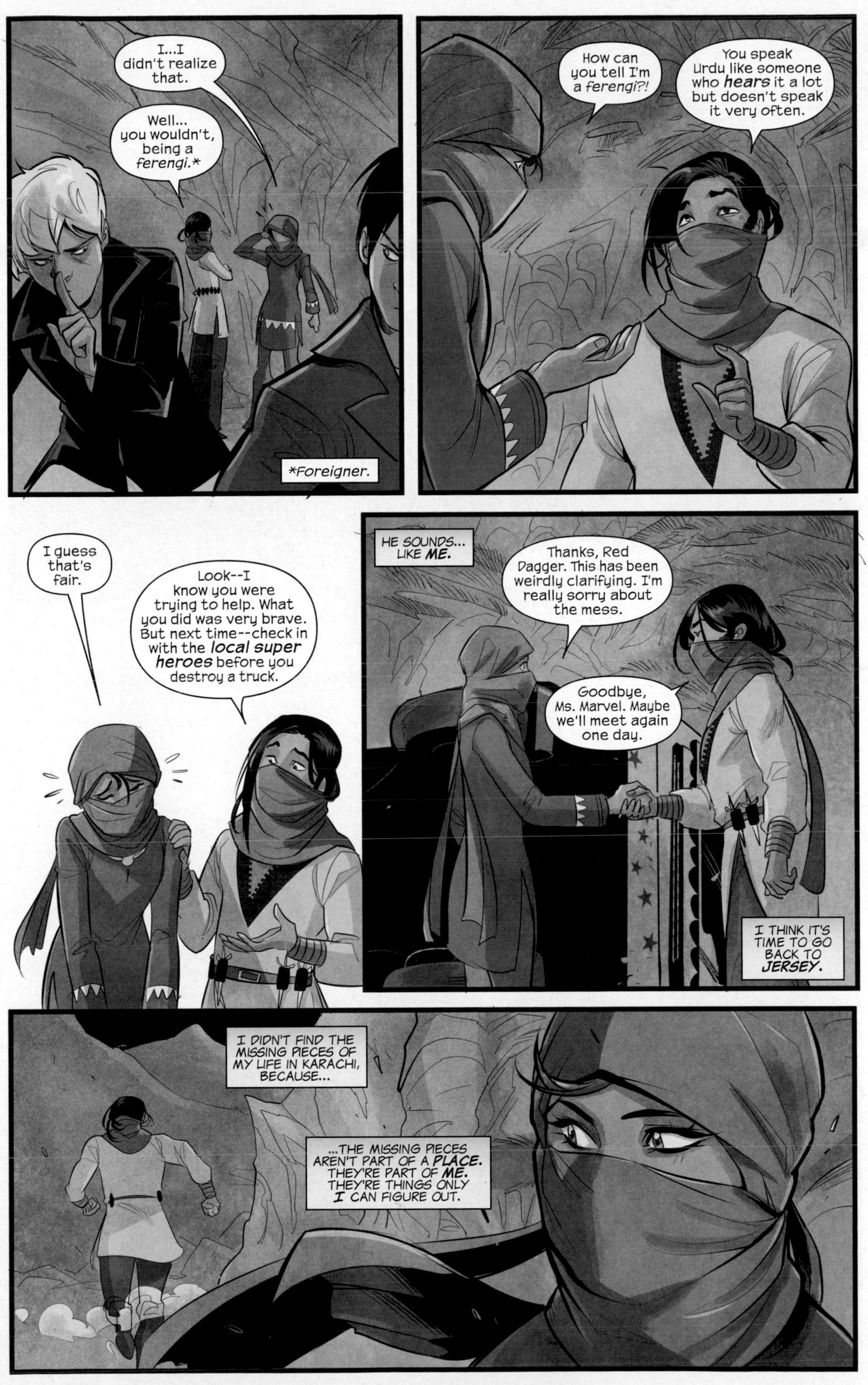

I...I didn't realize that.
Well... you wouldn't, being a ferengi.*
*Foreigner.
How can you tell I'm a ferengi?!
You speak Urdu like someone who hears it a lot but doesn't speak it very often.
I guess that's fair.
Look--I know you were trying to help. What you did was very brave. But next time--check in with the local super heroes before you destroy a truck.
HE SOUNDS... LIKE ME.
Thanks, Red Dagger. This has been weirdly clarifying. I'm really sorry about the mess.
Goodbye, Ms. Marvel. Maybe we'll meet again one day.
I THINK IT'S TIME TO GO BACK TO JERSEY.
I DIDN'T FIND THE MISSING PIECES OF MY LIFE IN KARACHI, BECAUSE...
...THE MISSING PIECES AREN'T PART OF A PLACE. THEY'RE PART OF ME. THEY'RE THINGS ONLY I CAN FIGURE OUT.

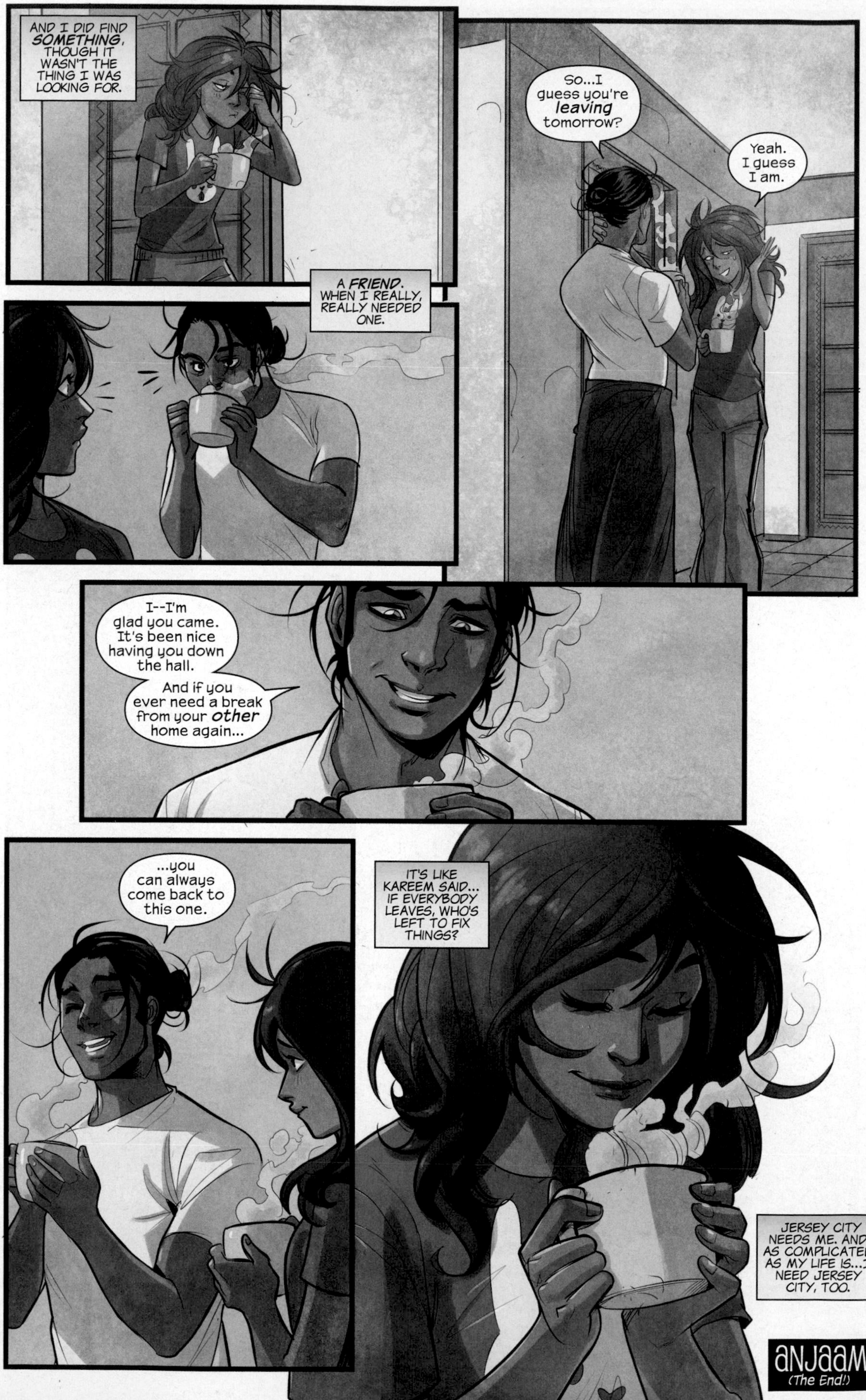

AND I DID FIND SOMETHING, THOUGH IT WASN'T THE THING I WAS LOOKING FOR.
So...I guess you're leaving tomorrow?
Yeah. I guess I am.
A FRIEND. WHEN I REALLY, REALLY NEEDED ONE.
I--I'm glad you came. It's been nice having you down the hall.
And if you ever need a break from your other home again...
...you can always come back to this one.
IT'S LIKE KAREEM SAID... IF EVERYBODY LEAVES, WHO'S LEFT TO FIX THINGS?
JERSEY CITY NEEDS ME. AND AS COMPLICATED AS MY LIFE IS...I NEED JERSEY CITY, TOO.
ANJAAM! (The End!)

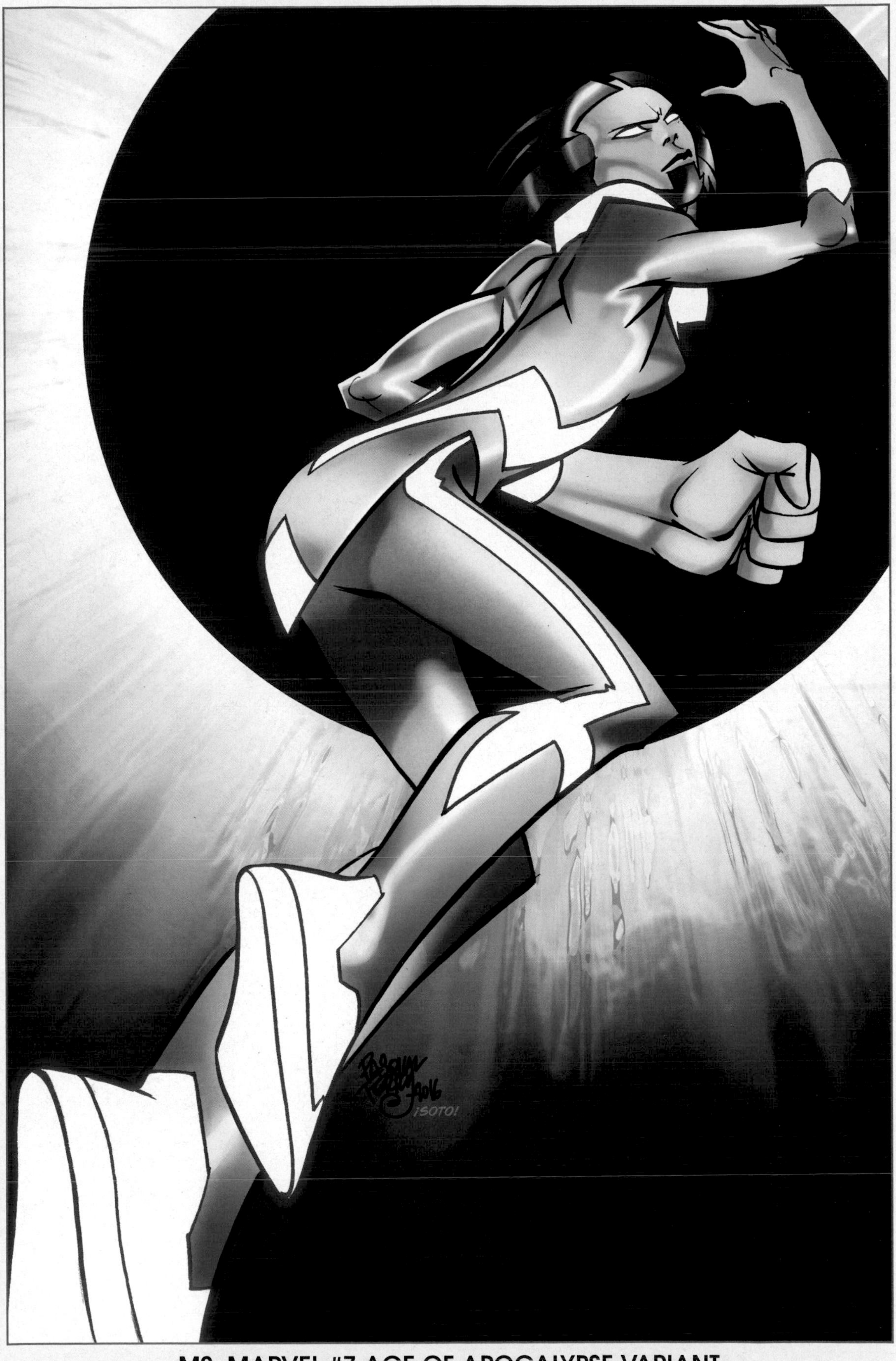
¡SOTO!

MS. MARVEL #7 AGE OF APOCALYPSE VARIANT
BY PASQUAL FERRY & CHRIS SOTOMAYOR

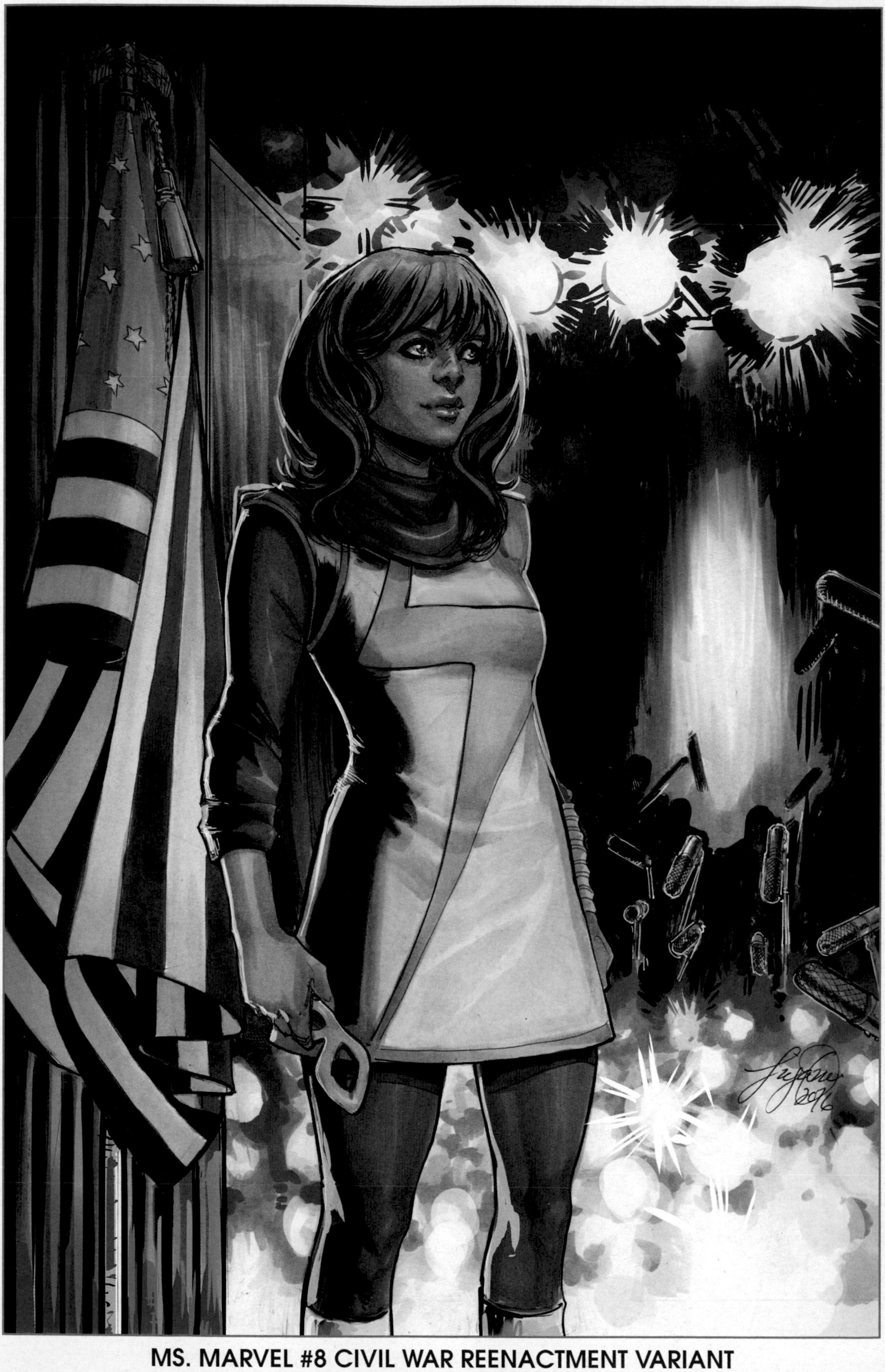

MS. MARVEL #8 CIVIL WAR REENACTMENT VARIANT
BY SIYA OUM

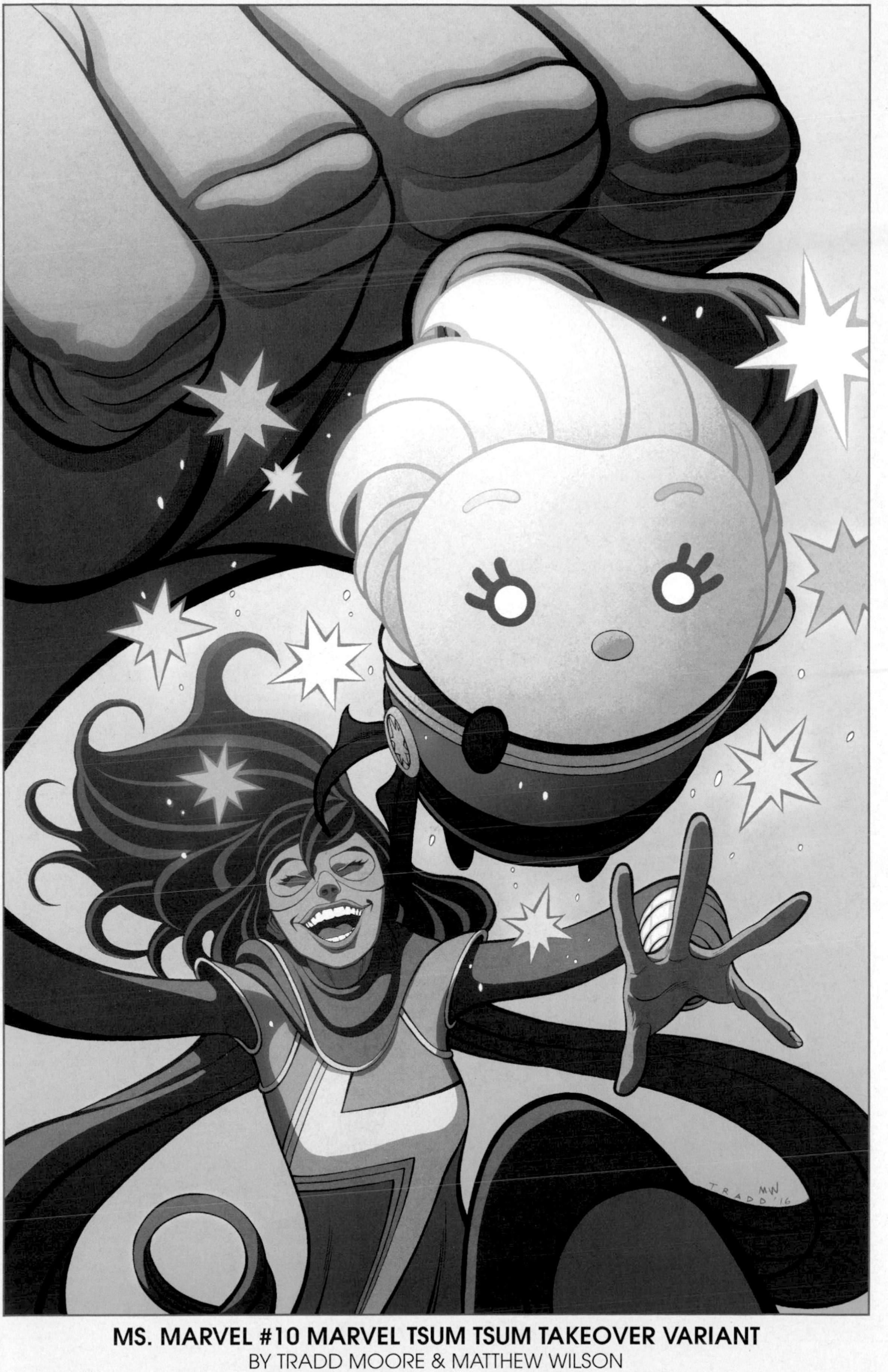
MW
TRADD '16

MS. MARVEL #10 MARVEL TSUM TSUM TAKEOVER VARIANT
BY TRADD MOORE & MATTHEW WILSON

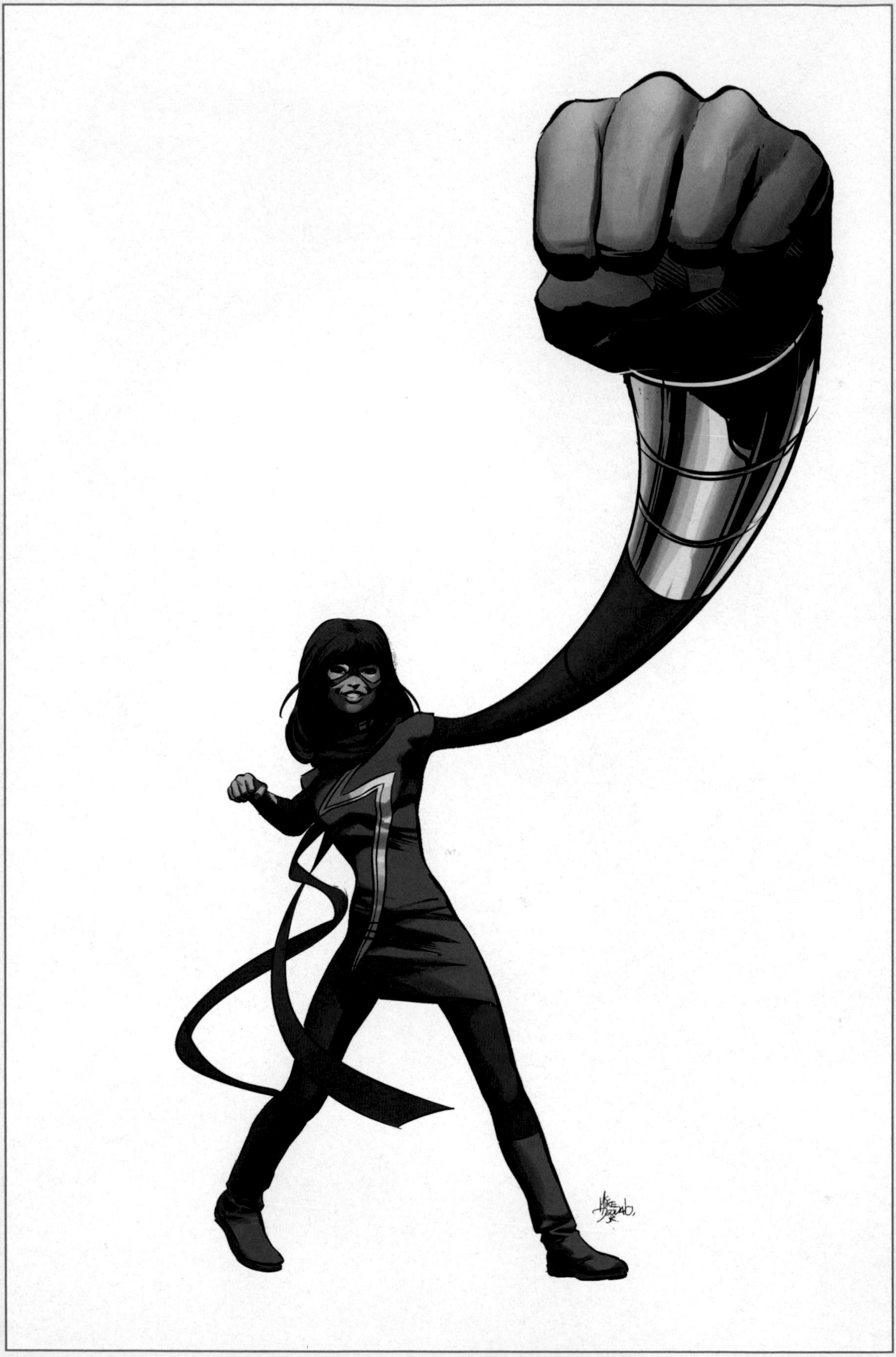

MS. MARVEL #12 TEASER VARIANT
BY MIKE DEODATO & FRANK MARTIN

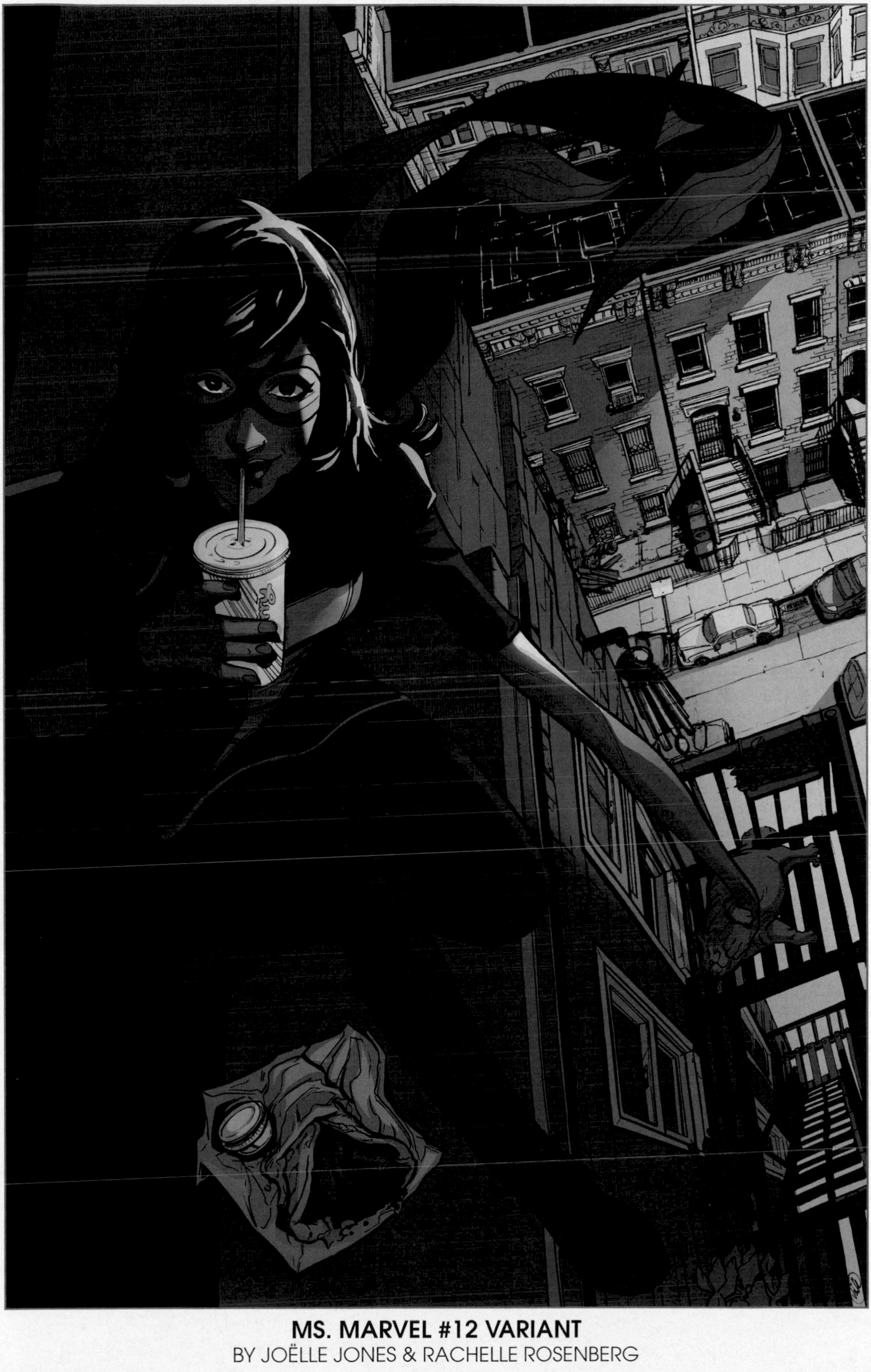

MS. MARVEL #12 VARIANT
BY JOËLLE JONES & RACHELLE ROSENBERG

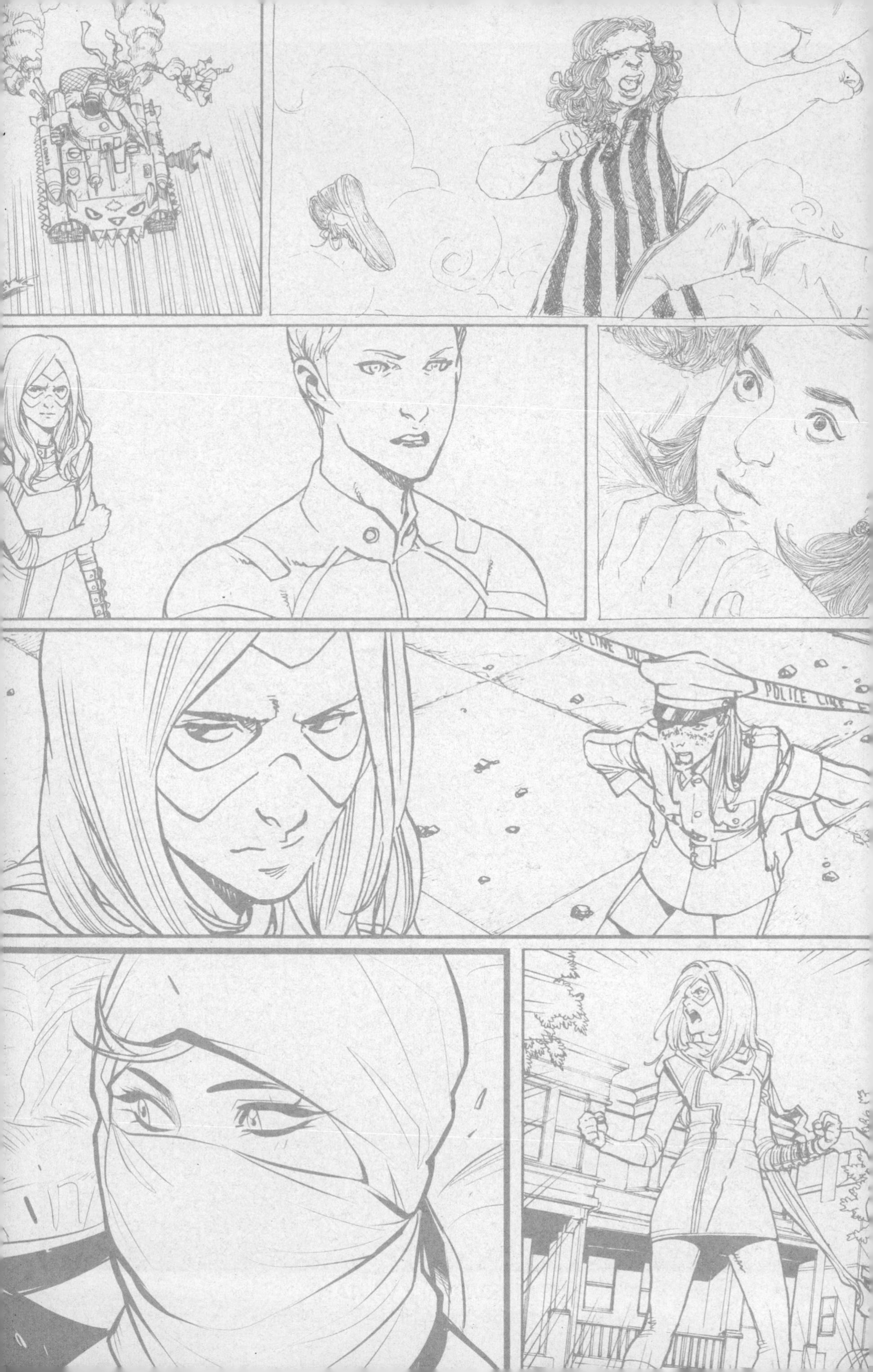
POLICE LINE